BEHIND
THE FRONT PAGE

The Author lovingly instructs a recruit.

A. A. DORNFELD

BEHIND THE FRONT PAGE

The Story of the City News Bureau of Chicago

with material supplied by
Tom Vickerman
including a memoir by
Archibald Leckie

Introduction by Mike Royko

Academy
Chicago
Publishers

Published by Academy Chicago/Publishers
425 N. Michigan Avenue
Chicago, Illinois 60611

Library of Congress Cataloging in Publication Data

Dornfeld, A.A., 1907-
   Behind the front page.

   Bibliography: p.
   Includes index.
   1. City News Bureau of Chicago. I. Title.
PN4899.C375D67 1983   070.4'35   83-11925
ISBN 0-89733-070-6

Table of Contents

INTRODUCTION

by Mike Royko

The first thing you noticed was the eye. I don't recall if it was the left or the right eye, but it appeared to be much bigger than the other one. Bulging, merciless, angry, all-knowing. And it didn't blink.

The eye had the effect of the harsh, blinding lamp that cops used to shine in the face of a suspect they were questioning. You wanted to confess, admit your sins, plead guilty—anything to make that unblinking eye turn away.

Next you noticed the clothes. They looked like something from a farmer-town rummage sale or a town Salvation Army outlet store. A soot colored flannel work shirt with the tail usually hanging out over baggy old pants that had a sagging seat and frayed cuffs that hung over ancient Sears Roebuck work boots. If you looked closely, you might see shreds of cow dung on the boots.

And, incongruously, a tie. Some colorless hunk of wool, with a lump of a knot off to one side, half-concealed by the upwardly-curling shirt collar.

Then you saw the body: tall, with stooped, powerful shoulders, like those of a man who had spent his life lifting heavy objects. Long, strong arms from which dangled big, calloused hands with knobby fingers and cracked fingernails. The body of a lumberjack or a merchant seaman. Or something put together out of strange parts by a mad scientist.

Topping it off was a large, weather-beaten head, with a firm jaw and a thatch of brown straight hair that looked as if it had been hastily wet-combed with fingers in the morning, and left to the whims of the wind the rest of the day.

Finally, the voice. Oh, God, what a voice. A klaghorn. A penitentiary escape siren. The screech of elevated train wheels rounding a sharp curve. It was a voice that made you jump to your feet, demanded your full attention, made your pulse race and caused acute hyperventilation.

Meet Arnold (Dornie) Dornfeld, editor, teacher and terror to big reporters, molder of some of the best reporters in the business, and a journalistic legend in Chicago and just about anywhere else where Chicago newsmen have wandered.

But don't be afraid. Despite his favorite admonition— "Spare me the bullshit, laddie"—I'll say it: a sweet and wonderful man.

A young reporter couldn't have been in better hands, whether he knew it or not. Unfortunately, the young reporters who went to work for the City News Bureau didn't always know it. Not in the beginning.

In the beginning there was fear. And fear is something that a reporter has to learn to live with if he's going to make it in the news business.

When you're a young police reporter, you have to overcome your fear of mean, tough cops who slam doors in your face. Later, you will run into politicians who can be hostile. Labor bosses can scare hell out of you. So can generals and admirals and ghetto gang leaders. And presidents of giant corporations, who threaten to get your job. Give them a chance, and they'll all try to intimidate a reporter, brush him off, or spin him around.

So Dornie's approach was simple: he wanted the young reporter to fear him, the editor, more than anyone with whom the reporter would have to grapple while covering a story. No thick necked Chicago detective who said: "Get the fuck away from me, punk," could scare us as much as the thought of going to the phone, dialing the City News Bureau, and telling Dornie: "Uh, I can't get the story." So you went eyeball to eyeball with the Chicago cop and got the story.

Accuracy? I don't know who said it first*, but Dornie is generally credited with the immortal lines: "If your mother says she loves you, check it out." And: "Don't tell me what you think—tell me what you *know*."

Accuracy. Speed. Determination. An eye for a story and an ear for a quote. The willingness to jump out of bed at any hour and rush out to a triple murder or a raging fire. He made you think it was a natural, normal way to live.

But Dornie was more than a drill sergeant. A high school dropout, he was once described by Howard Ziff, an Amherst College graduate, later a brilliant reporter at the *Chicago Daily News*, and now a journalism professor at the University of Massachusetts, as: "One of the best read men I've ever known. He knew more about more things than most of the professors I had in college."

An eclectic mind. He could discuss philosophy, pimps, poetry, history, prohibition gangsters, and the beauty of great sailing ships. Pity the presumptuous young liberal arts graduate who wanted to dazzle Dornie with his book learning. He'd be left sprawling somewhere back in remedial philosophy.

Not everyone could handle Dornie. Their natures were too sensitive. For example, the young Ivy Leaguer who was working in the "back room," the first job you did at CNB. You were copy boy, gopher, and listened to the police radio for any horror that sounded promising.

One night Dornie came in with a painful carbuncle on his foot. It had developed while he was hauling and chopping firewood—a business he ran on the side for the pleasure of the hard, clean work, and income to supplement the cheapo CNB paycheck.

That night, one of the Ivy Leaguer's back room duties were to keep a kettle of water on the hot plate and to pour it into the tin pot in which Dornie was soaking his foot.

* Ed Eulenberg said it first—Dornfeld.

After the third kettle, the dazed young man was muttering: "Is *this* what I went to college for? To pour water for his *foot? His foot?*"

When last seen, he had departed CNB for a career in an uncle's brokerage house.

But those who survived came to know the Mr. Chips side of Dornie's personality. Like any good professor, he got to know his pupils outside of the classroom.

There were Saturdays or Sundays at his old, frame house on a few acres of farmland in a distant rural suburban area. He built the house himself, and it looked like it. Legend has it that during World War II, when gas was rationed, he kept a horse and rode it each day to town, where he parked it in someone's yard while he rode the commuter train to Chicago.

He'd gather the young reporters and their wives or girl-friends around his Franklin stove for a day of eating thick slices of ham, potato salad, dark rye bread, drinking good German beer and listening to Beethoven. Who else but Beethoven for a man who could roar as magnificently as the Fifth? If you sat through all nine symphonies, and appeared to appreciate them, he might invite you back for all the concerti.

If you handled the beer and Beethoven, and had a strong back, the ultimate honor: he would hire you to help him haul and chop firewood.

And all the while you learned. About reporting, first, then about writing. About simplicity, brevity, clarity—but turning the phrase that gave a story that added touch of class. If you stuck around long enough, you learned about editing, guiding young reporters, and scaring hell out of them.

If you got to know him well enough to have a beer after work or visit his home, you might even learn about things like marriage and being a father. He was married to and loved the same superb woman most of his life. He lost her and we all ached for him.

More than two decades after I worked for him, I had a party at my home for another City News Bureau alumnus, who had returned from a long stint as a war correspondent in South-

east Asia. I invited about thirty other ex-CNB reporters—
now newspaper city editors, investigative reporters, columnists, TV news directors, a few Pulitzer Prize winners among
them.

Dornie arrived with a gift—a trunk load of firewood, which
he ordered us to haul into the house.

My teenage son began making the fire. Dornie watched
him for a minute or so before saying: "Laddie, do you know
the proper way to make a fire?" My son said: "Yeah, sure."
Dornie watched him for a few more moments, then fixed him
with that eye. His voice rose about an octave and a decibel.
And he said: "Laddie are you *sure* you know how to make
that fire?"

My son looked him in that eye, stood, backed away from
the fire, then said: "Uh, I think maybe you'd better show me,
sir."

At the far end of the room, the veteran war correspondent
giggled and said: "You know what?"

"What?"

"I'm still a little afraid of that sonofabitch."

I told him I was too. And a city editor said: "And so am I."

I'd better stop now. Or Dornie will be saying: "Laddie,
spare me the bullshit."

But it's not.

PROLOGUE

Anywhere today on the newsfronts of the world, from Hollywood to the Kremlin, where reporters gather after working hours to relax and swap trade talk, conversation is almost certain to turn eventually to the City News Bureau of Chicago: its iron discipline, its hardnosed insistence on accuracy and, most of all, its legendary tightfistedness.

Several of those present would probably have received their early training at the bureau; most of the others would have heard about it. As becomes quickly evident at such bull sessions, the CNB, apart from its function of gathering and distributing news, serves as a training ground for young men and women who want to become journalists, writers or communicators of any kind.

If we could tune in on this hypothetical journalistic conversation, held somewhere in, say, the Middle East—Beirut?—we would find the participants gathered in the one drinking spot in town that has the notable advantage of remaining open despite sporadic gunfire in the streets. It is one where food may be ordered too, but at the customer's own risk.

Half a dozen people huddle at a table considered safe because it is near a window protected by two-inch planks, as opposed to the half-inch plywood covering the establishment's other windows. The people, who drink as they talk, are well-dressed by local standards: they are wearing shoes, and their clothes have no holes in them.

A portly fellow complains about the Greek beer he is drinking. It comes from Piraeus, but he says it is almost as bad as the stuff he used to get at an all-night joint in Chicago when he was working the City News Bureau overnight. His wallet, containing Lebanese pound notes, lies open on the table. Conspicuous in it is the press card of a famous international news service.

There is a stir in the group.

"The City News? That weird place?" a woman says. She is a somewhat battered but still attractive blonde who writes for a Philadelphia daily. "Did you work there too?" She was there for over a year in the sixties. "I remember Gershman," she says reflectively. "He used to come out of his office and get the big city desk scissors. He cut his tuna fish sandwich into quarters with it. It drove the city editor nuts. What was his name...Larry Mulay..."

A shabby character in a threadbare sports jacket interrupts. "When I was at the bureau I remember the Coast Guard picked one of our guys up in a stolen sailboat. I think the charge was piracy. But he was after a story... Anyway someone else stole it first—."

Someone else interrupts. He has never worked at City News, but he heard a story about a reporter there who got a red-hot interview with Al Capone, and the city desk turned it down. Somebody said they were afraid Al would sue them for libel.

The Greek beer drinker sips moodily. "Some people think it's a great place to learn," he says, "It looks better when you haven't been there for forty years."

"It was a goddam sweatshop," the blonde says. "A Marine bootcamp."

"Well, you could learn there," a bearded reporter says. He has been silent up until now. "And they paid you. Not much money, but they paid you while you learned."

"A lot of penny-pinching slave-drivers," says a fellow with a handlebar moustache.

Memories begin to surface of CNB employees who achieved subsequent fame. Stories about how Mike Royko used to rewrite other people's copy, when he was the bureau's midnight desk man, just to make them mad; about what Charles MacArthur said he did with his pencil when he was confronted by a stickup man with a large pistol; about how Claes Oldenburg was terrified that he was going to get chewed out because he had to push the editor's frozen car by hand for more than two blocks before he could get it started, and how the same Oldenburg, the son of the Consul-General of Sweden, was able to get into the exclusive Swedish Club on the north side, something no other reporter had been able to do, to get information on a crazed gunman who was running amok in the building... Someone mentioned the rumor that Yellow Kid Weil, the famous con man, had been fired from the bureau for falsifying his expense account by thirty-seven cents.

The City News Bureau was originally called City Press. It is over one hundred years old, and for the first sixty years it was desperately hard up for money. There is a story that Walter Brown, who managed the Bureau in the 1920's, once spent half an hour with a newly hired reporter explaining that it was possible to cover all six police stations on the northwest side for a single seven-cent streetcar fare, if transfers were used judiciously. It was often said that a City News reporter who spent a nickel for a telephone call in the course of his duties could hope to get the nickel refunded only if he could draw a convincing picture of the buffalo on the reverse side of the coin.

But interwoven with complaints about the bureau's unreasonable demands are comments that a month after Gershman (or Mulay or Brown) was ready to fire someone for missing a triple murder in Hegewisch, he lined that same reporter up for a good job with Associated Press. A certain pride is taken too in the fact that CNB is the oldest news service still operating.

That there are contradictions in the reminiscences of ex-staffers is not surprising: the very existence of the bureau as a cooperative enterprise in a fiercely competitive field is in itself a contradiction. The Chicago dailies, as well as the wire services, the electronic media and the news magazines use

CNB to cover the same news sources that their own staffs cover. Thus, naturally, competition is lop-sided. In the unending struggle for news sources—both the pride and the bane of the communication trade—the bureau is more often the loser than the winner, since City News reporters are handicapped in many ways. If one of them unearths a promising lead he is under orders to telephone it at once to his office for instant transmittal to other media, which at once put *their* reporters to work on the story, often in considerable numbers. Everything else the CNB reporter finds is sent immediately to aid the other reporters who are working against him. Thus the CNB reporter is certain to be scooped on his or her own story, the one he or she had dug up in the first place. If you work on a newspaper, of course the treatment is entirely different. A reporter's story is kept quiet until it is pursued to its end; then it is printed. City News people, however, are obliged to assist the staffs who are busily at work cutting the bureau's own collective throat.

The CNB reporter's complete anonymity frequently rankles, but that is the frustrating nature of the job. There are other, worse, disadvantages. Usually these reporters are very young and completely inexperienced; they are, in fact, trainees. They have built no contacts among police, prosecuting attorneys, judges and deputy coroners with whom much local news originates, while opposing numbers on the newspapers enjoy many such contacts. Public servants have a healthy respect for the power of the press to build or denigrate them in stories and articles; naturally they favor representatives of that press over employees of the bureau.

Nevertheless there are heartening occasions when the youth and inexperience of these hapless recruits works to their advantage. The kindly impulse to call in the City News kid and let him in on something has saved many a bureau worker from being disastrously scooped.

AUTHOR'S NOTE

Because the City News Bureau has always been preoccupied with keeping up with the events of the past few hours, it has never paused to draw breath and record the story of its origins, its growth, its troubles and its triumphs. However a young City News editor, Tom Vickerman, was able to rescue a good deal of information about CNB's formative years from oblivion.

In 1937 when he was working on his thesis for the MA in English, Vickerman began a correspondence with Archibald Leckie, who had come to the bureau from the Chicago *News* as a star reporter, and who was eventually to inherit the bureau himself. Leckie had left the bureau years before and bought an interest in a newspaper in Rockford, Illinois. He sent his reminiscences to Vickerman, who included them in his thesis, which was unfortunately never submitted for the degree, because of the intervention of World War II.

When he returned to civilian life to work for the *Chicago Daily News* Vickerman carefully preserved his thesis, and much of it appears in this book.

The author also wishes to thank Edward Eulenberg and Walter Spirko and Larry Mulay for making available to him materials from the files of the City News Bureau and the Chicago Newspaper Reporters Association for use in this book.

PUBLISHER'S NOTE

We have chosen to edit this book in conformity with the style recommended in the City Press Association's own "Reporter's Note-Book": that is, generic nouns are not capitalized. This is somewhat archaic usage, but we thought it fitting in this case.

We wish to thank a good many people who have gone out of their way to help us with this project. First of all, Shirley Haas has read and proof-read the manuscript, catching errors, and has provided some photographs from the files of the Chicago Public Library. Second of all, Walter Ryberg came up to our office and shared his memories with us; his help was invaluable. Equally valuable has been the help offered by Alan Mueller, who has sent photocopies and made many suggestions. The doors of the City News Bureau have been opened to us, and we have had long conversations with retired General Manager James D. Peneff and General Manager Bernie Judge. City Editor Paul Zimbrakos has been good enough to come to our offices and answer endless questions and offer original material to us including photographs. We have had long conversations on the telephone with Edward Eulenberg, Larry Mulay, Marjorie Kriz, Walter Spirko and Gladys Wherity, for decades the " Ruby Ryan" of the City News switchboard. News Editor Ron Berquist kindly offered us many photographs, as did Gera-Lind Kolarik. Thanks are also due to Ellen Warren of the *Chicago Sun-Times* Washington bureau and ex-*Daily News* man Bob Gruenberg. In addition, we should like to thank the people who wrote to us with anecdotes and information, much of which is incorporated in this book. We are both touched and grateful by this outpouring of good will, and we hope this book lives up to the generosity of these people who made it possible.

1

Sutor's Bureau

The story of the City News Bureau of Chicago begins
somewhat inauspiciously in 1881, when a dapper, genial,
yellow-bearded man named John Sutor opened a modest
agency in a half-basement on Washington and LaSalle
streets. These premises had only recently been vacated by
the Atlantic and Pacific Telegraph company, and it is an
indication either of the casualness of Sutor's enterprise or the
lack of faith in it by the management of the building, or both,
that no one bothered during Sutor's tenancy to remove the
name of the telegraph company from the windows, or to add
any other name.

Sutor's intention was to supply the daily newspapers of
Chicago with chatty items of social interest gathered ran-
domly in the city and suburbs by reporters and free-lancers.
Sutor did not originate this idea: it had started during the
Civil War in many cities, where small newspaper staffs could
not cover all the local news themselves. These social notes
from all over were important to the city's newspapers: if a
paper failed to report a social gathering in a suburb, that
paper could lose prestige and, worse, subscribers. But it was
expensive for the papers to keep a finger on the sometimes
faint social pulse: Sutor offered a service that would lower
costs for them.

The journalistic practice of the day was to print these

items, called "personals", interspersed with fashion notes, clever sayings, funny stories and advertisements, in one column:

Wednesday evening a very novel entertainment was enjoyed by guests of the Woodruff hotel. The affair was a soap bubble party, a prize being awarded the individual who blew the largest bubble.

The good people, young and old, of the Leavitt Street Congregational church held an apron sociable Friday evening.

The Ottoman sofa-bed is both ornamental and useful and is sold only by J.A. Colby and Co., 216 and 219 South State street.

A very encouraging meeting of the Village Improvement Society was held Monday evening. There was a good attendance and a good deal of profitable discussion.

A cynical man says his wife is only half like a telescope; he can draw her out but he can't shut her up.

Dr. and Mrs. W.H. Phelps, née Lincoln, have returned from the south and will be glad to see their friends on Thursdays during April at No. 8 Oakwood boulevard.

Silver mounted ebony prayer books are the proper thing for this Lent, and they dangle from the belts of fair worshippers as they go to church at the end of silver chains. Elegance is thus carried into religion.

The citizens of Evanston will learn with regret that Dr. N.S. Davis and family have taken up residence in Chicago.

The recent storms have torn away the greater part of

the old Davis Street pier. The structure has long been considered unsafe by many people and its disappearance will be a relief.

The newspaper scene in Chicago in the eighties was a spirited one. Victor Lawson and Melville Stone had created a lively little contender in their *Daily News*: the *News*, for instance, had introduced the innovation of a front page devoted to news. The older papers still carried only advertisements on the front page; for, as an example, bargains in "Ladies kid gloves with 3, 5, 7 or 10 hooks", or a medicine which would cure "syphilis, catarrh, rheumatism, cold sores and eczema." The page makeup on the news pages of the papers was dull: print was small and crowded, and there were no illustrations. The daily news was segregated under general headings: Marine News, Railroads, Courts, Council, Congress. More sensational items carried headlines: "Extraordinary Robbery"... "Fearful Train Crash"... "A Pitiful Tale."

Behind this rather dull exterior, however, beat tumultuous emotions. There was sometimes violent competition, and the use of strong language. The *Tribune*, for instance, once demanded in a headline that something be done about Wilbur Storey, the unpredictable publisher of the Chicago *Times*:

Quite, Quite Mad
Mr. Storey Following in
Footsteps of Ophelia
Let Him Be Confined
Dying at Top

John Sutor, who was capable but easy-going, was not really up to the hectic pace of the city's newspapers. His agency was under-capitalized from the start; he had too few reporters, and, since it was the custom of reporters to float from paper to paper in a city anyway, his low salaries did not help him to keep good men. Charles Dennis, for instance, who was to become editor of the *Daily News* and the biographer of Victor Lawson, came to work for Sutor in the summer of 1881 when he was graduated from the University of Illinois. Dennis lasted at the bureau for three weeks before he pushed off for greener fields.

Sutor sought with his abbreviated staff to cover the whole city and all the suburbs; his reporters were not assigned fixed territories but floated around. He tried to eke out his news by buying items from free lancers—among them Clarence Dresser, who sold the *News* the famous interview with William Vanderbilt, in which the latter exclaimed, "The public be damned!" But Sutor was constantly being scooped, and the handwriting was on the wall. The papers would not pay a bureau to provide news that they were finding for themselves.

In 1888 Sutor decided that seven years of striving were enough. He sold his bureau to George Wright and John Russell, two of his reporters, and left both Chicago and the newspaper business for good.

2

Wright and Russell

Wright and Russell christened their bureau the Chicago
City Press Association and moved it to quarters in the rear of
the second floor at 162 West Washington street, diagonally
across from the new building of the prestigious *InterOcean*.
They took the business somewhat more seriously than Sutor
had; they were more business-like men, aware of the great
advances which were changing newspaper coverage methods.
There was electricity, and there was the telephone. Archie
Leckie, the reporter who was to inherit part of the bureau,
reminisced in the thirties about the methods of lighting in
the 1880's when he came to work for Wright and Russell:

> In the late eighties the electric light came to be more
> than an experiment. Gas was the general illuminant.
> Along the streets were lamp posts eight feet high, each
> carrying a single burner, protected from the wind and
> weather by four panes of glass held in a metal frame.
> The posts in the better districts were of iron. In some
> sections they were still the cedar posts brought over
> from the Michigan woods. They, like the iron pillars,
> were painted green. They were not ornamental, but
> were a boon to dogs and drunkards.
> Just before sunset a man with a torch on the end of a

stick, the flame protected from the wind by a tin can, topless and with holes on the sides, would trot down a street, zigzagging from side to side. He would poke his torch into the lamp, tripping the valve and igniting the flame with one movement. Sometime in the early morning hours, he would be around again, turning off the lights.

There were many attempts to dispense with the lamplighter. One was to ignite the gas with spongy platinum, all lamps on the circuit being controlled from a central point. There were other schemes, but none of them lasted. In the first place the lamplighter or someone else had to keep the glass reasonably clean. Then too, the small boy, curious to see what made it work, had much to do for conservatism.

When the electric lights were strung in the office, usually on pliable wires and held to desired points by a string attached to a tack in the wall, they were an improvement over the flaring gas jets. Still, Wright and Russell had much the best of it with a kerosene student's lamp on their desk. Then the gas people introduced the Wellsbach light in which the gas heated an asbestos fabric to incandescence, producing a hideously greenish but brilliant illumination. It was some time before the electric globe caught up. The little back office at 162 Washington street was the best lighted newsroom in Chicago...

Wright and Russell assigned fixed territories in the suburbs to the reporters, making each man responsible for all the news in his territory. Once or twice a day the suburban men sent in their news by train, giving the copy to a brakeman or a "news butcher"—young vendors who hawked newspapers, magazines, sandwiches and oranges on the trains. A messenger boy would meet the trains, pick up the copy and take it to the office. Occasionally stories were sent by telegraph, but this method was reserved for only the most important stories.

The telephone was coming into use, but it was not easy to place calls to the city from the suburbs. This was long distance, and connections with the Bell system had to be made through independent systems. The considerable amount of noise on the line caused misunderstandings, and consequent errors in the copy.

Apart from long distance there were difficulties on the city lines, but nevertheless the telephone was proving, in the eighties, to be most useful to newspapermen. Service at that time was completely informal: most of the desk men and reporters knew the operators by name, and relied on them to supply all sorts of information. It was the first duty of the afternoon city editor, when he came to work at 7:30 in the morning, to call "Central" and see if she had any news. Leckie recorded a typical early morning conversation:

> Editor: Hello, Annie, where have you been so long?
>
> Operator: My sister was sick over at St. Louis. I was with her.
>
> Editor: Hope she's better; glad you're back. Where is Ed Insley, do you know?
>
> Operator: He was at the Grove [Cottage Grove avenue police station] half an hour ago.
>
> Editor: Try and get him for me, will you?
>
> Operator: All right, Mr. Wilkie.

Annie finds Insley, who comes on the line, while Annie stands by in case of difficulties with transmission.

> Editor: I want you to go over and see Phil Armour... Armour, I said... A-R-M-O-U-R... Hell, no. Tell him, Annie, will you?
>
> Operator: All right, Mr. Wilkie.

A consultation with Insley, and then Annie returns.

> Operator: He says Mr. Armour is always in bed at eight o'clock.

> Editor: Does he think I don't know that? Tell him to get him up and say Old Hutch charges him with starting a corn corner. Have him get a statement from Armour.
>
> Operator: [very faint] Don't be a fool, Ed. [Louder] All right, Mr. Wilkie, he's going right over.

All this was part of the day's work for Annie. She probably knew John Wilkie and Ed Insley only through their voices on the telephone.

Annie's only reward was a box of candy or two from some of the newspapers at Christmas. But she not only helped to locate reporters, gave messages and translated murky conversations. She was able, in the course of her day or night, to pick up important news tips. Once the *Daily News* scored a notable scoop on the Chatsworth railroad wreck because of a conversation between an editor and "Central". After a while these kinds of leaks brought a ban on personal service from operators. By that time, of course, the service had improved and interpreters were no longer needed. But the early telephone girls had served an important purpose.

Wright and Russell worked hard, and soon brought their bureau to a standard of efficiency that the newspaper editors could not help but notice. They were relieved to be able to turn over routine news to City Press. This included listings of new suits filed in the courts, and marriage licenses issued and other minor information. Wright and Russell were anxious to provide more interesting news, and the time was growing ripe for them to do it.

There were six morning newspapers in Chicago in the late eighties: the *Herald*, the *InterOcean*, the *Times*, the *Tribune*, the *Morning News* and the *Globe*. Each paper kept from two to four police reporters on duty from ten p.m. to four a.m. These men scouted the city's police stations for exclusive stories breaking, as police stories usually did, at night or in the wee hours of the morning. Each paper's reporters were sharply in competition with all the others.

Or so the editors and publishers saw it. The reporters

themselves worked out a somewhat different arrangement. Certainly every reporter wanted a scoop. That was what he was there for: to beat out the other papers. If he did that, he was congratulated sincerely by his bosses, and sometimes even given a raise in pay. On the other hand, if he were scooped he could quite often, in those days, lose his job. Nevertheless, as the reporters sat around playing poker on Monday nights in the reporters' room in City Hall, they came to agree that the loss of an occasional scoop was not worth the risk of getting fired for missing other people's scoops. The poker games came to be played every night, and every night two or three men took turns prowling the city's police stations. They returned to share their news with the others. This arrangement created pleasant social evenings, and relieved the reporters of tension and stress. Nobody scooped anybody on police news.

After awhile, as was inevitable, the city editors became aware of these "love feasts". Most of them had been police reporters themselves once, and they kept aware. They cracked down heavily on their men and saw to it that the scooping resumed. But as soon as the heat lessened, the poker game would resume. Finally the editors had to confess that they could not beat human nature.

They decided that as long as they were not going to get scoops anyway they might as well get their police information through City Press and save money. At the same time they could slap back at their recalcitrant reporters. As long as they were at it, they made arrangements for City Press to cover not only police stations, but other city departments as well.

Now Wright and Russell could expand their staffs; this was the sort of arrangement they had been waiting for. They wanted the best reporters they could get for the bureau; theirs was not to be the training ground for cubs that it became under their successors. They hired Joseph Watson away from the telegraph desk at the *News* for general assignments, and Edward Emery from the *Times* to take over civil courts. Edward Barnard, one of the best police reporters in the city, covered Central and south side police stations for the bureau; Archie Leckie came from the *News* to cover criminal court, and Harry L. Sayler, who had arrived in Chicago from Indianapolis only a few weeks before, was assigned to City Hall.

Other able reporters were easily hired, because Wright and Russell were paying salaries higher than those the newspapers were paying. City Press thus had a strong, experienced staff. The editors had been afraid that the absence of competition would make the bureau men slack, but this was not of course the case.

The fact was that there was no absence of competition. The newspapers were really not content to let the bureau do all the work for them: they were constantly sending men into the city departments, where City Press was hired to do the work, in order to dig up exclusive stories. Sometimes editors of newspapermen had special tips; sometimes the editors wanted to see what was going on, and sometimes the newspapermen on their own initiative tried to scoop the bureau. When a paper succeeded the bureau heard about it quickly from the other, scooped, papers. Consequently the bureau men had to stay on their toes, as Archie Leckie put it:

> Scoops in the departments became rare. The bureau men were all competent newsgatherers, and, being on the job all the time and every day, became so thoroughly acquainted with the officials and clerks, the record books and filing systems, that it was matter of minutes to find information on the search for which an outside reporter might have to spend the entire day. Indeed, it was impossible for the outsider in the courthouse, for instance, to get what he was after without soliciting aid from the clerks and these were sure to inform their friend, the bureau man.

The news had never been so promptly and thoroughly gathered. The partners were making good money from the bureau. But in 1889 a cloud appeared on their horizon; it would not be fair to say that it was no bigger than a man's hand. It was a considerable cloud, and it began to darken the landscape around City Press.

Victor Lawson, ever active and seeking for improvements, had long felt that the city's newspapers should band together and form their own news-producing bureau, to ease the strain of salaries, the tension of constant scoop-seeking, and, undoubtedly, to cut down on the costs of Wright and Russell's expensive seasoned newsmen. It was difficult to make the strong, suspicious individualists that ran the Chicago newspapers agree together. But on September 26, 1889, Lawson did get five newspaper publishers to come to a meeting in William Penn Nixon's office at the *InterOcean*. It was a preliminary discussion. Lawson, who had bought into Melville Stone's *News* in July of 1876 and through perserverance and excellent administration brought that ailing little sheet into a condition of health and prosperity, had earned the respect of his peers. He was not only interested in forming a local news bureau, but was considering the foundation of an Associated Press; in a few years he did actually create the Associated Press of Illinois, by resolving disputes between the Western Associated Press and the New York Associated Press. He saw a local and a national bureau working in tandem, and this was eventually what he did achieve.

At the 1889 meeting, Nixon was chairman and Lawson acted as secretary. Present were Dunlop, Hesing of the *Staats Zeitung*, and Sullivan of the *Journal*. Lawson's motion was adopted unanimously: that eight papers, and no others, be invited to join the new association. The papers were the *Tribune*, the *Times*, the *InterOcean*, the *Morning News*, the *Herald*, the *Journal*, the *Staats Zeitung* and the *Evening News*. Lawson presented a draft of the Articles of Association for the proposed bureau. These were not of course accepted as they stood. It was agreed that Lawson would rewrite them, adopting various suggested modifications, and the publishers would meet again.

The next meeting took place on April 8, 1890, over six months later. The publishers came together again. There was still a lot of skirmishing; these men were intensely afraid of one another. More argument and changing of Articles ensued. Finally, on June 19, 1890, eight publishers of ten Chicago newspapers signed stock subscriptions. The new bureau was called the City Press Association of Chicago, a name uncomfortably similar to Wright and Russell's Chicago City Press Association. Obviously, Lawson did not expect any confusion between the two bureaus to be very long-lasting. In addition to the eight papers represented at the 1889 meeting, subscriptions were taken by the *Post* and the *Mail*, both evening papers. The *Post* had been founded that year by John Walsh, a noted local banker, and his aide James W. Scott.

On July 1, 1890 the publishers announced formally the formation of their bureau and notified the partners that their services would no longer be required by the newspapers which had come together in the new agency.

This was, of course, a death knell for the Wright and Russell bureau. The publishers further announced that any men who wished to leave the old bureau would be actively considered for the payroll of the new one.

Russell had no stomach for a fight. His health was not good, and he sold his interest in the bureau to Sayler. So for a short time Sayler and Wright were partners. But the bureau could not make money with most of its subscribers drained off, and Wright clearly saw the handwriting on the wall. Archie Leckie was not afraid of the publishers, and he and Sayler were friends. Leckie was willing to take over, so Wright was glad to sell out to him and follow his ex-partner in leaving what was now only the shell of their prosperous bureau.

Between them Sayler and Leckie paid about six thousand dollars for the business, which consisted of a dilapidated desk, four old kitchen tables, a few wooden chairs, two typewriters, a stock of "flimsy" paper on which reporters in those days wrote their own stories, and some carbon paper. No one could call it a promising investment.

3

The New Bureau

Among the agreements reached by the newspaper publishers when they banded together to create their new
bureau, was one signed on August 13, 1890, which read:

> The undersigned publishers of Chicago morning
> newspapers agree with one another that they will
> depend upon the City Press Association for night police
> news and each agrees that he will not permit anyone
> representing his paper to be put on night police work
> except as may be agreed with all those signing this
> paper. This will not be binding on anyone signing it
> unless signed by the publishers of all morning papers
> that are members of the City Press Association.

The agreement was duly signed by representatives of *The
InterOcean*, the *Herald*, the *Morning News*, the *Tribune*, the
Staats Zeitung, and the *Times*. The idea, of course, was to
stop expanding staffs and wild scoops which often involved
blowing a minor story up out of proportion because it was an
exclusive.

John Ballantyne, the managing editor of the *News*, was
appointed manager of the new bureau, which took large
quarters in the Western Union building at 110 S. LaSalle

13

street, adjoining the Western Associated Press office. Lawson intended that the City Press should sit side-by-side with the Associated Press, the one to cover local, and the other to cover national, news.

The new enterprise, with its supporting subscribers, began to thrive at once. Ballantyne started off with twenty-five men, but by September 30, 1890, not even four months after its foundation, City Press had thirty employees on the payroll, which added up to a weekly salary toll of $516, including the manager's salary of fifty dollars a week.

One problem that began almost immediately was the violation of the agreement by morning newspapers not to compete with the bureau in night police work. City Press had commenced to cover night police work on August 19, six days after the agreement was signed, and Ballantyne noted that the *Herald*, alone among the papers, seemed to be making no attempt to live up to the agreement. They had two to three men assigned to night police work, and the first night they did their work openly. Ballantyne reported this breach to Lawson, and after that the *Herald* men made an unsuccessful attempt to camouflage their work. Ballantyne reported the situation to Scott, and the *Herald* men lay low for two or three nights, doing most of their work by telephone. But then they came boldly forth once more, and Ballantyne reported to Lawson that there had been an attempt by a *Herald* man to bribe a City Press police reporter to furnish the *Herald* exclusively with any important police news he unearthed.

This charge of dastardly behavior was mitigated somewhat several days later when Ballantyne discovered that the *Herald* man had not requested exclusive news, but had asked the City press man to keep quiet about the fact that the *Herald* was engaged in night police work. "It was nevertheless," Ballantyne said primly, "an attempt to bribe." The possible reason for all this underhanded work may have lain in Ballantyne's mournful admission that "the night police work of the City Press Association has not been thoroughly satisfactory either to the papers or to me..."

This low standard was obviously not Ballantyne's fault.

The publishers had dropped Wright and Russell's practice of hiring the best men they could find at wages higher than the newspapers paid. They were actively seeking to cut costs, and they had an ambivalent attitude toward City Press that was to continue throughout its life: they resented to some extent the association's encroachment upon their own staff. Ballantyne could not go into what he called "the open market" for his staff, but was compelled to select the best men he could find "from the unemployed who drift into the city" or from those men whom the newspapers chose to drop. Since the newspapers as a rule did not drop their best men, Ballantyne felt he was handicapped in trying to perform his best work. Many of the men he hired were cubs, new to newspaper work, and many were new to the city itself, which caused delays in coverage.

"I think this association should be placed on a footing with the Associated Press," Ballantyne wrote to Victor Lawson, "and be permitted to engage any man whose service seems desirable, provided he is willing to accept the assignment."

Needless to say, this request was futile. Ballantyne had better luck with another request, which was to acquire free passes for reporters from the local railway and street car companies. It had been his intention, Ballantyne said, when the association was organized, to handle suburban work through the men on his city staff:

> I thought that by 'planting' them around in the various suburbs they would be in a position to gather important suburban news stories in the morning before coming to the office and in the evening after their city work was done.

He was forced however to reconsider this plan.

> My city men have to report in the morning between 8 and 8:30 and do not finish their work until 6 in the evening, and frequently later. Before 8 a.m. it would be possible for them to collect very little news; during the

day the suburbs would be entirely uncovered; in the evening they could devote very little time to the work without robbing themselves of necessary sleep...

Because of these considerations, which were only marginally humanitarian, Ballantyne had to hire reporters who were stationed in the suburbs. He began with the north suburbs as an experiment and found that the reporter averaged three columns of news a week, some of it very worthwhile news. But the expense for street car and railroad fare was $6.51 in that week—too heavy to be borne. It is interesting to note that Wright and Russell had, in addition to hiring seasoned reporters at good wages, paid the travelling expenses for suburban men out of the bureau, and had still done well financially.

In any case the Chicago City Railway co. agreed to allow the bureau 600 rides per quarter, which Ballantyne estimated was "equivalent to car fare for one police reporter." The Chicago West Division Railway company, and the North Chicago Railway company, both owned by Charles Yerkes, allowed transportation for eight reporters, two more "if necessary." Ballantyne made agreements with the Illinois Central, Milwaukee and St. Paul, Grand Trunk and Rock Island railroads, and a limited agreement with the Burlington line. The Pittsburgh and Fort Wayne, Eastern Illinois and the Northwestern railroads refused to allow free transportation "except upon a definite advertising contract." Ballantyne suggested that the newspapers divide expenses on the Northwestern among themselves, because the "drain" for three reporters riding the Northwestern line was very great.

Ballantyne appears to have been an excellent manager, conscientious perhaps to a fault. He was willing to admit mistakes, and did not try to cover them up, although he was quick to defend his reporters if he thought they had been unfairly accused of sloppy work. On December 24, 1890, when the association had been in business for barely six months, Ballantyne did not allow Christmas festivities to keep him from writing a long letter responding to a list of complaints from the newspapers:

The complaint of Mr. Dennis, regarding our report of the assets and liabilities of S.A. Kean & co. was well-founded. Our reporter, as well as the reporters for the *Tribune, Herald* and the old City Press Ass'n [Wright & Russell] made the mistake of entering only the equity in one million dollars of hypothecated bonds in the assets, and placing the entire debt of one million dollars in the liabilities...all the reporters [were misled] except Mr. Rhodes, of the *Daily News*.

I do not understand Mr. Dennis's statement that there is nothing in our report of a crusade by the Citizen's League against the downtown saloon keepers. Proceedings were begun before Justice Wallace...against Potter Palmer, J.B. Drake...and warrants have been issued for a number of others. I have not personally examined the records...but my police reporter assures me that such is the fact and gives Justice Wallace, his clerk and Mr. Albertson (of the Citizen's League) as his authority.

The report of the Baptist ministers' meeting was undoubtedly inadequate. The Baptists do not admit reporters to their meetings... Last Monday the secretary was unable to give our reporter any information... Heretofore he has frequently contrived to secure the manuscript of the paper forming the basis of the discussion, but in this case it was secured by the reporter of the *Daily News*. The secretary has promised to use his influence with the ministers to allow our reporter to be present at their meetings... If he succeeds in this, we will be able to give better reports.

Although you have made no complaint of the report of the Congregational ministers it was just as inadequate as that of the Baptist ministers and for precisely the same reason...

We do not, and never have reported meetings of the Park Boards except a few, relating to the World's Fair.

Liaison between the publishers and Ballantyne was good, and everyone was determined to maintain a professional, hard-working agency as cheaply as possible. Ballantyne's reference to the "old City Press Association" shows clearly that no one expected the older bureau to survive, as the virtual appropriation of their name had already attested. And the old bureau was in the throes of a mighty struggle.

4

The Sayler and Leckie Bureau

When Sayler and Leckie took over Wright and Russell's bureau, they pooled their resources, offered one-sixteenth interest in their company to those three capable reporters who had chosen to stay with them rather than go to the publisher's association and hired a few cubs. Both men were in their twenties, and filled with optimism. They cut their own salaries to $14 a week apiece in order to be able to pay the reporters more money. And since they were both young they did not hesitate to cover beats in addition to doing desk work: Leckie took the court beat and Sayler took City Hall.

They worked eighteen hours a day, but they still could not handle the mass of routine news that the bureau was responsible for: the lists of new court suits and marriage licenses. Consequently they trained boys to take care of some of these things, so that the rest of the staff, experienced reporters as most of them were, could concentrate on the fight for exclusive stories for their shrunken clientele.

The *Times* had deteriorated after the death of Wilbur Storey and had been taken over by former mayor Carter Harrison, who had been severely criticized by the city's moneyed citizens for his failure to take stern action against the anarchists. He wanted to use the *Times* to answer his critics. He did succeed in being reelected in 1893, so that he could run the

19

city during the Columbian Exposition, but the publishers association wanted no part of him. They did not consider him a legitimate publisher, so the *Times* came to Sayler and Leckie at a slightly higher assessment than the publishers levied. The *Globe*, reputedly owned by a gambler named Mike McDonald, also remained with the bureau despite the higher assessment, and the partners kept the *Abendpost*. After a short while the *Staats Zeitung* deserted Ballantyne and returned to the partners.

This was hardly an impressive roster of subscribers, but the two young men persisted. They had covered city departments for a long time, and had made many friends. One day a court clerk whispered to Leckie that a sensational bill for receivership had been under discussion with a judge, and would be filed the next morning. Ordinarily such information was not privileged, but through a lucky coincidence— lucky for Leckie, that is—a routine assumpsit suit for $500. had been filed that day against the same company.

With the assumpsit suit as the basis for a projected three-column story, Leckie dropped in on Herman Reiwitch, city editor of the *Herald*, and told him that he had "a whale of a scoop." He offered to sell it exclusively to the *Herald*, which could then scoop the *Tribune* and the *InterOcean*. It was just the kind of story that the *Tribune* liked. Reiwitch protested feebly that the *Herald*, along with the other publishers, had made an agreement not to patronize Leckie's bureau. But he could not hold out against the temptation, and he finally bought the story for fifty dollars.

When the *Herald* and the *Times* appeared with the story Ballantyne's line was flooded with calls of complaint. There was of course nothing he could do about it. This was part of Leckie's strategy, apart from the much-needed money.

Leckie recalls another incident:

> The suicide of a lumber tycoon, resulting next day in a crash in the lumber trade, was through influence kept off the coroner's blotter until the following morning. A deputy sheriff notified Sayler and there was another

first page spread, this time to the *Tribune* and *Times*, while the other editors tore their hair. And so it went. The *Morning News* alone got the worst of it every time, for Mr. Lawson would not have permitted his men to violate their agreement. But this, too, was useful in the end.

Public officials knew about the competition, and they could not help rooting for the underdog. When things had been pretty well stirred up by a series of different scoops, alternating between all the papers except Lawson's, Leckie began to call on the publishers once or twice a week. Although they were cool to him at first, eventually most of them became friendly. One of these was James W. Scott of the *Herald*, a kindly man who sympathized with the young partners. R.W. Patterson of the *Tribune* was also won over.

"There is no sense in all this, Leckie," he said one day. "Why don't you give it up? We'll give you a good job."

"We can't just give it up, Mr. Patterson," Leckie said. "Every dollar we have is in that business and we must keep going."

That angle had not occurred before to Patterson, Leckie says, and the thing appealed to his sense of sportsmanship.

Of all the publishers, the most difficult for Leckie to deal with was William Penn Nixon of the *InterOcean*. While he was tolerant enough in his day-to-day associations, Nixon was strongly opposed to anything that could cause dissension, and he believed that "unconditional surrender" on the part of the two reporters was the only answer to the conflict between the two bureaus. James Scott tried his best to defend the partners at the publishers' meetings which were held in the Union League Club, but more than once he told Sayler and Leckie that he did not believe it was going to be possible to change Nixon's mind.

Christmas of 1890 was not a very happy time for the two men. They were tired and discouraged. Every Christmas it had been the custom of the bureau to put together a page of stories of the season—Christmas at orphan homes, hospitals and similar heart-tugging institutions. Leckie describes the stories as "all rot of course, sob stuff about the old tramp in jail who hadn't tasted turkey for ten years when he last ate dinner with his dear old mother, and the little crippled Bobby who fondled the velocipede Santa had brought and said he would ride it next week while the sweet-faced nurse behind him sadly shook her head. But the papers always printed the page. And after all, the institution trustees were among the best people..."

This year the partners had no heart to collect poignant stories; they were feeling too sorry for themselves. They decided they would give the staff a well-deserved rare holiday and treat themselves to Christms dinner for a change. As they sat in their office, moodily planning their day, the door opened and the assistant editor of the *InterOcean* hastily entered.

"Say," he said, "are you fellows going to cover the hospitals tomorrow?"

Leckie did not blink. "Of course we are," he said. "Why?"

"Well, that damned bureau of ours isn't going to do it," the editor said, "and Harry Ballard sent me over to see if we could get it from you."

"Sure you can," Leckie said.

"How much do you want for it?"

"Oh," said Leckie, "let's say fifty."

"Hell no," the editor said. "Ballard said twenty-five. I'll take a chance and make it thirty."

Christmas dinner was forgotten and everyone buckled down to some hard work.

When the *InterOcean* and the *Times* printed the "old bureau's" Christmas contribution, Mr. Nixon heard a lot of complaining from the other publishers—complaining that went on for months. It was the turning point.

On April 24, 1891, Sayler and Leckie were summoned to the publisher's office in the *InterOcean* building. There, before the assembled publishers, William Penn Nixon threw in the towel, and Sayler and Leckie were appointed co-managers of the "new" City Press Association. They were in effect bought out, for three thousand dollars. As joint managers they were each given a weekly salary of $40, a considerable improvement over their earlier income.

The merger of the two bureaus firmed the name of the resultant organization into the City Press Association of Chicago, stopped confusion and put an end to wasteful competition. The best men on both staffs were retained, and John Ballantyne, possibly to his great relief, returned to his job at the *Daily News*. In lieu of proper notice he was given four weeks' salary—two hundred dollars.

5

Leckie's Reminiscences

At this point we must give a moment to Archibald Leckie's own memories which he sent to Tom Vickerman in the 1930's, of the Chicago of the eighties, and especially of the Chicago newspaper world of the eighties.

*   *   *   *   *

There was much truth in the assertion made by Easterners that Chicago was a provincial place. Indeed, the competent newspaperman of the eighties had to have a working knowledge of the city as it had existed a score of years before because development had been so rapid that many of the pioneers were still active in urban life. Joseph Medill was one, even more potent than in Civil War days. His old friend, "Long John" Wentworth, was still doing quite a bit of real estate business in the Summit and Lemont districts, where the drainage canal was to create a boom. John B. Drake, the nationally celebrated and genial host of the Tremont House built the magnificent Grand Pacific hotel at Clark and Jackson streets. It was opened the day the wonderful depot at the foot of LaSalle street was dedicated by the Lake Shore and Rock Island railroads, aided and abetted by the entire community. Joe Stockton, the industrious young man who drove a truck, hauling goods for the merchants, listed the Joseph

24

Stockton Transfer company, with its hundreds of trucks, on the stock exchange. Potter Palmer had turned his dry goods business over to his young partners, Marshall Field and Levi Z. Leiter. Mr Palmer thought there should be a Democratic hotel to offset Drake's Republican hostelry, and built the equally grand Palmer House, which was good business toward making Chicago a convention city.

Frank Parmalee had given up his seat on the box of his bus, long used in transporting commercial travellers between hotels and depots. He was now head of the Parmalee Transfer company. Philip D. Armour and Nelson Morris no longer spent all day at their packing houses, grown from small beginnings to mammoth institutions. H.H. Honoré [Bertha Palmer's father] had gone out of minor real estate transactions and was looking after his business property, such as the Honoré block in La Salle street. Superintendent of Schools Hanford had been shot and killed by Alexander Sullivan who was acquitted after a trial which had split the city into two factions along lines which were erased by the strenuous efforts of the wiser citizens. But Sullivan, a dour figure, and his wife, Margaret, were still active in city life.

The influence of the social life of a few years past was very strong: the sleigh races, at the first snowfall, and the "game dinners," perpetuated at the Grand Pacific from the old Tremont House days when hunters were sent up to the Skokie marsh and the Desplaines valley for wild fowl, rabbits and bear meat. To these functions were invited all Chicago's notables until about 1898, when the increased numbers of notables forced the discontinuance of the honored fete.

The annual Charity Ball was a great event. Bertha Honoré, afterward Mrs. Potter Palmer, beautiful, accomplished and gracious, reigned first as the acknowledged belle and then for many years as social leader and dictator.

There was a great social competition, each division of the city striving to establish superiority. Around Union Park and Ashland boulevard on the west side the Carpenters, Stones, Plamondons, Carter Harrison and other of their associates built fine homes, usually "marble fronts".

Prairie avenue and 22nd street was at first the center of south side activities. In this section dwelt George Pullman, Marshall Field, the Badgers, Van Schaacks, and Keans among others. Indiana avenue, with its single track horse car line and shade trees, became popular and led the social growth gradually out to 35th street and Grand boulevard, where editor Wilbur Storey of the *Times* built a marble palace.

The north side, severely hit by the fire, had a bad start in the new era, but the Ogdens, C.H. McCormick, Leander McCormick, the Stevensons, Potter Palmer and others who remained steadfast, lived to see it come into its own. Among these, C.H. McCormick was one of the greatest leaders in building a new Chicago after the fire of 1871. He erected the splendid McCormick, Reaper and Ashland blocks, the first buildings to have elevators, which were propelled by little steam engines built in Robert Crane's works in Clinton street. [The City News Bureau was quartered on the seventh floor of the Ashland block from 1917 to 1937.]

Mrs. Palmer and other social lights of her generation scorned the sneers of provincialism and just rode over them. There continued a remarkable loyalty to old customs. If there was a great public function, Joseph Stockton was always in charge of transportation arrangements. John B. Drake looked after entertainment. To H.M. Kinsley, who in the old days catered at social affairs, but had long since doffed his apron and had established an excellent and exclusive restaurant in Washington street, west of State, was relegated the task of arranging excellent banquets. Johnnie Hand, who had fiddled the Virginia Reel at most of the old time parties, found himself in charge of the great Charity Ball after the opening of the Auditorium at Wabash avenue and Congress streets. He too arranged the music for the balls and receptions attending the World's Fair functions and a prouder leader than he never waved a baton at a great stringed orchestra, alternating its dance numbers with the music of the Marine band. Mrs. Palmer overruled all objections that Johnnie was not capable or was getting too old.

It would be difficult to imagine a better qualified leader in any social circle than Bertha Honoré Palmer. A regal beauty even in her advancing years, she was an executive of the first order with great intelligence and the ability to get at the root of any controversy and settle it. In her relations with newspapermen she was brief but courteous, and quick to recognize the news and the proper occasion for giving or withholding it. She made enemies but never feared to do so and her friends were legion...

Whether the city limits had or had not been officially extended at that time, the practical limits of the city [in the 1880's] were circumscribed by 39th street, Western avenue, Fullerton avenue, and "Government pier", then half a mile or so east of Michigan avenue and forming a harbor for yachts and "bum boats".

Black Jack Yata was king of the bumboat folk and his barge was a center of battle, murder and sudden death.

Along the shore, or lakefront, Dirty Cavan, Clabby Burns and other notables of the day sought bucolic victims and sold them the Masonic temple or city hall.

Entirely beyond the practical city district lay the important suburbs of Hyde Park, the Town of Lake—which included Englewood and the Stockyards—Riverside, Austin, Oak Park, Jefferson, Rogers Park and Evanston.

Beyond these, but almost as distant as Detroit is today, lay such outlands as South Chicago, Blue Island, La Grange, Hinsdale, River Forest, Winnetka and Lake Forest. All were reached by fairly good train service but the schedules often failed to meet the needs of travellers.

It took just an hour to reach 39th street by horsecar. In emergencies the Herdic cabs were available, two-wheeled affairs with a folding apron over the laps of the passengers. and the driver overhead and behind in a dinky seat.

One night there was a destructive fire in the Stockyards and Joseph Medill, publisher of the *Tribune*, was dissatisfied with his paper's account. When Mr. Medill was dissatisfied others were made fully aware of it, and for long years thereafter the *Tribune* responded to a 4-11 alarm at the "yards" with four men in a cab. As almost every fire in the grease-impregnated packing houses was a potential disaster, a "4-11" was turned in at the slightest provocation. The *Tribune's* cab bill over the years must have been appalling. A few all-night cabbies were virtually supported by the news-papermen.

The great morning paper, when the *Daily News* was founded in 1876, was the *Times*, whose publisher, Wilbur F. Storey, had to recover from the setback of his "secesh" attitude during the Civil War. Since Storey carried a telegraphic service superior to that of any other paper in the West, and sent special correspondents to cover major events, his paper achieved many noteworthy beats.

But the *Tribune* was coming along and pressing hard on Storey's heels, and the *Times* reverted to "yellow journalism" years before the "Yellow Kid" was born. For a time it ran one-word top decks on its display heads, preferably verbs, but adjectives or nouns would do on occasion. The front page might bristle thus:

Damned	Hell	Horrid	Busted
Is Smith Bill	Breaks Loose	Mormon Rites	Grain Firm
in Congress	in Milwaukee	Scored	Goes Under

Storey did things that started talk about his mental condition, particularly the erection of a magnificent mansion in Grand boulevard for which it was considered he could have no use. The building proceeded slowly and there were years for the rumors to grow.

Then the *Times* grew still more sensational. A murderer on the scaffold in Cook County jail confessed his guilt and repentance and his confidence that Jesus was waiting to receive him. The *Times* headed its story "Jerked to Jesus." It climaxed a crusade for safer theatres with a graphic account of the burning of McVicker's theatre the previous evening, giving all details of a catastrophic theatre fire and ensuing panic, including a list of prominent persons who had perished or been injured. The last line of the story was: "What if all this had happened?"

This fabrication thoroughly shocked Chicago, and even Storey, with his fading faculties, must have realized he had gone too far. He became very ill and guidance of the paper passed to more discreet but less successful hands. Many readers were to remember the McVicker's story when on December 30, 1903, the Iroquois theatre fire took 596 lives.

The *Times* essentially was Storey and when he became incapacitated his splendid organization seemed to disintegrate and the brilliant staff appeared to wilt without the Chief. He died in 1884.

By the mid-1880's the *Times* had sadly fallen from its high estate. It was still published at the northwest corner of Washington street and Fifth avenue [now Wells street]. In Washington street, half a block west of LaSalle, was a modern building housing the *Herald* of John R. Walsh, the banker. The *InterOcean*, with William Penn Nixon at the helm, was at the northwest corner of Madison and Dearborn streets. Many considered it the leading morning paper. But the *Tribune*, diagonally across the street on the southeast corner, was coming on strong.

Half a block south of the *Tribune*, on Dearborn, was the *Journal*, a five-cent afternoon paper whose history went back to 1844. It had had a strong hold on home circulation in the days before street sales developed. The paper had only recently abandoned its pioneer Hoe press on which the type was locked on an enormous cylinder against which four men from two platforms on either side of the press fed the single sheets. That press had been a wonder of Chicago a few years before. The *Journal* never seemed to recover from the shock of stereotyping.

The *Mail* was on the west side of Fifth avenue, half a block south of the *Times*. For awhile it was the only real competitor of the *Daily News* since the *Journal* disdained to dismount from its five-cent high horse to notice Stone and Lawson's contemptible little penny sheet.

The *Mail* was a fine, decent paper with an excellent staff.

Stanley Waterloo was managing editor and politely declined my services when I was seeking my first newspaper job. He had a glass eye and, in a later period, after the third drink, would put his arms around my neck and weep with the good optic as he told me it was the regret of his life that he had not hired me. Of course, the only thing to do then was to buy him another libation. But he was a competent editor and for a time set the *News* a fast pace.

Next to the *Mail* was an equally shabby building occupied in succession by struggling newspapers, including the *Dispatch*, which was to become notorious under Joseph Dunlop. At one time Dunlop was city editor of the *Inter Ocean* and I can only imagine the circumstances of his leaving that eminently respectable and staid publication. He went to the *Times* and started crusades that always seemed to end abruptly. It didn't take much money in those days to start a newspaper, but Joe must have been thrifty to save the necessary capital to take over the *Dispatch*.

Each day the *Dispatch* appeared with little news but several scare heads, one at least being a scandalous yarn. Rumor had it that he got something on Marshall Field and did not hesitate to tell him how much advertising suppression would cost. Field, according to gossip, turned slowly in his swivel chair, faced Dunlop and replied, "Well, its publication will cost you your life. If you print a word of that I'll shoot you down like a dog."

That story, unprinted, was about Dunlop's last. He was indicted, convicted and sent to the "big house". His paper folded.

Believe it or not, the *Staats Zeitung* was once a tremendous power in the Chicago newspaper field. The city had a large German population, immigrants during the Civil War. Because of their military training they were of great value to the Northern forces and when President Grant began the distribution of political loaves and fishes they did not hesitate to seek their share. Their influence was strong enough to have German included in the curriculum of lower school grades. While they spoke English they did not read it well, so when A.C. Hesing started a really good newspaper in the German language it was an instant success.

After Hesing's death and the succession of his son Washington Hesing to the throne, times had changed. War gratitude had waned and the new generation of German-Americans preferred to use English. Factional views also encouraged William Michaelis to establish the rival *Freie Presse* and, later, Fritz Glogauer to launch the *Abendpost*. From this time I fear no German language newspaper enjoyed great prosperity.

In 1885 the *Staats Zeitung*, with considerable loss in circulation, was still published at the northeast corner of Washington and Fifth. The *Freie Presse* was just north of the *Times*. A Swedish language paper also circulated in Scandinavian parts of the city.

The *Staats Zeitung* was included in the clients of the publishers' association bureau but we had no difficulty in getting it to desert to us—at a price. I think Mr. Hesing's defection was a deep mystery to the publishers until the day they took over our bureau and we listed our contracts which we insisted must be carried to the end of the year. My statement that the "Staats" was paying $10 a week brought out a roar of laughter and the comment: "Wash couldn't resist that."*

The *Abendpost* also took our service at a very small price, as did a Swedish paper whose name I have forgotten.

Many newsmen would put the cradle of the modern newspaper in two equally shabby buildings between Washington and Madison streets, south of the alley on the east side of Fifth avenue, or Wells street. Each building was of 26-foot frontage, four stories high, and without elevators or other modern conveniences. Here in the mid-1880's was the home of the *Chicago Daily News*, grown since 1876 from a struggling one-cent sheet to independence, financially as well as editorially.

In the basement of the south building were two presses, each with a maximum capacity of 32 pages. The contrast

* Leckie and Sayler's agreement with the publishers stipulated that the *Staats-Zeitung* be serviced for twenty dollars a week until January 17, 1892.

with the mammoth machines of later years is not exactly what it seems, for then the papers were all handset and it was not possible to fill more than that number of pages. Irving Stone, cousin of Melville E. Stone, the editor, presided over the pressroom and was always in the forefront of advancements in newspaper mechanical devices.

On the first floor, somewhere in the rear of the business offices, Victor F. Lawson, the publisher, had his quarters. The newsmen did not know a great deal about Mr. Lawson. Many were there for years and never saw him. From his newspaper one would not know he existed. Yet no good movement in Chicago was without his powerful influence. He was a master of detail and organization.

Editor Melville Stone's office was on the second floor. The staff saw plenty of him when big stories were on. Sometimes he would accompany a reporter to the scene of a story and write the lead himself.

The newsroom was on the top floor. Those flights of stairs were terrifying to the casual visitor. It took technique to conquer them. You did not go up one at a time. You took a running jump at the third step, catching the balustrade at arm's length, then you pulled in as you reached the second-next step, and so swung up in no time at all.

The newsroom was possibly 125 feet long by 25 feet wide. Near the stairway was a kind of box for the afternoon city editor and one copyreader. Dividing the front of the room into spaces six feet wide by eight deep, were partitions which at one time separated in order Henry Ten Eyck White, managing editor of the afternoon paper, Ed Cowan, city editor of the morning sheet, Eugene Field, who retained possession of his cubicle against more or less serious opposition from Charles H. Dennis [later Victor Lawson's biographer], John Ballantyne and F.W. "Doc" Reilly, each of whom seemed to have a clouded title to the fourth cubicle.

Henry "Butch" White had been on the *Tribune* where he conducted a column known as "Lakeside Musings" and other good work. Coming to the *News* it seems he had some slight friction with Joseph Medill, the *Tribune* publisher. Thereafter it was White's delight to dig up some embarrassing controversial point in the *Tribune* and send a reporter to interview Mr. Medill on the subject. Not that he ever embarrassed Medill, for the old war horse could take care of himself. He was very deaf and at first inclined to be crabbed. On the reporter's second visit he became very gracious, welcoming subsequent calls and furnishing excellent copy, none to his disadvantage. There was no real enmity on White's part.

White was as nearly like a bulldog as humanly possible. He was gruff and surly in contacts with his men except on rare occasions after hours when he would surprise a reporter credited with good work by becoming delightfully companionable. "Friends are no good," he would say. "They only borrow your money." He was strict on the subject of free advertising. A lawyer's name must not be mentioned in a story except that of A.S. Trude, a leading criminal attorney. For him the *News* conducted a consistent "build-up" and in exchange secured many exclusive stories.

One day a big box was brought to White's office. It contained a typewriter, the first seen in a newsroom, and on this machine the editor pecked away with one finger until he became quite proficient.

Below the editorial room was a mysterious loft. The entrance was barred by a massive door, locked and bolted when not in use. But everyone knew that the "typesetting machine" was under experiment. Printers were close-mouthed and there were rumors of impending trouble. It never developed, and day-by-day the orders to send copy to the machine increased. Still it was a long time before the door was unlocked and the first Merganthaler was erected in the composing room.

In the art room Joe Sclanders produced illustrations on chalk plates with a staff attired like surgeons at an operation. A cub artist, John T. McCutcheon, turned out some daily sketches to embellish the produce market reports from South Water street. It didn't look like a promising field, but the pictures of potatoes crying their eyes out in shame at low prices or carrots dancing with glee on the upturn, caught the public fancy.

George Ade began turning out "Fables in Slang." Finley

Peter Dunne, then just plain Pete, produced Mr Dooley's first remarks on Fire Chief Sweeney...

From the time I came in contact with newspapers as a cub reporter, my observations took on a more vivid character. For the next few years I dealt with the rank and file of the folk who were merely cogs in the wheels. The "great" men who I glimpsed occasionally in the Press Club, were the managing or city editors I had unsuccessfully approached in seeking a reportorial job. These were: W.K. Sullivan, managing editor of the *Journal*, Fred Hall, famous city editor of the *Tribune*, Joseph Dunlop, city editor of the *InterOcean*, Stanley Waterloo of the *Mail*, and Ed Cowan, then city editor of the *Morning News*. H.T. White, managing editor of the evening *News*, was the one to acquire my services. He always claimed to be unlucky.

I have an impression of two generations of reporters when I was admitted to the circle in the reporters' room in the City Hall basement. While some of us frequented this center regularly in line with our plebian duties, everyone dropped in occasionally, even the city editors. Among the seniors, those who most awed me as men who had achieved fame, were the members of the *Times* staff such as Charles Diehl, whose exploits in the Sitting Bull Indian uprising were still comparatively fresh, Sam Steele, Guy Mainwaring, Jack Klein, who became my mentor and friend. Then there were: Billy Knox of the *Morning News*, Teddy McPhelim, the brilliant dramatic critic of the *Tribune*, John E. Wilkie, a star police reporter who became city editor of the *Tribune*, Frank Vanderlip, Charlie Chapin and Leo Canman, also of the *Tribune*. There were Florence Sullivan and the insufferable Frieberger, both of the *InterOcean*, the latter Chicago's only male society editor.

Jack Pratt and Edward Insley were in turn city editors of the *Tribune*; Harry Ballard took the city desk at the *InterOcean* when Dunlop went. I remember a long procession of talented youths, some of whom became famous, like Vanderlip, George Ade and Peter Dunne. Charlie Chapin's sad story ended after his years of service as the really great city editor of the *New York World*, in Sing Sing where he died: he had murdered his wife because he knew he was losing his grip and could not keep her in the luxury which his large salary had permitted.

Ballard went East and became managing editor in New York. Insley, Pratt and Klein went to San Francisco. Klein went on to Samoa and figured spectacularly in a native war which just escaped being a serious international incident.

John Wilkie, son of the noted Frank B. Wilkie of the old *Times* staff, left the *Tribune* to become chief of the United States secret service.

A principal rendezvous for newspaper editors and reporters when payday relieved the usual money stringency, was Billy Boyle's all-night restaurant in the alley from Clark to Dearborn streets, between Washington and Madison. There was many a joyous gathering "in the chophouse in the alley when the paper'd gone to press." Politicians, first-string gamblers and men-about-town generally were to be found there and many a story was told off the record in the wee small hours.

The night police reporters seemed to lead charmed lives. Only a few beginners carried weapons, yet they went constantly into the haunts of the Market street gang, into Little Hell and Goose island where it would be imagined a well-dressed stranger would be in serious danger. These haunts often were productive of good stories if discreetly written. There was Joe Hunt's saloon on Kinzie street where many confidences might be exchanged with some plug-ugly over a game of pedro. "Dapper Danny" Considine in his place in Market street, with a two-carat diamond glistening in his bosom, his oiled hair parted in the middle, always had a sparkling and friendly eye for a stranger. His other eye, less conciliatory, was on the nondescript gang in the backroom, entrance to which was reserved for the elect, except when a couple of policemen rudely broke the rules and emerged with a struggling and expostulating member of the gathering.

But best of all, to those who had entree, was old Tom Carney's place at Market and Illinois streets. There were no pretensions here. The very sawdust on the floor was dirty, the air reeked with the odor of stale beer. The whole interior was dim, as light could not penetrate the dirty windows. Tom Carney, with bleary eyes that seemingly could see very little, saw everything as he sat with a dirty pack of cards playing "farty foives" with some disreputable old neighbor. "Big Andy" Garvey stood behind the bar with a gun on a handy shelf at his right hand and a bung starter in similar position at his left. But Andy was a suave, if sardonic and discriminating extender of credit, as became an employee of Tom Carney.

One night a reporter [Leckie himself] was held up in Market street. He told Tom Carney and mentioned his loss of $3.50 and a watch. Carney was sympathetic but critical of one who would hold out such temptation to the "byes". A couple of days later Tom motioned the reporter to the most remote corner of the saloon and slipped into his hand the missing watch and $2.40 in currency. Those who learned of the incident later were divided on whether the $2.40 was the actual amount taken, or whether $1.10 was retained by Carney as a proper commission.

About the time of local elections Tom Carney's was a busy place. Few aldermanic candidates got through without his goodwill. His relations with the police department always seemed cordial.

Mr. Carney had one soft spot in his heart and that was for poetry. He could recite it by the yard, mostly the most sentimental verse. It was for his benefit that a reporter [Leckie again] perpetrated a story when a drink-besotted mother managed to lie on her twin babies in bed and smother them. In the story all the sordidness of the occurance—the unkempt room, the liquor-permeated atmosphere—was deleted. The mother appeared a lovely and grief-stricken bride, and a little wisp of crepe floated from the door in a sob-rousing manner to guide the coroner's man to the scene. That beastly two sticks of type haunted the reporter for years. Its last appearance, as far as he knows, was in a St. Louis paper, credited to the *Atlanta Constitution*, and that was five years after it was written. Only the street location differed from the original.

But the relatives of the infant decedents were well known along Market street and the author was glorified as the greatest of writers, and was pledged the friendship of all the gang. Had he desired his enemy's blood it probably could have been arranged. As he didn't, he merely used his honorable position for the acquisition of news. Furthermore, he was never again molested.

The heart of things was in the reporters' room in the old city hall, on the ground floor, opposite the fire alarm office and adjoining detectives' headquarters.

Thence the reporters scattered for their tours of the city and there they gathered to contribute to the "love feast" of news or to write their "scoops" when the love feast was off. When news was popping as it usually was, the center of activity was in that shabby room with the one long table and the *Tribune* man's roll top desk, a dozen chairs and a telephone as its only furniture. Once in a while either of the two joint chiefs of detectives, Horace Kipley or John Shea, would drop in with a tip that sent the whole assembly scuttering to the telephone and then en masse to some murder or robbery.

During the anarchist troubles, the East Chicago avenue police station, in charge of Captain—afterward Inspector—Michael Schaak, was a center of excitement. Schaak was a fine police officer with a Teutonic temperament ideal for dealing with anarchists who were mostly of German extraction or birth. He took a major part in the apprehension and conviction of anarchists.

He had trouble, however, understanding the Gaelic frame of mind, and when an international incident concerning the Clan-na-Gael's proposed invasion of Canada was referred to him on a complaint from Washington, he turned the matter over to his subordinate, Detective Dan Coughlin, one of the foremost Chicago policemen. With his colleague, Jake Lorch, Coughlin had done some noted work in crime detection. It was understood that Lorch and Coughlin could have had lieutenancies had they desired them.

At this time, while attempts at "fine writing" were discouraged, a reporter, who then was required to write his own stories, had the opportunity, when inspired, to get in a soul-moving human interest yarn. One reporter in particular [once again, Leckie] had acquired a reputation in this direction, perhaps not fully appreciated by his city editors, but raising him to empyresh [sic] heights in the minds of his friends on the police force as well as in other and less reputable circles. One day this reporter was told at Central police station that Dan Coughlin had been trying to reach him from Chicago avenue.

It looked like a story and the reporter was on his way forthwith. At the station the desk sergeant said Dan was over at Jake Lorch's flat around the corner in Wells street. There the story developed. Jake was lying in a blood-stained bed, with a surgeon working on him. He had been shot by his beautiful but neurotic wife, and in what he supposed to be his dying gasps, was determined that she would not profit by inheriting his property. That was his one thought, and with Coughlin's persuading, the reporter wrote Jake Lorch's will, distinctly disinheriting the lady as far as the law would permit and setting forth that there never had been a ceremony which would give her a dower right. Coughlin and Lorch were more confident than the reporter himself that the will would hold. Jake immediately began to breathe more easily and, by reason of an iron constitution, subsequently recovered.

There was trouble in the Clan-na-Gael. One faction wanted to invade Britain's Canadian provinces, while the other faction, being somewhat stuffy, insisted that the time was not ripe. It is not clear to which faction Dr. Cronin, a prominent north side physician, belonged. He was treasurer of the organization and presumably gave funds to his faction. It developed later that there were charges within the organization of misappropriation of funds.

Dr. Cronin disappeared. His wife and friends insisted that there had been foul play. Dan Coughlin, in charge of the police investigation by order of Schaack, could find nothing to justify the charges, and insisted that Dr Cronin would turn up when he was ready. Cronin did finally turn up, in a remote sewer catch basin, evidently having been dead for some weeks. A call was made for Coughlin to appear before Schaack. But there was no Coughlin. He had vanished into thin air forever, as far as the Chicago public was concerned. It was freely charged, though never proved, that Dan Coughlin himself was the avenger of the clan's treasury.*

Another who completely disappeared was Willie Tascott. Willie was a none too bright youth whose one ambition in life was to be a newspaper reporter, and, with no definite plan to this end, he haunted the reporters' room and became more or less of a pest with his offers of aid.

One night, February 8, 1888, Louis Houseman, then on the *InterOcean*, called up one of his colleagues in the reporters' room (it was not a love feast that night) and said there had been a murder at Madison and Sheldon streets. It was a childish but often perpetrated practical joke designed to send the opposition on a wild goose chase. It worked. Half a dozen reporters threw down their cards and hustled to the location designated. There was no excitement, no murder.

A few hours later it developed that at the moment the phone call was made by Houseman, Amos J. Snell, millionaire owner of the old Chicago and Milwaukee toll road, was shot and killed in his home at Washington and Sheldon streets, just a block away. He had heard a noise downstairs and surprised a burglar who had opened a safe kept in the "front parlor." The burglar promptly shot the aged man. It was shown in the investigation that the safe had been opened with the combination. An apparently keen but somewhat unsatisfactory search was inaugurated by the police. In the course of this, Houseman's telephone call developed, and Louis had the fright of his life in making a satisfactory explanation. Of course he knew nothing of the murder and his fool call was just a peculiar coincidence.

William Tascott was a distant relative of the murdered man and somehow the murder was attributed to him. No

* Coughlin later was tried for the murder of Dr. Cronin, convicted, sent to prison for a few years and acquitted after a second trial.

reporter on the case believed that Willie did the job or had brains or nerve enough to do it. However the public found a "goat" and was satisfied. But Willie Tascott had disappeared, and, although it seemed that not even one of Mark Twain's elephant hunting sleuths could help finding a youth of his well marked features, his gold front teeth and an ingenuous personality that would lead him to discovery if there was a chance, Willie disappeared permanently in the port of missing men. There was no further determined investigation of the Snell murder.

The first contact the newspapers had with the group subsequently known as the anarchists was through the efforts of the group itself, which sought publicity for some meetings which were held on Sunday afternoons in a shabby little hall in Randolph street, east of LaSalle street. The then strange and quaint doctrines pertaining to the rights of the "working class" and the various methods proposed for obtaining "equality" made more or less interesting copy. As meeting after meeting developed increasingly violent cures for existing evils, the public curiosity grew, but it was some time before the well-attended lake front meetings with the orators demanding the seizure of property and the death of capitalists aroused the people to something more than mild interest, often sympathetic, for the unbalanced theorists.

At the early meetings, the most prominent figures were Albert Parsons and his dark-skinned wife, Lucy. Parsons was a natural demogogue and publicity seeker. He had "the gift of gab werry galloping" and could talk a crowd of enthusiasts into a state of wild enthusiasm. He lacked logic and perhaps brains, but Lucy, no mean orator herself, had plenty.

Michael Schwab seemed to be, with the exception of Spies, the only one of the radicals possessing ability and common sense. He was a kindly, thoughtful man, comparatively at least, soft-spoken and gentle. "Direct action", a term recently coined, presumably fitted in with his theories, but he was an opportunist and held to a course of moderation until the time came to adopt violent measures. Schwab was a student with a philosophic mind and was patient in expounding Marxian theories for the benefit of any questioner.

Oscar Neebe also was about as gentle a man as ever attempted to scuttle society and it was difficult to understand how he would engage in a wholesale murder plot. Engle and Fisher had no dealings with capitalistic newspaper reporters.

August Spies, editor of the radical *Arbeiter Zeitung*, or *Worker's Gazette*, was best known to newspaper men, with whom he was generally friendly. He was a scholarly man, always neatly dressed and of gentlemanly demeanor. After the arrests of the alleged conspirators, he had to bear the brunt of the attack because his editorials, in the light of the Haymarket bombing, formed an irrefutable record against him.

But the arch anarchist of the group was Louis Lingg, said to have been the actual bomb maker. Certain it was that he had made a study of explosives and had the nerve to use them. He was a handsome, big fellow with a powerful physique and a mass of curly, waving hair. He would talk to no newspapermen, but declared to the jailers that he would never die on the gallows.

One dull day in the criminal court building, Jack Klein, a *Times* reporter, suggested to another that the latter go up to the court room on the second story while Klein went over to the jail which stood across an areaway and was entered by an iron staircase on the outside of the building. As the second reporter, a few minutes later, was coming down the stairs, he glanced through the window toward the jail and saw an excited-looking deputy jailer dashing down two steps at a time. The reporter rushed across to the jail and, through the barred door, glimpsed wild excitement within. Jailer Ben Price, after first refusing, opened the door just far enough to let the reporter slip into the jail office. At that moment, several men, one of whom was Klein, staggered in from the cell block and laid what was left of Louis Lingg on the floor. Lingg had taken the fulmination cap in his teeth and held a lighted cigarette to it until it exploded, shattering his head.

As he lay on the floor, his great chest heaved and at each

moment the blood spurted over the dying man, and Klein was on his knees holding Lingg's head. A doctor came rushing in and in a minute Lingg, still breathing, was carried into the bathroom and placed in the tub; what for, no one could guess as it was too late to conserve the cleanliness of the jail floor. The placing of the dying man in the bathtub always seemed one of the most gruesome gestures imaginable. Probably it was just nerves. Anyway, Lingg died in the bathtub in a few minutes.

Jack Klein always was falling into big news. He seemed fated to be right there when something broke. A little after the hanging of the anarchists, he with three other Chicago reporters was engaged by M.H. DeYoung to work on the *San Francisco Chronicle*. From there he went to Samoa, under an arrangement with the *New York World*, to cover the native civil war, supposed to be incited by the Germans on the one hand and the British on the other. Klein had a narrow escape when captured by the Germans and accused of being a German renegade. He was able to prove his American citizenship and escaped.

Many men who have achieved success and fame in newspaper work and other walks of life, attribute it in a large part to the training they received on the City Press association, or City News bureau. Frank E. Rowley, long the gifted assistant publisher and managing editor of the *Chicago Chronicle*, was in turn reporter and desk man for the City Press association. Charles Dillingham, the New York theatrical producer, was an alumnus. Charlie Dryden the beloved and talented originator of about all baseball jargon, was given his start in newspaper work there. Hector Elwell, managing editor in the Hearst service, used to hang flimsy on the hooks, was promoted to be a reporter and became one of the best. James Bicket, long manager of the *Chicago American*, was a City Press cub, and afterward for years day desk manager. O.O. McIntyre was a City Press reporter. There are scores of others.

6

Love Feasts and Scoops

The slogan of the *new* new bureau was "Up On Your Toes."
This expressed the attitude of the managers: they and their
thirty-five employees ran, rather than walked, through the
office in their shirtsleeves. It has been said that Leckie's
telephone conversations consisted mostly of stuttering and
yells. Once, when he was having trouble getting through to
the County building man that he had been fired, Leckie
stormed out of his private office in a rage, fired the deskman
on the spot and took his place for the rest of the day.

It is appropriate here to print a memoir of those days by
Otto McFeeley, which was sent to Isaac Gershman in September, 1951, and which has reposed in the City News files
every since. It describes vividly life with the two managers:

> After working as a boy reporter on daily newspapers
> in Marion, Indiana, having a hand in starting two daily
> papers in that town (one of which sold for two hundred
> thousand dollars in 1935), working with a surveying
> party in Central America and a year in the army during
> the Spanish-American war and ensuing events, I came
> to Chicago to be a news writer.
>
> I applied at all newspaper offices, then more numer-
> ous than today... At the *Journal* office the dapper city
> editor sat on a table when I applied. He obviously sym-
> pathized with me. He said he had no openings but might
> have. He handed to me paper and pencil and asked me

43

to write my name and address to be used in the event he needed another reporter. I did this and he continued to talk to me, the while cutting the paper, on which my name was written, into small pieces. He did this absent-mindedly as he tried to encourage me with talk of newspaper work in the city. This city editor, as all others, suggested I apply at the City Press office, then in the Western Union building at Jackson and Clark...

I had never heard of the City Press association and feared it was some sort of a racket. I did apply and was hired after a few minutes' conference with Mr Sayler.

I did not know it then but soon was to learn that I was serving with an outfit as tough as any I had ever known with tough men in tropical jungles and in the army. The Press association was ruled by two men, Sayler and Leckie, of concurrent jurisdiction. Both were gentlemen of the old school, always polite, always calling reporters by the title Mister, to dignify them and no doubt impress upon them the responsibility of a man who wrote for newspapers. They did not use the language of disciplinarians of the jungles nor of the army but they were more devastating. When either one, reading my copy, asked: "Mr. McFeeley, how could you gather so much misinformation in so short a time?" it was like being struck by a whip as they pointed out politely that you had neglected your responsibilities, leaving the impression that you were ignorant, lazy, and only semiliterate. Some young men may have been so discouraged that they became salesmen, bank clerks or ad writers but many of them learned the trade and became noted in newspaperdom from coast to coast.

In 1900 the City Press office was inhabited by a crew that included Bicket, Bill Clarke, George Wharton, Eddie Raferty (then office boy but destined to become a star reporter), Jimmy Murphy, Snively (...later chief of police in Los Angeles), a man named Bowman, who soon was elected president of a college in Iowa... A reporter named Preston, who was a flame of fire. Everyday he was in the thick of some startling events. He disappeared and I have never heard of him since.

Then there were the three Johnson brothers, products of Chicago and each one noted among his professional brethren and fondly remembered by all who worked with them.

When Mr. Sayler hired me, in an early forenoon of July, 1900, he directed me to be in the office at 6 p.m. I was there. He introduced me to Mr. Johnson, one of the brothers, but I can't remember his first name.

"Mr. McFeeley," said Mr. Sayler, "you are to visit northside police stations tonight with Mr. Johnson who will show you around. Call up every hour or oftener from East Chicago police station."

Johnson and I left the office. I was sure it was a racket. I knew the lake was on the east side of the city so East Chicago avenue must be out in the lake. If the kindly Johnson had shoved me into a coal hole or hit me with a pair of knucks and robbed me I would not have been surprised. I was on guard and alert for violence.

Happily, I was misinformed.

It seemed to me and other new reporters that if Sayler hired a man, Leckie hated him and if Leckie hired a reporter Sayler hated him. At this distance of fifty years I now realize that this was not true. Both Sayler and Leckie were kindly men and whipped reporters with their vast vocabularies only because they believed such discipline was the only way to teach young men to be news writers and editors. All newspapers were carefully clipped and if any report contained information not in the City Press copy, it was marked a scoop against the reporter on that story or field, such as police and the courts.

I lasted until January of 1901. I was on the verge of being fired often because Mr. Leckie was there when I wrote my stuff. He seemed to be infuriated by me, of course in the most polite manner. One Sunday afternoon a missionary from China who was to lecture that night in the large Presbyterian church in Austin was trying out his magic lantern. A terrific explosion occurred, blowing an arm off the missionary and the entire east wall of the stone church out into the street. I wrote the report and said that the explosion was caused by acetylene gas. The report was published in all Chicago newspapers and most of those of the USA, via the AP.

There was then an association of acetylene gas manufacturers, rich and powerful. National officers of the association were alarmed. They feared their business had been damaged, if not ruined. They soon learned the City Press was responsible and Mr. Sayler of course knew I was the offender. He sent for me and said:

"Mr. McFeeley, we have ruined the acetylene gas business of the United States. Hundreds of newspapers are to be sued for damages running into millions. I wish you would at once investigate this matter, not to justify our report, but to get the facts. Find out what did cause the explosion."

I soon learned that it was not acetylene that caused it. Then I knew I was finished at the City Press.

When I went into the office there were the great rich men of the acetylene business and Mr. Sayler, all grim. Being certain I was to be fired, I was arrogant, even insulting to Mr. Sayler and the acetylene moguls. I sat quietly, planning to return to Indiana, to do my stuff and quit Chicago. The acetylene men raged and threatened for some time. Then I spoke, with amazing courage.

"Gentlemen," I said, in the manner of a brave and informed man, "you haven't a leg to stand on. You have no ground whatever for damage suits. You are entirely misinformed. Acetylene gas is not a patented or proprietory product, any more than hydrogen is."

As I talked I thought Mr. Sayler for once was a little bit proud of me. The acetylene men were abashed. They uttered a few more words and departed. I heard no more about the matter and I do believe even Leckie thought that perhaps there was some good in me.

That was in December. I survived until January. I reported a fight in a hotel. The cook stabbed a waiter. I wrote the story and then Leckie called me in. The stabbed man had died and it was a murder. I had neglected to call the County hospital to learn the results before writing the story.

The next day Mr. Sayler informed me that they could get along without me. "I see no reason why you can't get a job on a newspaper," he said with something of sympathy in his voice. "Don't say you resigned here. They will know that is not true. Say you were discharged. That is considered a recommendation by most city editors in Chicago."

In getting fired I did a great thing for Chicago newspaperdom and the government of the city. Strange as it may seem, just as I was leaving the City Press office forever, low in spirit and doubtful of my ability, if any, I passed another young man just entering. It was easy to see that he was looking for a job...

I had been assigned for some weeks to cover western suburbs with headquarters at Austin police station. The man who passed me in the hall found favor in the sight of Mr. Sayler and was hired to take my place in the suburbs. I lived in Austin and that night I met the man who had taken my job.

I later learned to know him well and today, 1951, I realize what a fortunate thing it was that Sayler hired my successor. If he had not, the man, in all probability, might have taken his talents and energy to Kansas City, St. Louis, or even New York. My successor...is one of the most distinguished and useful citizens of the city. His name is Oscar Hewitt. After a noted career as reporter and foreign correspondent he was appointed, 18 years ago, to be commissioner of public works of Chicago...

I did get a job on the *Evening Post* where I spent seven

delightful, lazy years working beside Percy Hammond, the gallant Eddie Weslake, Francis Hackett, Joe Sheean, Boswell Field, Gene Morgan, Babe Durand and others.

Sayler and Leckie accepted willingly the penny-pinching custom of hiring no seasoned reporters and did not fight against it as Ballantyne had done. They saw their function partly as a training school for cub reporters. And obviously they were good at it, as Mr. McFeeley attests, since he himself proved the truth of Sayler's statement that a firing by City Press was considered a recommendation by most city editors.

In 1891 the service had fifteen subscribers. Beside the original ten newspapers which had founded the publishers' press association, there were the *Globe*, the *National Zeitung*, the *Abendpost*, the *Tageblatt* and the Western Associated Press. For a short time, when United Press joined, the number of subscribers to the bureau rose to sixteen. (This was not the United Press of today, but an earlier organization which folded in 1894 after a bitter struggle with Lawson's Associated Press, founded in 1892 to replace the Western Associated Press. During this period of struggle, John Walsh's *Post* and *Herald* remained members of City Press, although Walsh himself was a strong partisan of the UP. This was true, too, of the *Tribune* from 1893-94 when that paper also refused to join Lawson's AP. Lawson made no attempt to make subscription to AP a prerequisite for service from City Press, although he could easily have done so.)

On May 23, 1894, besides Leckie and Sayler, City Press had a staff of thirty-four people: there were two day copy readers; four court reporters; seven police reporters of whom three worked days and four worked nights; four reporters with specific assignments: hotels, the Federal building, the County building and real estate transfers; three suburban reporters, one each for Town of Lake, Evanston and Hyde Park; three general reporters; two men to look after the pneumatic tubes; three "typewriters" and seven boys: two day copy boys and two night copy boys, one day office boy, one court boy and one City Hall boy.

Marian Heath, one of the general assignment reporters, was the first woman reporter to work for City Press. Some time after 1894 she was joined by Katherine Leckie, a cousin of Archie's.

Perennially columnists dig up the fact that Joseph "Yellow Kid" Weil was employed by the bureau briefly in January, 1895. But this was long before his confidence games had earned him his nickname.

Charles Carpenter, who was a cub reporter for the bureau in the winter of 1892-93, recalled the old days:

> There was a small office occupied by Leckie and Sayler and another room for the reporters who wrote their stories on a sort of board shelf, all on flimsy paper, several sheets at a time, on the bottom of which we put a piece of heavy tin or metal of some kind... The staff was small and we did not use typewriters.
>
> Boys were employed to carry the copy to the different newspapers and if I am not mistaken they received five cents a round trip. I remember Joe Herricks, who covered the criminal court building, then on the north side. Heck Elwell's first job was carrying Joe's copy from the criminal court building to the office. I believe he got four dollars a week for this work.
>
> ...One day a notice was posted on the wall that typewriters were to be installed and that after a certain date all reporters would have to hand in typewritten copy. We all got very busy picking out our stories on the machine and it sure was tough for some of the boys...
>
> I first was sent out to Hyde Park to cover police news and when the old World's Fair was opened, early in 1893, I remained there covering police news of the fair. There was plenty of it. Nicholas Hunt was the police inspector in charge of the district...
>
> After the close of the fair they sent me to Evanston to watch for the finding of the vessel named *Chicora* which went down in Lake Michigan with twenty-one men aboard and all were lost. This was in the dead of

winter and the boat was enroute from Milwaukee to St. Joseph, Michigan, with a cargo of flour. We reporters never found the *Chicora* but I covered the north shore territory for a year or two before I was transferred back to Chicago and put on day desk work. There I remained until Rowley took me over to the *Chronicle* doing south side police work for him...

...I might say that of all the training schools for newspaper reporters, the City Press and the City News Bureau were the best. Those who were fit for the work went ahead while others, not adapted, soon fell by the wayside and sought employment in other fields...

There were many matters to sort out. The board of directors held regular meetings to discuss bureau matters, and the editors of subscribing newspapers met monthly to assess the performance of the bureau and its value to them. This assessing was to continue throughout the life of the bureau; it was a constant source of faint anxiety to the staff, like a dull toothache, constantly giving rise to rumors of dissolution.

At a meeting on May 4, 1891 the board of directors added society events and City League baseball games to the departments marked out for coverage originally by Ballantyne: that is, the City Hall, County and Federal buildings, Army headquarters, law, criminal and police courts, hotels, police stations and police news, fires, inquests, races, strikes, and suburban news. There was no special sports department, but each reporter covered sports events in his district. In 1896 special wires were rented so that City Press could cover the Decoration Day races in the suburb of Wheeling. For a time a race track which lay north of Waukegan, just over the Wisconsin line, was part of the north shore reporter's regular assignment. In the early nineteen hundreds out-of-town correspondents were paid fifty and seventy-five cents each for box scores of the Three-Eye League and other minor league baseball.

Before they sold the bureau, Wright and Russell had begun the compilation of election returns from the suburbs. Under

Leckie and Sayler this coverage was extended to the city precincts. The early attempt to tabulate the returns during the presidential election of 1892 was a complete failure. But City Press learned, and eventually developed a system that depended on the use of police both in the city and in country towns and the hiring of hundreds of messengers and telephone men to bring in fast and accurate information.

Invariably complaints came to Sayler and Leckie from the editors' monthly meetings. The bureau had to be alert for the bootlegging of news: a copy boy for the bureau was discovered to be furnishing his reports for two dollars a week to a paper that did not subscribe to the bureau. The boy was promptly discharged. But there were other problems: one newspaper believed it was being put last in the order in which bulletins were telephoned to the members. Another editor said his paper was getting the worst of the paper flimsies: these were, as we have noted, stacks of very thin paper interspersed with carbons, on which reporters wrote out their notes in longhand, ten copies at a time. The copy boys were supposed to shuffle the stacks before delivery, so that each client would get a fair number of legible top, and nearly illegible bottom, sheets.

The partners were kept busy checking complaints and writing explanatory letters. One of the latter went out to C.E. Chapin, city editor of the *Herald*, on May 18, 1891:

> In regard to your complaint that this office did not handle the news of the Reidell murder as promptly as it should, would report that we have made an investigation of the matter.
>
> The murder occurred at 10:05 o'clock and at 10:15 o'clock Mr. Chamberlain, our Central station reporter telephoned the Deering street station. The news had not yet been received. Mr. Allen, who relieved Mr. Chamberlain at that time, did not again call up Deering street station for about an hour and at 11:30 o'clock learned of the affair, consumed a few moments in securing some few details and then notified the office. At 11:40 o'clock

our Mr. Leckie commenced to telephone to the papers a bulletin of the affair. He telephoned in the following order: *InterOcean, Tribune, Herald,* and the bulletin was taken over the wire by your Mr. Browne not later than 11:45 o'clock.

It does not appear that there is much excuse for Mr. Allen not hearing of the murder in the hour between 10:30 o'clock and 11:30, but he accounts for that by saying there is so little news at Deering street that he is accustomed to call there less frequently than at more important points.

Yours very truly

Leckie & Sayler, Mgrs.

An explanation went to William Penn Nixon on July 7, 1891 of a late report of a Rockwell street car collision:

...the scene of the accident was 2½ miles from the Desplaines street station where the west side night police reporter is located at that hour in the morning. It was necessary to travel this distance for which 20 minutes at least must be allowed. After procuring all the facts obtainable under the circumstances no telephone service was to be had nearer than the County hospital, nearly 1¼ miles from the accident. The accident was telephoned from this place to our office and written at 4 a.m. At 4:05 a.m. all copy had left the office by special messengers. One of your own boys was entrusted with the *InterOcean* copy. When he reached the *InterOcean* office the door of the city editor's room was closed and locked. He could find no one to whom to deliver the copy and put it under the door.

The papers had made an agreement with Ballantyne to withdraw their reporters from those city departments which the bureau had been assigned to. However, the papers flagrantly violated this agreement. When the managing editor of the *Post* complained that a bureau reporter was "dogging the heels" of a *Post* reporter who had been sent out for an exclusive story, and that the bureau was not doing a good job of covering hotel news, Leckie and Sayler released some of their resentment and tension in a letter to him:

Replying to your esteemed favor of yesterday would say that we do intend to cover hotels from and after this date to the best of our ability as we have done heretofore. We will inform you in case we should so far be seized with dementia as to willingly slight or wholly abandon any of our work, including hotels...

It will be idle to discuss the allegation, utterly unfounded, that any employee of this association in his search for news "dogged the heels" of a *Post* reporter. The allegation that we have at any time abandoned the hotel field with or without warning is evidently based on misinformation, but has the following slight foundation:

At the time you complain of the excellence of our hotel work we were so situated, after much planning, to put upon the service a man eminently fitted for the position. That his work was excellent we agree with you. He was a man who would have no need, even had he the inclination, to "dog the heels" of anyone.

Through one of the complaints which occasionally reach this office and which was not dissimilar to yours, we were obliged to transfer this man temporarily. We afterward gave him a vacation, but he will soon be back at work. In the interim, we have filled his place as well as we could in the emergency. Observation of the morning papers will show you that there has been little in the hotel field of late and we cannot say that the change at this season was particularly disastrous.

We beg to take issue with you on the assertion that your charges as to the work in the city hall, government building or north side are well founded. We do not expect our one man working in each of the departments referred to, especially the city hall, can at all times hold his own against a dozen reporters from as many afternoon and morning papers. In this connection we would say that by a peculiar coincidence we had but a few days ago a very similar complaint to yours in which the court service was attacked as being abominable, while the same critic said the City Hall and government service was good. We attempt in the City Hall, government building and north side, as in all departments, to cover the territory as would any first class newspaper. That our reporters have this to do they understand. What the *Post*, the *News*, or the *Journal* wants, we want. Our men are moved by the reportorial instinct that makes a valuable man. He cannot see another reporter in the field without conscientiously endeavoring to ascertain his business.

It is a matter for sincere regret that you should make such an allegation as your last. That the managers of this association are incompetent may be. That they are so insane as to deliberately antagonize and wilfully annoy the *Post* will not be credited outside your office... Among reporters we are aware that the bureau has not now and has never had a kindly feeling; but we shall not go so far as to impute what the *Post* editors may feel to this source...

In early 1893, before the opening of the Columbian Exposition, City Press moved to new quarters in the Phoenix building on Jackson boulevard, east of the Board of Trade. This building had been purchased by the Western Union Telegraph company, and the Associated Press was moving into it; therefore, since Victor Lawson insisted that City Press and the AP stay together, City Press had to move, too. Their rooms adjoined the AP rooms on the seventh floor of the Phoenix building.

The new location was not as close to the newspaper offices as the old one had been. The members of the City Press staff most affected by the new location were therefore the copy boys, who had to run the copy on foot from the important news centers (City Hall, Criminal Courts building, Harrison street station) and act as messengers to the newspapers. They were important to the functioning of the bureau: in addition to picking up and delivering, the boys sorted the flimsy in the "back room" after it had been written and corrected at the desk. Often there were not enough copy boys for the work, and it was necessary to hire extras from the American District Telegraph company, which furnished messenger service in those days.

On the night of May 24, 1893, editors and managers began to notice that the copy boys appeared to be loitering much more than usual. They were walking out with copy and showing up at the newspaper offices an hour and a half or two hours later. When the papers began to complain it was discovered that the boys had gone on a kind of slow-down strike. In those days there were no agonizing reappraisals or discussions: all the boys were immediately fired, and replaced by ADT messengers.

Even before this contretemps, the managers and the publishers had been discussing a means of doing away with the need for so many copy boys. In late December, 1892, Leckie wrote to J.W. Scott, the publisher of the *Herald*, about an underground pneumatic tube service for communication between the City Press offices and the newspapers. Leckie had been attempting to get estimated costs on the tube system for Scott, but final prices could not be gotten together without competitive bids from construction firms not only in Chicago but also in Detroit and New York. It was not even definite that City Press would move to the Phoenix building and this too would affect the costs.

Leckie was most anxious for this system to be installed:

> The need for such a device becomes more impressive daily and if it can be arranged so as to handle both ours and the telegraphic report it would be decidedly economical. There is little doubt that if located in the Phoe-

nix building an arrangement could be made to handle all newspaper specials for the Western Union in consideration for the use of power for the exhaust blower, thus saving the telegraph company much in messenger wages and the papers in time.

Leckie estimated that messenger service for City Press and Associated Press was costing $3,000 annually, $1,500 apiece. In addition Associated Press had an operator at the *Journal* office for $600 a year and an operator at the *News* who cost $480 a year. This was a total cost of $4,080 annually. The annual cost of the tube service he estimated would be roughly $1,500 for interest at 6% on the $25,000; there would also be $500 for power, $350 for repairs, and $1,150 for the four office boys who would still be needed. He guessed that Western Union service would deduct about $500 from the cost, bringing the total to $3,000 annually, a clear saving of $1,080 a year.

Leckie wanted the system ready before the World's Fair opened. Even with a board of directors dominated by the fast-moving, energetic Victor Lawson, this was an unrealistic goal. Lawson himself was fond enough of the bureau to want to start a "bureau of correspondence" which would furnish City Press service to papers across the country. Although the idea never got off the ground, probably because it would have brought City Press into competition with Associated Press, it nevertheless shows that Lawson was satisfied with the bureau concept, and it is therefore no surprise that the tube system was in operation by the fall of 1893. Leckie says:

> It was a tremendous task to place the tubes beneath Clark, Washington and Dearborn streets to the newspaper offices. Water and gas mains, sewers, and wire conduits had to be moved or evaded. Space for the necessary vaults was difficult to find but in the end the tubes were put in operation at a cost slightly within the estimate of $100,000. This was only possible because of the cooperation given the newspapers by the city and

public utility companies. There was not an injunction or other legal obstacle. Frequently the utility companies went to considerable expense in the moving of their pipes or conduits to expedite the work.

The traffic situation in the Loop then was probably even worse than it is today. There were streetcars and horse-drawn wagons clogging intersections, and there were no traffic lights. The messenger service was really too slow for the newspapers, and dispatches were generally too long to be read over the telephone. The pneumatic tubes could propel canisters containing the copy at speeds of thirty to seventy miles an hour. When the system first started, propulsion was provided by steam jets under pressure of 125 pounds to the square inch. The copy was sucked to its destination, where it landed with a loud report.

At first the three-inch tubes were set in trenches. Problems with this occurred however, when leaks developed in the tubes or when the carriers holding the copy became jammed at curves. When that happened, whole lengths of tubing had to be dug up to free the carrier. This difficulty was overcome when the tubes were incorporated into an elaborate system of tunnels which had been dug beneath the business district in 1899 by the Illinois Telephone and Telegraph company. These tunnels were taken over by the Chicago Tunnel company and expanded to a sixty-five mile network to haul freight, garbage, coal and ashes underneath the city, and City Press took fifteen miles of that system for their tubes, which, once in the tunnels, could more easily be opened and repaired than when they were in the trenches, and canisters could be easily fished out when they were stuck.

Thus there were fifteen miles of solid brass and copper tubing channelled into an underground railway system, running in a network from City Press and Associated Press to the County building, the Board of Trade and the newspaper offices. The steam propulsion caused tremendous amounts of moisture to condense in the tubes, so that there were times when the system delivered material that was literally soaking wet. When vacuum pumps were substituted for the steam pressure, this moisture problem was solved.

Getting clear copy remained a problem. The papers complained constantly that the sheets they were getting were illegible. Leckie describes the flimsy system:

> The duplicating process by which each newspaper was furnished with [copy] was the same as used by the Associated Press—yellow flimsy. This was a tough tissue paper made up in "books" of one hundred sheets. Between each two sheets of tissue was placed a sheet of carbon paper, double-faced, so one sheet of tissue would show writing from the back, while the next would have the imprint on the front, and so on for a dozen sheets. A sheet of tin was slipped beneath the last sheet, and the writer, with a stylus under great pressure, transcribed on this pad his message to the newspaper reader. It was possible under good conditions to produce legible copy but in practice the results, especially on the last sheet, was calculated to make the copy reader tear his hair and drive the compositor mad.

The bureau was anxious to correct this situation. They experimented first with reproduction on gelatin, but this did not work. Something was badly needed that could turn out duplicated copy quickly and cheaply. Some newspapers used a process that involved a wax stencil; the process was expensive and not fast enough for the bureau's needs, but Leckie saw something in the basic idea, and discussed it with Addison C. Thomas, western manager of the Associated Press, Irving Stone of the *News* and Cassius M. Hamilton, superintendant of the new tube system. Leckie describes the results of the discussion:

> Hamilton was an excellent mechanic and with much collaboration produced the first of a series of machines for printing duplicates from a wax stencil. The machine printed from a continuous roll of paper, each sheet

being cut off like the sheets in a web press... Improvements were made until a thoroughly practical machine was developed and manifolding was revolutionized. And then came a shock. The A.B. Dick people owned basic patents and when they learned about the new device shut down hard. They made a price for a license which was absolutely prohibitive and it seemed that all the work was for nothing. Then arrangements were made to turn over rights to the new machine in exchange for the right to use it and manufacture wax sheets in Associated Press offices and their subsidiaries. The emancipation of the newspaper offices from flimsy was even a more important step than the introduction of the tube system.

This machine was known as a Cyclograph. For years this revolutionary system of manifolding was used both by City Press and Associated Press. Even after the AP went to teletype, City Press clung to the Cyclograph. It was a practical and economical system.

In the mid-thirties Vickerman estimated the value of the tube system at two million dollars. By 1954 its value had escalated to five million, according to an article in the *Quill* about Frank T. Fitzgerald, who spent his days underground as superintendent of the "news subway". Fitzgerald had been dispatching news through the tubes since 1900, when the system was at 111 West Jackson boulevard. He had helped to move the system to new quarters in 1917 and again to 188 West Randolph street where it was located in 1954.

Fitzgerald and his staff operated the set-up twenty-four hours a day. There were four pairs of tubes going to each newspaper: in 1954 the papers were the *American*, the *Daily News*, the *Sun-Times* and the *Tribune*. The tubes still served the Associated Press, the Board of Trade, the County building, and the law department of the *Tribune* at 33 North LaSalle street. Fitzpatrick remembered clearly the days when the tubes served thirteen Chicago newspapers.

Stories were phoned in to the bureau office from reporters stationed throughout the city. These stories would be rewritten at breakneck speed by skilled rewrite men and then placed in the Cyclograph for duplication. A strong-armed copy boy cranked the Cyclograph and as the duplicated stories emerged they were placed in canisters and dropped in a tube which led to Fitzgerald's central tube room far below the city's streets. From there they were dispatched to their destinations.

The copy which travelled through the tubes had first been typed on parafin-covered stencils. A carbon paper backing protected the stencil when it was in the typewriter; an extra-thin sheet of tissue paper kept the parafin from clogging the typefaces. Copy people, mostly new employees deemed too young or too green to be put out on a beat at once, were obliged in their spare time to assemble backing, stencil and tissue sheets into what were known as "books". "Make book!" was the call issued by the boss of the back room. Desk men, reporters and rewrite men might enjoy moments of respite from the flow of news. But the copy staff had to "make book" in the slow spots.

The Quill reported in 1954 that 268,281 pieces of copy, including pictures, news releases and messages, were sent through the tubes in a year. As each piece of copy was relayed in its envelope, a record was kept of its size and the time it was relayed.

Copy was not the only thing that came through the tubes. In 1950 an eight inch water main broke under Clark street, and the nearby newspaper tube picked up the water and sent it gushing into the press room of the Board of Trade building, effectively damping down trading news for the rest of the day. Given the kittenish nature of many newspapermen, other things—hats, billiard balls and even on one memorable occasion a white mouse—came skidding through the tubes. Once a newspaper complained that there were bugs in its canisters, and duly received a small bottle of roach powder.

One copyboy tried to send change for a dollar to a tube

room employee. The canister arrived empty, the copy boy was told. Tension resulted: accusations flew back and forth, and there was a dispute over the wherabouts of the coins. Finally they were found, floating around in the air under fourteen pounds of pressure at the top of a curve in the tube. When the air was shut off for a moment they slid safely to their destination. The bureau was forced to ban this sort of activity eventually. It caused too many costly repairs.

In 1961 the inexorable march of progress caught up with the pneumatic tube system. The underground railway had been abandoned by the city, leaving the tunnels to rats and casual water. And City News had switched to Teletype, so the tubes supposedly were no longer needed, although Walter Ryberg maintains that the tubes were much faster than Teletype and most people at the bureau thought abandoning the tube was a step backward. In any case the system was believed to be archaic, and was discarded.

7

Hard Times in the Nineties

The bureau covered the World's Columbian Exposition of 1893 with ten extra men. Three men were hired as "type-writers" to rewrite the reports. The Fair's swarms of visitors, meetings, and inevitable police news—to say nothing of the "hootchy kootchy dancers" and other absorbing exhibits on the Midway—provided reams of copy. It is interesting as contrast to note that for covering the World's Fair of 1933 the bureau added only four extra employees.

On the evening of October 28, 1893, a City Press copyboy was sitting in the operator's chair at the Harrison street police station, calling the "run" on the police telephone for an acquiescent reporter, when the operator, John Sweeney, rushed in and reclaimed his chair, sending the boy sprawling. In reply to the boy's anguished complaint Sweeney said that Mayor Carter Harrison had just been shot.

This was the tragic event which marked the close of the Columbian Exposition. When John Eugene Prendergast, the man who had killed Harrison, was put on trial, City Press, in a special service to the newspapers, hired stenographers and furnished a verbatim account of the testimony. This was the first big trial to be handled by the bureau on an extended scale. It was certainly not the last.

Despite the success of the Fair, times were hard in 1893. And after the Fair was over, thay did not get any better. The winter of 1894 has been called a winter of despair: homeless people slept in saloons, in the public rooms of City Hall and even in police station basements which were infested with vermin and rats.

The depression hit the newspapers hard. The *Globe* went into receivership. The *Abendpost*, which was not served by the pneumatic tubes, withdrew from the service to keep down expenses. In 1895 John Walsh, the banker, sold his interests in the *Herald* and the *Post* to James W. Scott and founded the *Chronicle*, a morning paper. Scott bought the *Times* and merged it with the *Herald* to form the *Times-Herald*, just a few days before he died. At that point H.H. Kohlsaat, who had earlier taken over the *InterOcean*, took over both the *Times-Herald* and the *Post*. The *Morning News*, the name of which had by then been changed to the *Record*, was involved in the fierce fight for increased circulation. The *Record* chose to fight by printing mystery fiction rather than expanding news coverage.

These combinations and mergers wore away the newspaper presence in Chicago: the city's heyday as a newspaper town was over. The field was finally narrowed to five dailies in English: two morning and three afternoon papers.

City Press was able to weather the loss of all these papers, but not without severe retrenchments. The payroll was trimmed. And on June 21, 1894, the board of directors laid down a ten point program to cut back service and confine it to routine matters until the times improved.

Hotel service was curtailed, although ordinary meetings at hotels were still to be covered; running reports of city council meetings were dropped, but resolutions were to be reported; important trials were not to be covered unless there was special agreement with the newspapers beforehand; grand jury proceedings were to be given briefly and factually, omitting gossip and speculation; descriptive work was to be dropped from fire reporting; detective investigation and description were to be dropped from crime news; the board of education would no longer be covered; reports were not to be founded in gossip, and as little "descriptive work" was to be done as possible; but coverage of county board and parks and townships boards was not to be curtailed. Reporters were not allowed to comply with special requests from city editors unless the request was connected with routine bureau work.

Many of these proscriptions were dropped when times got better. The hotel beat was restored in its entirety to remain until the depression of the 1930's forced the bureau to drop it again, for good this time. All court trials now, unless there is special agreement with the newspapers, are fully covered by the bureau. Running stories of city council meetings are required, and the same is true of school board meetings. Gossip and rumor are supposed to be eliminated from City News reports, and all news is to be based on an authoritative source. When rumor or similar information is carried at all it is segregated in a "Note to City Editors".

The taboo on description remained until the early 1920's when there was a puzzling murder in which the police were studying all details for clues to the solution. The young man on the desk on last watch at City Press was an aspiring playwright. He was moved to describe the victim's room in detail, and he put the description in the form of dialogue.

It was well done, and was consequently printed verbatim in the early editions of the *Daily News*. Victor Lawson read it and thought it had been written by one of his own reporters. He sent a word of commendation to Henry Justin Smith, his managing editor. Smith in turn telephoned Walter Brown who was then in charge of the bureau. This was a lucky thing for the desk man, because Brown had been about to discipline him for disobeying the rules. Instead Brown raised his salary. That young desk man was Isaac Gershman, who was to become general manager of the bureau in 1931. From the time of Gershman's dialogue, a reasonable amount of description has been allowed by the bureau.

The publishers had a necessarily ambiguous attitude toward City Press. They needed the service, but each publisher hesitated to help give a really excellent product to his rivals. What each publisher probably wanted was a local bureau so weak that it could be beaten out on the occasional good story by the publisher's own staff, but strong enough to prevent the other newspapers from getting scoops. This kind of unreasonable, perhaps subconscious attitude, brought pressures to bear on the bureau staff.

For one thing, as we have noted before, the Leckie and Sayler management was restricted to hiring only inexperienced men. There were no schools of journalism to provide promising youth, of course; the bureau managers had to deal with beginners who knew nothing at all about the profession. It developed later, when schools of journalism did send graduates to City News, that they did not do appreciably better than any other novices. But in any case, experience was always the best teacher, and the publishers were shrewd enough to realize that even knowledgeable reporters from out of town made costly mistakes before they learned the ropes of the city. The publishers used City Press as a place to train newcomers cheaply.

On the other hand, although the bureau could not hire reporters away from the papers, there was nothing to prevent the papers from hiring competent reporters away from the bureau. John Ballantyne had been most baffled by this situation, since of course the newspapers offered better salaries and other inducements, including the possibility of advancement. Ballantyne kept losing his best men, and finding himself with drifters and cast-offs.

Leckie and Sayler chose to go with the tide, so to speak. They hired inexperienced men in key positions. Promotions were almost routine: if a man did well he moved onto the staffs of the newspapers. It was understood even by the managers that City Press was a stepping-stone to newspaper jobs. And, as a result, City Press training has always produced the "heavy men" on Chicago newspaper staffs. And many who have gone to other parts of the country hold similar positions on newspapers around the world.

The system had its defects, of course. Certainly City Press coverage never equalled that provided by the team of experts put together by Wright and Russell. And although Leckie and Sayler took a genuine interest in their young employees, their tolerance was sometimes strained. There is obviously something wrong with the story about a three-month-old baby who ran into the path of a streetcar and was seriously injured. Somehow this story escaped the notice of a harassed desk man. There was also the news story, which got into print, of the desperate citizen who shot and killed himself, and then turned the gun on his wife. There was the reporter who was stationed at a police station where reserves had been assembled in anticipation of labor violence. This reporter, later called on the carpet because he had managed to miss the disturbance when it came, confessed that he had moved on to a quieter station because there were too many noisy policemen at that one.

8

Sayler's Bureau

In 1901 Archibald Leckie bought an interest in a newspaper in Rockford, Illinois, and resigned from the bureau. He and Sayler had worked together as a team to establish the agency as an aggressive, dependable organization, patiently training each set of eager cubs, who "graduated" in turn, to make room for another batch. No other organization had worked quite this way. New and untried reporters were able, after only a few weeks, to hold their own to an amazing degree against older reporters with years of experience and many valuable friends.

In honor of Leckie's departure a banquet was held for the entire staff at a downtown hotel; it was the first such celebration in the bureau's history, and it remains a rare one, because of the difficulty of logistics. It was hard to assemble the staff. During their years as co-managers even Leckie and Sayler had alternated monthly as day and night managers: everyone was almost never in the office at the same time.

Leckie was the dynamo of the bureau, a newsman to his fingertips, with tremendous drive and energy. Now Sayler was assuming control. He was a massive man, six feet tall, with a deep chest, black hair and moustache, and an imposing manner. He had come to Chicago from Indianapolis in 1889 and, although he had had newspaper experience and had graduated from De Pauw University, had looked for work for a long time before he had been hired by Wright and Russell.

Sayler was perhaps more ruminative than Leckie. His

Indiana roots were important to him: he was the historian of the Indiana Society of Chicago, which claimed George Ade, Meredith Nicholson and John T McCutcheon as members. He was also the author of several series of children's books, among them *The Airship Boys* and *The Aeroplane Boys*, written under his own name, and the *Big Game, Boy Scout* and *Girl Scout* series, written under various pen names, of which "Gordon Stuart" was one. He wrote adult novels too, but did not have the courage to submit them to publishers.

Sayler's books were innovative, and successful enough to be widely imitated. He took great pains to be accurate: since aviation was a new field in his day, he wrote away for books and magazines, and even contacted manufacturers to be sure that he was familiar with the technical side before he began writing. One of the *Airship Boys* series was called *The Ocean Flyer, or New York to London in 12 Hours*—a prophetic title. His outdoor books were set in the Lake of the Woods in Canada or the Evangeline country of Louisiana, both places where he spent vacations. As time went on and publishers pressed him for a schedule, he often sketched out the plot and gave the book to someone else to write: Frank Honeywell and Winfred Whitcomb of the *Daily News* were two of his ghost writers.

Sayler's manner was somewhat aloof and some of the staff found him intimidating, but he was proud of the bureau and backed his staff with the same vigor with which he attacked them when he thought they had fallen down on the job. He held an open house for them every New Year's eve in his house at 7124 Euclid avenue.

His forcefulness is clear in this letter, which he wrote on September 29, 1902, in reply to a complaint from a city editor:

> I concede that the T---- is the most particular paper in Chicago as to the correctness of its statements. Despite this I won't stand second to any paper in my own contempt for errors or intentional fakes. Therefore when I get five complaints from you within a few days they have a double significance in this office.

As a result of those of Saturday night and two others almost as recent I have come to two conclusions: That in two stories sent you there were statements that were not well founded and that in two other stories someone in the T---- office made unjustified complaints and that in one story we were excusably at fault.

In the gypsy story we said that three girls had been brought from Egypt and that a triple marriage would take place Sunday. Both statements were in error. It is now said the girls were from Bosnia, and that the weddings will take place Tuesday. Aside from these errors the investigations of two papers yesterday seem to confirm our story. In the "silk hat" burglary we were wholly at fault and the fact that the error was due to a misunderstood word over the telephone does not help matters.

In the Rohfling story at Desplaines street I think developments show your information that night was at fault. I criticize the story not for any errors but because it contains an implied "roast" of the police that should not have crept into it. In the South Chicago beat story your information, it seems to me, was also at fault as the columns of your paper since then attest.

The story in which I believe we were excusably at fault with two newspapers was the Murray rescue story at Evanston. In that I believe our man was "strung"...

Three of five errors chargable to the bureau was probably not a bad record, as news went in 1902. Still, five complaints all within a few days from one paper would throw any bureau into turmoil.

On January 5, 1903, Sayler wrote to A.L. Clarke, city editor of the *American*:

I have made the natural attempt to find some palliating excuse for our missing the Barrett-Palmer case, with but poor success. We cover Hyde Park and Englewood at night with one man, but a live one. In spite of the fact that headquarters are officially at the Hyde Park station, he finds it usually to his advantage to work in the main from Englewood and the stockyards. Now and then he does not go to headquarters. That evening was one of the misses.

Perhaps you would like to know the man's version of what took place that evening as he reports it to me. It illustrates one phase of reportorial work, if the story is true, and I believe it is. I give an extract from the man's story:

'Friday,' he says, 'I called up the Hyde Park station regularly. Frank Moss, the desk sergeant who booked Miss Barrett at 5 o'clock in the afternoon answered me on two of these occasions and said that there was nothing doing. When I asked Inspector Hunt about the matter last Saturday he said that outside of himself, Lieut. Sullivan and two detectives, other attachés of the police station were ignorant of the facts in the case. He told me he was looking for me all evening, but that he was busy and did not call me up, expecting I would show up later in the night. He said that I made a mistake in not making Hyde Park my 'hangout' instead of Englewood.

'Frank Moss explained that he and the rest of the fellows behind the desk were unacquainted with the facts in the case. Beyond the booking of the woman he knew nothing until a reporter of the name of Scott for the T---- called late in the evening and commenced to ask questions about the shooting affair. Then Frank Moss became impressed with the fact that he had a newspaper story in the booking of the young woman. He said he started for the phone to call me up and had expressed the determintion to do that when Scott caused him to abandon his purpose by saying that I had the story. According to Desk Sgt. Moss, Wagonman Wolf and Detective Breen, who were there at the time, Scott explained that I had the whole story as he had met me down at the doctor's office.

'He told them, they say, that I had landed everything and had started into the office to write the story when he left me for Hyde Park. Satisfied with this information that I would not be scooped nothing more was done to notify me, he says.

'At 12 o'clock I made another call over the phone. Desk Sgt. Donovan answered and said that there was nothing in sight. The next day he came to me and told me that of course he thought that I had the story for the reason that the booking occurred in the afternoon. Other friends of mine, who were on the late watch that night, were also of the same opinion, though it was not until the next day that they knew the story of the shooting in full.

'As a precaution against a repetition of being scooped on an open story in the future, I intend to move to Hyde Park a week from today and make that station my 'hangout'.'

This man is still a live one and I do not think anything is to be gained by more action than I have taken, which was a heart to heart talk on carelessness.

It can be seen that Sayler tried to be fair. He had a quick and rather frightening temper, but he also had a good bit of charm which he used on occasion to advantage. One evening the criminal court reporter was leaving early for a party at the Bismark Gardens on Addison and Halsted streets, a northside spot which was frequented by judges, bailiffs and clerks. The desk man, however, held him up by insisting on clearing some item on the schedule. The reporter protested that the records were locked in the vault. The desk man would not be dissuaded: in his day, he said, the reporters knew the combinations to all the vaults on their beats. The reporter finally lost patience, told the desk man to go to hell, and left for the party.

The next morning he had Sayler to deal with.

"I'm quitting," the reporter shouted, before the conversation had really begun.

"You can't quit," Sayler roared. "You're fired."

"I'm not. I quit."

"You're fired!"

That was that. Sometime later, after the reporter had gone to work for one of the newspapers, he met Sayler, who held out his big hand.

"I'm glad to see you," Sayler said. "You know, it was a shame you had to quit us after all those years."

"I didn't quit," the reporter said. "I was fired."

"No, you weren't," Sayler said. "you quit."

Suddenly both men remembered their last conversation and burst into laughter. Sayler was able to melt away grudges.

In 1900 William Randolph Hearst entered the Chicago newspaper field with the *Evening American*, and two years later he added the *Examiner*, a morning paper. All sorts of changes ensued about this time. In 1901 Kohlsaat sold the *Post* to John C. Schaffer and bought the *Record* from Victor Lawson, combining it with the *Herald* as the *Record-Herald*. Lawson had the paper back on his hands within the year, and hired Frank B. Noyes, the Washington publisher, to run it.

In 1897 Charles Yerkes, who controlled the Chicago street railway lines, had taken over the *InterOcean* and was also in the midst of a feud with Lawson, whose newspapers, he said, did not accord fair treatment to Yerkes' proposed program of improvements in local transportation. Lawson replied that Yerkes' cable systems were both faulty and badly managed. Yerkes brought George Wheeler Hinman to edit the *Inter-Ocean* from the editorial staff of the New York *Sun*, whose proprietor, Charles A. Dana, was strongly opposed to the Associated Press, and announced that the *InterOcean* under its new management would oppose "the Chicago newspaper trust" and advocate supplying AP news to all papers that wanted it. The *InterOcean* began to refer to Lawson as "Rice Water Lawson" (in a reference to the free nursing care that the *Daily News* offered to tenement babies) and also as "the Baal of the newspaper trust."

Yerkes moved to London but the *Inter Ocean* continued to bait Lawson, and in 1900 sued the Associated Press, which had banned the *InterOcean* from service because it was employing another news service, the Laffin service. The *InterOcean* contended that the AP was acting in constraint of trade, and the Illinois Supreme Court found in favor of the *InterOcean*, declaring that AP was actually a public utility since it was chartered to build telephone and telegraph lines. Lawson fought this decision by organizing a new Associated Press in New York as a New York corporation. The old AP was allowed to cease existing on December 31, 1900.

In 1904 John Eastman gained control of the *Journal*, and in 1905 the *Chronicle* folded, close on the heels of the sensational crash of the John R. Walsh banks. This was the last major change in the Chicago newspaper scene until 1914 when James Keeley, who had become managing editor of the *Tribune* in 1898, bought both the *Inter Ocean* and the *Record-Herald*, and combined them into the *Herald*, a paper which did not survive the first World War.

Archibald Leckie did not remain in Rockford, but went to Joliet, and then in 1904 moved to Philadelphia, to try to establish a City Press association there. On February 15, 1904 he wrote a letter to "Messrs. Sayler, Jones, Wharton, Brown, Johnson, Watkins, Harshman, Elwell, Ash, Tavenner and All the Others" on a letterhead of the Philadelphia Press Association which carried an address of 911 Walnut Street, and listed *The Daily Bulletin, The North American, The Record, The Telegraph, The Press, The Inquirer,* and *The Public Ledger* as clients. The time he wrote the letter was, rather significantly, 3:15 a.m.

> I can't end this "first day" without acknowledging your kind, cheering and very welcome telegram. It struck me just when I needed it as badly as I ever did a big drink at the breaking of the cold gray dawn of the morning after election day.

The institution of a C.P.A. by whatever name it may be called, in a conservative city like this is no joke, and the fact that one of the papers, one of the most enterprising and energetic, has taken up a fight against it does not lighten the task. I have had to get together a new force of men who never saw a stylus or a sheet of flimsy and to jump into every department, including marine and markets, without any breaking in process.

I have wished a hundred times to-day that I had the old Chicago force with me to show them what Johnson used to call "many things" but even you fellows would have your own troubles with the system in vogue here where everything is done to tie up news. There are over forty police stations and police boats and there is not a telephone in any one of them; each has to be visited at least twice each night. Fires are struck only at the engine house and city hall and everything is on a similar plan. I have fourteen men on night police work alone and a total staff of forty-two.

On February 25th Leckie wrote again. His letters are interesting because they point up the differences that obviously existed between Chicago, apparently a city open to new ideas, and Philadelphia, where it was difficult to make headway. The letters also point to the very warm feeling that existed between Leckie and Sayler, and Leckie's warm feeling for the Chicago bureau. Leckie's commendable optimism in this second, and apparently last, letter is unfortunately misplaced; his attempt to open a bureau was a failure.

In this letter the letterhead is new, and *The Inquirer* has been replaced by the *German Daily Gazette*. The letter is addressed to Sayler alone:

I have had no time for social correspondence in the past ten days and consequently no opportunity to tell you of my thrilling experiences. My copy has not blown out of the window as it being winter time the windows are closed. Were it not for this fact I am convinced that my experience would in this respect as in most others have paralleled that of poor John Ballantyne. I have certainly had a fierce game and you have no conception of the difficulties I have to meet. I had none myself or I doubt if I would have had the courage to tackle the job. However by sheer force I am getting the best of it and can with reasonable certainty predict success. I have been conducting a continuous old-fashioned "election" stunt almost as much in the dark as we were that never to be forgotten night when we first grappled with returns.

I have a big force, which was at first the scum of the town, without the slightest conception of what was expected of them and little inclination to do what was wanted when they had it drummed into their thick heads. My twenty district or police men are of all degrees of incompetency or indolence, the few experienced men I have being more aggravating than the cubs. I don't know the city myself and though I have been at it day and night, catching a little sleep on a couch you can believe it has been enough to make a quitter quit. The city editors are with two exceptions against me and are constantly kicking about the service on the most trivial pretexts, as usual missing the many really good grounds for complaint. My men are refused news at the police stations, through the machinations of the other reporters and on the pretext that they have no police cards, which here take the place of badges and are all-powerful.

My cards in turn are held up and I am unable to get them put through the necessary red tape at the city hall. My market men have been ruled off the Bourse and the Commercial and produce exchanges and I am making up a kind of report from the brokers' offices and bucket shops.

But things are clearing up... I to-day got word from the director of public safety that he would see that I got my cards and that in the meantime he would discharge or degrade any police official who refuses legitimate news. Such a remark when made here means more than it does in Chicago. The Commercial Exchange reopened my matter today and had a stormy board meeting, adjourning until to-morrow. I have hopes.

I am left to fight it out alone but have all kind of moral support. The publishers say they will, if necessary, shut off the publication of market news. They have raised their subscription voluntarily and told me to go ahead regardless of expense and not to lose my nerve...

Not the least of my troubles is the Messenger service. The little imps will turn my head if I don't find some means of getting some good boys.

My financial arrangements are most peculiar. I met the payroll last week with my own money, owing to slowness in the publishers coming up with their subscriptions. I am carrying three bank accounts, personal, personal no. 2 which I use for office matters on my own capital—and A.S. Leckie General Manager, which is my office account, which I have not yet touched.

I haven't drawn a cent myself yet and haven't any definite knowledge of what my salary is to be. I had to leave my name off the last payroll and don't see how I can get it on the next...

...I would like to have another 250 yellow books and 1,000 carbon sheets to fit them. If you can spare the former and order the latter for me, shipping them by express, you will add to the obligations under which you have placed me...

In those years around the turn of the century many people came to work for City Press whose names later became famous in the newspaper world. Walter Brown came back from the Spanish-American War in 1899 to join the organization, of which he was to become general manager. Junius B. Wood, who would become one of the most noted of the *Daily News* foreign correspondents, started as a bureau cub in 1900.

Percy Hammond, later a well-known newspaper drama critic, was a City Press reporter and desk man. James P. Bicket, who was for years managing editor of the Chicago *American*, had risen by 1900 from a beginner to desk man at the bureau. And Walter Howey, who was to be made a legend by Hecht and MacArthur in their play *The Front Page*, began his career at the bureau. Philip Kinsley, later a *Tribune* writer, earned what was possibly his first two dollars in newspaper work as a bureau helper in the judicial election of June 1, 1903.

Clare Snively, a reporter of the period who became police chief of Los Angeles and then a parole officer for the Department of Justice, wrote to Vickerman in the thirties:

> My first work with the bureau, because I was unacquainted with Chicago's streets, was covering downtown assignments. I had been a general news gatherer on my dad's paper, a p.m. daily, Canton, Ill., and went to Chicago in October, 1899, with somewhat of an inferiority complex following a long period of drinking. I had my mind made up I'd keep away from reportorial work because of convivial associates and tried my hand at soliciting subscribers for the old morning *Record*. Didn't know the paper was under boycott, so had several thrilling, unhappy experiences when I solicited wives of laborites—was roller-pinned, cuffed and bootjacked from top floors to the street. Ten days of that strife with strikers and their wives caused me to search out my cousin, who was an AP editor, just across the hall from the bureau office, and he, with the assistance of George Ade and John T. McCutcheon, persuaded Harry Sayler to give me employment.
>
> I was a pencil pusher; knew a typewriter when I saw one, but never had tinkered with one. When Mr. Sayler learned I had no typing experience he indicated I could not work for the bureau. I pleaded for time and he gave me an old machine, stationed in a rear room to practice on. I worked all night on the keys and acquired suffi-

cient practice to pass into employment, going to work the next night.

After a few weeks training in the downtown district I was shunted to the old territory of Austin, Oak Park, Cicero, Harlem, Maywood and towns adjacent, making headquarters at Austin, which had just been annexed to Chicago... I covered this territory, via street cars and elevated services until I formed acquaintance with police and justices; then I purchased a bicycle on instalment plan and covered the beat on the wheel. I must have made good as a newsgatherer as my salary was increased once or twice for my coverage.

Next I was called into the office and was directed to take charge of the Criminal court beat. Old Joe, last name forgotten, a veteran bureauman, who covered this beat, had died or was on a tear, I do not recollect which, so I was transferred. I worked this beat for several months, and was transferred to the City Hall beat, bucking such men as Guy Cramer, Harry Young and veterans of those days. I "jumped the gun" on a bullet proof jacket test in order to scoop Davy Barnes, *News* police reporter and was on the carpet before Mr. Leckie when City Editor Harry Bird of the *News* complained. Chief Kipley, Billy Pinkerton and others—even Mayor Carter H. Harrison—intervened for me, but it did not avail. Mr. Leckie, instead of bouncing me outright, gave me six weeks in which to find other employment. Through Harry Chamberlain, I landed on the old *Record*, and the day before the *Record* was disposed of I landed on the *Daily News* with the assistance of Jimmy Gilruth. I had many interesting experiences while with the bureau, but covered more important stories while on the *News* staff...

On the afternoon of December 30, 1903, a relatively new reporter was walking to his assignment at City Hall when he noticed an accident involving a fire cart, and thereby stumbled onto one of City News's greatest scoops. It was the Iroquois theater fire.

The Iroquois had just opened on Market street, now Wacker drive, north of Madison street, and had been issued a license without proper inspection. There was a matinee that day for a performance of *Mr. Bluebeard* with Eddie Foy Sr. and the Seven Little Foys. Unfortunately the audience consisted largely of children. The fire apparently started in the area of the stage. Attendants attempted to open a skylight, when the flames swept out over the audience, so that the fire could be diverted upward, but the window was not yet operating and would not open.

Most of the dead were found on the main floor: the exit doors opened inward to the auditorium and consequently bodies were piled up around them. It was an unparalleled catastrophe; from it came new laws requiring a fireproof curtain between the stage and the audience, and exit doors that opened outward. All other news was squeezed out of the newspapers, which kept the presses rolling for lists of the dead, eyewitness accounts, statements by city officials, stories about acts of heroism and biographies of the noted dead. The entire City Press staff was kept at work all night. At 4 a.m. one youngster telephoned James Bicket, who was still on the "day" desk.

"I'm going home, Mr Bicket," the young man said. "My work is all done."

"The hell it is," snapped Bicket. "Get out to an undertaker's and watch for identifications."

But it was weeks before some of the victims were identified. And for at least ten days the newspapers grappled with the story. At Hearst's *American*, the staff worked around the clock catching naps on desks under the lights or on top of stacks of old newspapers in the reference room. Most of the men stayed in their clothes for a week. Out of gratitude for their selflessness Hearst gave each member of the staff an unprecedented bonus of three weeks' extra salary.

Eventually, largely because of press agitation, five men were indicted by the grand jury for neglect leading to the deaths, but when public hysteria ceased to be enflamed, the indictments lapsed.

We are fortunate to have discovered in the City News files Walter Howey's own story of his scoop, and some of his other experiences, written apparently for Isaac Gershman in September, 1951 and sent to Chicago from Hearst offices in Boston:

It took a year at the Chicago Art Institute for Walter Howey, born in Fort Dodge, Iowa, to discover he could never become an artist.

Howey decided to try the newspaper business. He went up the stairs of the Fourth avenue building of the old *Daily News* and told Harry Smith he understood George Ade, the humorist, was sick. Howey told Harry Smith he was a versatile writer and felt he could fill this vacancy. City Editor Smith told Howey Ade was not sick. Howey said, "If anybody else is sick, I might fill in."

Smith asked Howey if he knew his way around Chicago. Howey told him he knew it like a book. Smith asked, "How long would it take you to get to the corner of State street and Wabash avenue?" Howey told Smith he thought he could do it in about ten minutes because he was a runner. Smith told Howey to run and call him up from that corner. A traffic cop informed Howey that these two streets ran parallel and never met and had no corner. Howey walked around a few blocks and then returned to see Smith. He complimented Smith on his great sense of humor. He told Smith that this proved that Howey also had a sense of humor because "Howey had to run to make the joke good."

Smith then called Harry Saylor, then Manager of the City Press Association, and Howey went to work at eight bucks a week.

One day he was walking toward the City Hall at Randolph and LaSalle streets when he heard clanging firebells and saw a fire horse run into a loaded truck and fall.

Instead of caring for the horse, the firemen rushed down the middle of the block to the Iroquois theater foyer through a broken glass door. Howey followed them in.

Lorgnettes, feather boas, opera glasses and pocketbooks were strewn along the aisles, marking the frantic escape of first floor theater patrons. A company headed by the late Eddie Foy, was presenting a New Year's matinee.

The firemen heard groans from the balcony and climbed the smoke-filled stairways to where piled-up victims had died from inhaling smoke and flame from burning scenery drawn into the theater by a powerful exhaust fan in the theater roof.

Howey encountered Bill Sallers, city fireman assigned to the theater, who was blistered and burned. Sallers volunteered the belief that at least 25 people had been killed in the fire.

Howey went to Eddie Dreyfus' saloon, adjoining the theater, dropped a dime in the wall phone box and pressed a button for a telephone operator who was slow to answer. He then went to a bookmaker having a rolltop desk and an unlimited telephone at the rear of the saloon and offered the bookmaker what money he had saved, about $20.00 for the use of this unlimited telephone for the afternoon.

The bookmaker agreed to the deal provided he could sit at the telephone and keep the wire in touch with the City Press office then run by Walter Brown.

Howey brashly told Brown that he had taken charge and asked him to have all reporters report to him at Dreyfus' saloon for fast news communication.

Howey then had a boy get a paper of pins and go around to all public telephones within several blocks of the Iroquois theater and stick a pin into the shielded wires of each telephone.

Howey knew it was not necessary to cut a telephone wire to render the telephone inoperative. The pins set up a short circuit.

This is how Howey's telephone provided about all the news concerning the Iroquois theater fire that all Chicago newspapers could print up to late in the evening when the late Harry Powers volunteered the startling information that there were 800 or more people in the balcony and he doubted if any of them got out alive.

For this stunt Howey's salary was raised from eight dollars to twelve dollars a week. This income in 1904 made a millionaire out of a newspaper reporter because he could get a choice of roast beef, roast ham, potato pancakes and young onions with a glass of beer for five cents and still save enough money to take a girl out seven nights a week.

Howey was introduced to the late Jim Bicket, formerly of the City Press, but then assistant city editor of the *Chicago American*, and he went to work for Mr. Hearst.

Howey has been with Mr. Hearst ever since except for a brief period on the *Chicago Tribune* and *InterOcean*.

Howey's reference to the *Tribune* here is deliberately low-key.

It is interesting to note, as an addendum to this story, that there are various versions of Howey's discovery of the Iroquois theater fire. The version given here has a strong claim to legitimacy, as we will see. But in other versions we are told that Howey noticed a trickle of smoke from under the front doors of the theater, or that Howey saw a trickle of smoke from a nearby manhole. The manhole appears again in this imaginative re-telling printed in *Time* magazine in 1950:

Hearst Executive Walter Howey...was only a City Press cub on routine assignment in 1903 when a blackened figure in stage costume suddenly popped out of a nearby manhole and gasped a few frenzied words.

Another City Press reporter who worked on the Iroquois theater fire was Frank Carson, who became nearly as much of a legend in his own right as Walter Howey. Carson had been a reporter in Chicago since 1904, and he was not always delicate in his methods of getting news. When John McPhaul met him in 1923, Carson was managing editor of the *Herald-Examiner*, having succeeded Howey, who had moved to New York to become managing editor of the *Mirror*. Carson and Howey had been on the *Tribune* together before that. Howey had left the Trib after a dispute with the owners, Joseph Medill Patterson and his cousin, Colonel Robert McCormick, vowing undying enmity against that paper. He began by giving a party to celebrate Carson's accession to Howey's job as city editor of the *Tribune*. Sometime during the festivities Carson gave Howey his autograph and learned the next morning that he had actually signed a contract to become city editor of the *Herald-Examiner*. Since this involved a raise in pay, Carson joined Howey to get news and to embarrass the *Tribune* whenever possible.

McPhaul noticed that Carson had a desk drawer full of badges in his office: coroner's badges, health department badges, fire department badges, building inspector badges—he could gain instant entrée anywhere for his reporters.

On October 12, 1902, a newcomer was added to the City Press payroll under the name of "Hartsman". He was actually Thurman Harshman who, as "Mr. H", ruled the bureau night staff from the city desk for more than thirty years. He always had a keen eye for idiotic copy. Many a cub whose efforts he sent back to be recopied squirmed with anger at the "old man", but many eminent figures on newspapers and magazines later gave him unlimited credit for helping them learn how to write. One of these was William L. Chenery, who wrote to Vickerman in the thirties when Chenery was editor of *Collier's*:

> The grim insistence of Brown and Harshman and their assistants at getting details right regardless of the effort required has, I think, been highly useful to me. I

remember also that Harshman had a lively appreciation of literature and he was always ready to encourage
a reporter who might turn in a good story or compose a
bright line.

Chenery started with the bureau in 1910, when he was a
dark-haired youth living at Hull House. He helped to cover
the sensational trial of Lee O'Neil Browne that year in the
case involving the expulsion from the U.S. senate of William
"Billy" Lorimer. At that time members of the senate were
chosen by state legislatures: the 17th amendment, authoriz-
ing senators to be popularly elected, had not yet been passed.
Lorimer was a Republican who had been elected with the
help of votes from fifty Democrats in the Illinois legislature.
Charles White, a Democratic state representative, gave Jim
Keeley, the editor of the *Tribune*, details of a scheme of bribery which had elected Lorimer. White admitted that he had
accepted $1900 to vote for Lorimer; but he wished to confess
in order to restore ethical conduct to the Illinois legislature.
He asked Keeley for $50,000 for his statement.

Keeley spent $16,000 on a two-month investigation of the
charges. He chewed White down to $3250 and found two more
legislators who were willing to confess that they had sold
their votes. The *Tribune* ran sensational headlines. However
a senate committee exonerated Lorimer after a months-long
investigation of their own.

There was a lot of political celebration: a band was sent
round to Tribune Tower to give a mock serenade. Lorimer's
friend William Hale Thompson referred to Col. McCormick
as a "pipsqueak", thereby guaranteeing a permanent lack of
positive publicity for himself in the *Tribune*. Lee O'Neil
Browne, one of the legislators named in the newspaper as
having accepted a bribe, was tried in county court and
acquitted. This was the trial covered by Chenery and other
bureau reporters.

Browne filed an enormous libel suit against the *Tribune*.
There were strong threats of other libel suits: Keeley had

implied that the money for the bribery had come from big business, and especially from the packing and lumber industries. Thus the czars of those companies threatened suits too. However, while McCormick and Patterson were panicking at the prospect of financial ruin, Herman Kohlsaat, who was in charge of the *Record-Herald* through Victor Lawson's dispensation, wrote a thoughtful editorial in which he commented that it was a sorry day in this country when $100,000 would be used to buy a senate seat.

Emotions exploded all over again. Kohlsaat said he had been told about the bribery at lunch by Clarence Funk, the general manager of International Harvester, owned by the Cyrus McCormick family. Hearings were reopened in the U.S. senate and the Illinois legislature. Funk testified that Edward Hines, the lumber tycoon, had asked him for $10,000 and had said that $100,000 had already been put up to ensure Lorimer's election. Lorimer was expelled from the senate by a vote of 55 to 28, and the libel suits were dropped. The *Tribune* was saved.

The Colonel, however, continued to quake for some time after the danger was past, and he did not apparently find it in his heart to forgive Keeley who, because of various snubs, left the *Tribune* and bought the *Record-Herald*, which Lawson had taken back from Kohlsaat, who could not make it pay. Keeley could not make it pay either, possibly because he needed to satisfy his financial backers, who were Samuel Insull, Julius Rosenwald and Charles Crane, representing the utilities industry, Sears Roebuck and Company and the plumbing equipment industry. After four years, in 1918, Keeley sold out to Hearst and became a vice-president of public relations for the Pullman company. Hearst merged the *Herald* with his *Examiner*. And Chenery left the bureau and went to the *Evening Post*.

Harshman had come from a small town in southern Illinois to make his fortune; his widespread interests included history, philosophy, sports, finance, politics, astrology and spiritualism. For years he kept a forecast of the grain market, and a number of traders fell into the habit of dropping by the office at night to consult him. One of his former night crew wrote:

> Harshman is fixed in my memory for two things: (1) his constant analyzing of the grain market on huge and numerous charts with but little noticeable financial improvement to himself and (2) his passionate discussions in the late hours of the evening on various topics, including religion.

George Clarke, city editor of the New York *Mirror*, added:

> (3) The T-bone steak he ordered every morning at one o'clock from the restaurant.

Harshman had a soft heart: he lent money to always-broke reporters, and frequently "lost" the dreaded blue envelopes in which Sayler's and then Brown's dismissal notices were left for the night desk man to pass to the staff.

One night during a heartbreaking family crisis Harshman was alone in the office except for a switchboard boy. There was a 4-11 fire alarm sounding, and the relief desk man was late. When Harshman finally was able to leave the office his desperately ill daughter, about whom he had worried all evening, had died. Each afternoon after that before coming to work at seven p.m. he visited her grave. He was a devoted family man.

Opposite Harshman on the night desk, from 1904 on, sat a little man with a green eyeshade and a long cigar drooping from his lips: Joe Levandier. He was Harshman's assistant.

"Does Joe still chew on that damn stick?" was the inevitable inquiry of the old-timer.

The eyeshade helped to cover a deep scar on Joe's forehead. A good many explanations have been offered for that scar. One was that he was struck by a piece of "iron confetti" thrown by a cheering bystander while he was covering a parade in a tough district. Joe himself said that a brick fell on him when he walked past a building that was being demolished.

"Joe and Harsh" worked together on many important news stories. Not many nights after Joe was hired, he was assigned to cover a sewer explosion at Root and Halsted streets, where a number of unidentified workmen were trapped and killed. Joe obtained a full list of the employees, and set out to visit their homes, on the assumption that if they were not home they had been killed in the sewer. Breaking bad news is a delicate business, of which Joe had had no experience.

He rang the doorbell of one house and asked for the man whose name he had on his list. The woman who had answered the door said that her husband wasn't home.

"What is it?" she asked. "Something wrong?"

"I'm sorry, Madam," Joe said. "He's dead."

The woman fainted into his arms.

At that moment a husky laboring man came strolling through the front gate, strongly interested in the sight of his wife clutched in the embrace of a young stranger. Joe had some difficulty explaining, and then he learned that it was the husband's night off and he had been downtown celebrating, and had thus escaped the explosion. Some were led to believe that such experiences with women had made Joe a bachelor by preference.

His imperturbability was as widely known as his bachelorhood. Since he took over the desk late in the afternoon he was often caught in a rush of bulletins, flashes and staff checking in and out. One day the frantic switchboard operator moaned,

"Joe, I've got seven telephone calls waiting for you."

"Put them on," Joe said imperturbably. "One at a time."

One of the earliest of the Harshman-Levandier news partnerships involved the crash of the John R. Walsh bank, of which Walsh, who owned the *Chronicle* and a large newspaper distribution agency, was the president and principal stockholder. On the night of December 18, 1905, a banker called the bureau and asked that a reporter be sent to the bank at once. Joe sensed something big, and bulletined the papers. He went looking for Harshman, who was at lunch.

The elevator wasn't working, so he ran hastily down the stairs, and nearly collided with Harshman, who was running up. He had heard Joe's footsteps on the stairs from the lobby, and knew at once that something was happening. Together they got the story started. George Bryant, then on the "last watch" at the detective bureau, was the only reporter available, so a police reporter was sent to cover one of the greatest financial stories of the new century.

The Walsh bank failure is usually credited as a *Tribune* scoop. McPhaul gives one version of it:

> Leaving the *Tribune* in the after-midnight hours of a cold December night in 1905 Jim Keeley observed a patch of lights in the First National Bank Building. A guard recognized him and in answer to Keeley's question explained that a meeting was going on. At the conference room door Keeley nodded imperiously to a second guard and was nodded inside. A quick glance told him that he was in the midst of a gathering of downtown bank presidents.
>
> "Well, gentlemen," he said briskly, "you have sent for me and I am here. What can I do for you?"

There was none among the bankers who did not recognize the *Tribune's* editor and each, evidently, assumed he had been summoned by one of their number. Keeley got a fill-in: John Walsh's bank was on the rocks. The editor nodded sagely, made a few non-committal remarks and excused himself to powder his nose.

He found a pail and slid out the door, explaining to the guard that he was going for coffee. At the *Tribune* he stopped the presses and, while the delivery wagons waited, dictated a story on the impending bank failure.

It has not been noted that the City Press bureau had the information on the bank failure before the *Tribune*. While Keeley was hurrying into the composing room to dictate the story to a linotype operator, bureau copy was going through the tubes to the *Tribune* and to other morning papers as well.

However at the *Examiner*, the *Record-Herald* and the *Inter Ocean* the carriers remained untouched in the basket until morning because the staffs had gone home for the night.

Walsh was convicted in federal court of diverting two million dollars of bank funds to his other enterprises. He was sentenced to two years in jail, and in the uproar the *Chronicle* folded.

R.W. Patterson was elected president of the City Press Association in 1903. He was succeeded by Medill McCormick, and then by James Keeley. Victor Lawson remained secretary during these changes.

During the early 1900's a ticker system was installed for sending bulletins to the newspapers. The message emerged in the news rooms on a tape, in a manner similar to the stock market tape. A woman operator was hired, but the system was too slow. If there were a rush of heavy news the bulletins would begin to pile up. The bureau returned to telephone bulletins. It was necessary to provide news quickly, especially after Hearst opened his newspaper in 1900, and the battle for circulation heated up. There were routine but bloody fights among the men who delivered the major newspapers, and much of the blood spilt belonged to newsstand operators. In 1900 the bureau began to keep a police reporter on duty all night: before that, the reporter had gone off duty at 4 a.m. leaving the city uncovered for three hours.

Everything had speeded up: there were automobiles on the street, some whizzing along at eighteen miles an hour. When they broke down, as they inevitably did, horse-drawn police patrols were sent out to retrieve them and haul them to the stations, somewhat impeded by the fright the hulks gave some of the more nervous horses. By 1905 electric streetcars had been in use for more than ten years. But money was tightening, and reporters who had once ridden for nothing and made free telephone calls began to find their privileges sharply curtailed. Bicycles were expensive and were considered rich men's vehicles: only a few reporters could afford them. One of these lucky ones was Otto Pompel, a bearded newsgatherer for a German language paper, who pedaled swiftly behind the police patrols, his whiskers ruffling in the breeze.

Another progressive reporter was the bureau's Norman A. Lee, an Englishman, who wore high top boots and had a revolver strapped to his hip. Lee carried the first portable typewriter ever seen at the bureau. He carried it with him to all assignments. If he were covering a fire he would sit down on a convenient curb and thump out his story on the spot, much to the delight of the neighborhood ragamuffins.

But the era of the "leg man" was already at hand. The number of rewrite men was increased at the bureau, and the office telephones were equipped with headgear, as reporters began to dictate their stories. Assignments had to change, since the old courts with their much bewailed injustices were replaced by the modern municipal court system. Juvenile court was established in 1907.

Libel suits were a constant problem for newspapers in those days, and the bureau itself was open to them as well. In a report to Lawson, Sayler wrote on April 20, 1901:

> The question of libel suits against the newspapers based on our reports seems to be a matter which must be taken up soon. While we have been particularly fortunate and have been involved in very little trouble on this score, the situation is becoming more threatening. With all possible care the collection of the large amount of matter from the police courts and other sources of minor news involves constant danger of error. With the experienced lawyers we have been successful, but a number of the young attorneys seem to have concluded that a promising field for fees lies in this direction...

Seven years later, in another report to the board of directors, Sayler wrote:

> Since I have been in sole charge, over seven years, ninety-one libel suits, aggregating $9,406,000 have been begun against the papers using this service. Of this

number, only eight suits were attributable either directly or indirectly to errors of ours...

On June 15, 1910, City Press was split into two organizations. The editorial department was incorporated on a not-for-profit basis as the City News Bureau of Chicago, and the old name of the City Press Association of Chicago was retained only for the tube system and its valuable assets. James Keeley was president at the meeting where the agreement was reached, and Lawson was of course secretary. It was a technical reorganization, done chiefly to save money on taxes, and made no appreciable difference in the operation of either unit. At the same time, however, the bureau's field of coverage was restricted to Cook county.

On May 31, 1913, Harry Sayler died suddenly at Indianapolis where he had gone to attend the 500 mile Decoration Day automobile race. He was survived by his widow and two children: a son, John, whom he had asked not to take up the grind of newspaper work, and a daughter Margaret. A tribute was given to him by the agency:

Under Mr. Sayler's direction these cooperative agencies (the City Press Association and the City News Bureau) doubled in scope and numerical strength and became established institutions of the Chicago newspaper field. To the development of the service Mr. Sayler contributed greatly and it became one of the most efficient services of its kind in the country, and especially notable for the speed and accuracy with which it performed the difficult and trying task of covering election returns. Harry Lincoln Sayler was an accomplished newspaperman, a most capable organizer and director of news collection, an expert of national fame in the compilation of election returns, a good citizen, a faithful friend, and a good man.

In Memoriam
Harry Lincoln Sayler.

"Scores of newspapermen, authors, and playwrights owe their first start to Mr. Sayler," said the *Tribune*. "He has probably corrected the faults of more budding writers than any other journalist in the country."

"He was not only an exceptionally capable newspaperman, but he had a high order of literary ability and was unquestionably the best writer of juvenile fiction stories of his time," said the Indianapolis *Star*.

Walter Brown became general manager at Sayler's death, and served until his own retirement in 1931.

9

Journalist Bootcamp

Accuracy! And details! The insistence on these has driven many a City Press neophyte to distraction. To the average cub it does not seem to matter whether one gas burner or three were open when pretty Jean Smithers was found unconscious in her room. But the extra burners are indications of suicide rather than accident. Many a disillusioned youth has found himself discovering that reporters and door-to-door salesmen have much in common. Both encounter the same rebuffs, doors slammed in their faces, drudgery and disdain. Reporters may encounter more threats and more actual physical violence, and they are supposed to maintain a professional bearing and harbor no resentments. If a reporter finds himself constantly getting into scrapes he will be replaced before much more time passes.

In primitive times, recruits came mostly from the ranks of newsboys and helpers on newspaper trucks: lads already bright, with a high polish of street smarts, but innocent of any academic gloss. Few beginners had university degrees in the early days. Pasted high on the wall of the copy room at City News for many years was a newspaper cartoon showing a downy, sheepskin-clutching youth confronted by a tigerish editor who snarls: "And what, may I ask, is a school of journalism?"

Young men seeking work at City News were commonly given test assignments, a few hours of actual work which could demonstrate almost instantly to a management with vast powers of discernment the applicant's journalistic potential. The test assignments were low-grade ore indeed. The new hand was sent to neighborhood pet shows, high-school debating society finals, or conventions of the National Association of Paper Clip Manufacturers. Since the bureau seldom covered these events anyhow, bungling the assignments would hardly matter.

When the job seeker stumbled into the office with a pocket full of notes and a head filled with confusion, he was invited to sit down at the typewriter and commit his findings to paper. The youth's personality, his capacity to make any sense at all out of the dreary crud he had been sent to cover, and his ability to get it down in understandable fashion determined his fate. Management placed great reliance on this process of "sniffing at" the applicant's first effort.

When hired, the newcomer was sent out on a police beat with an experienced hand, often a "veteran" of a full year on the job. The veteran taught him to telephone the six or eight stations on the beat every hour and to ask routine questions like "What's doing, Sarge?" in a friendly and interested voice. His mentor also explained that the youth must conduct himself in an unobtrusive, pleasant fashion among news sources—namely coppers—but never allow himself to be bullied or slighted in favor of competing reporters from the papers. This was not always easy. Particularly when the competitors were on first name terms with the policemen who controlled the flow of news.

The beginner soon learned that these newspaper representatives were more than competitors; they could become teachers and friends. On an "open story" when everyone knew roughly what had happened, reporters helped each other in getting details. But when a newspaper reporter had a quiet tip-off he disappeared to work in solitude. He showed up again only when his epic had been printed—perhaps even with a headline.

Three days (sometimes more, more often less) were allotted for breaking in the novice. Then he was sent out to cover a beat alone. Crime was most active at night; so night reporters were usually busier than day men. But on days there were police courts to watch, where the cases of wifebeaters and petty thieves were heard. It was the day man's job to attempt to isolate odd bits of news from this material. Upon reporting for work each day, the newcomer was confronted with clips of stories he had failed to get the day before. His explanation that the story must have come from tipsters—the papers were known to have dozens of these—met with pointed scorn. It was equally futile to plead that the policeman who gave out the story was an old buddy of the newspaper reporter. (The *Tribune* even handed out a substantial reward each month to any policeman deemed to have performed a meritorious act.) There was no defense for the crime of being scooped.

Although criticism and threats of firing were sharp at the bureau, no one seemed to notice when a beat man successfully covered a big story. Unspoken but religiously adhered to was the principle: "Perfection is acceptable. Wordlessly acceptable. Anything less cannot be tolerated; it will be excoriated."

A bemused reporter wrote to Vickerman in the thirties about the problems he encountered:

> Most of our stuff came from heavy-fisted coppers who had never learned to spell and who couldn't read their own writing anyway. The police might have a name spelled one way, the hospital another, the coroner a third. Probably it wasn't in the telephone book. Even members of the same family might spell it differently. That sometimes happens.
>
> But that was just a name. The age might be wrong. Or maybe Mrs. Jones was Miss Jones. Or Sam Jones in a scrape was Sam Jones Jr. The police seldom worry about such things. Or Jumbo street could be North Jumbo Street or South Jumbo street. Maybe it would turn out not to be in Chicago at all. Then maybe it was

one of the suburbs, but which one? Probably it would end up in Jumbo place. Jones was a laborer, according to the police report. But the police call everyone who works a laborer. The wife of a bank president is a mere housewife to the police. As likely as not Jones was a superintendent.

If it was an accident there might be a dozen names, ages, addresses, occupations to get right. Maybe a good many more. As likely as not you had to get them by telephone from a busy desk sergeant who was sore anyway about the story we printed last week of him falling into the lake while fishing. It was hot, the windows were open and streetcars were pounding by outside; a dozen noisy cops were laughing and talking at your elbow; the testy sergeant hung up when you asked him to repeat a name; the office was on the wire every three minutes wanting to know what the hell was holding up the story...

And it was supposed to be accurate! The readers of a newspaper never guess when they see a story so neatly in print, how much sweat and worry and mental agony went into putting it there. And the next time a reporter wakes them up late at night or annoys them when there has been a death in the family, are they sore!

Co-workers coached the beginner; news sources were often eager and willing to supply tips. And—perhaps most useful of all—competing reporters sometimes went out of their way to give pointers. One United Press reporter, Robert Klockau, later to become a prosperous attorney in Rock Island, was particularly known for this form of generosity. Bob tried to show by example how language should be used with clarity and color to avoid the deadly dullness which too often infects news writing. At one neighborhood horse show, he tapped out on his portable typewriter:

The winner of the bareback riding event was a veritable razorback hog of a horse, a sort of two-by-six plank on edge with a leg at each corner. Extremely flatulent too—his flatulence was so noisy that he seemed to be jet propelled. It was a mystery how his rider stayed on at the turns. Perhaps he was equipped with a prehensile posterior.

It did not go quite that way on the sacred UP wire, of course. Bob was just showing how it *should* be done.

Almost as important to the learner was the very atmosphere of the detective bureau, from which he picked up, seemingly by osmosis, the principles and practices that made the place tick. These were something like the British constitution—unwritten, seldom mentioned, but potent in a mysterious way.

Though disillusion awaited neophytes expecting to find high adventure in becoming reporters, they did "see life" though commonly of a tawdry and pathetic sort. They also saw death: bullet-torn store owners slumped over cash registers they died to protect; sodden, limp forms dragged dripping from the river. But, interspersed with all that, reporters often got in on the ground floor of interesting events: rescues from burning buildings by men who got themselves critically burned; collections to aid an evicted widow by neighbors who themselves were not far from eviction.

Such front row seats did much to alleviate the sheer misery of digging into dull records. Some reporters found such satisfaction in being the first witnesses on the scene that they passed up chances for advancement to more dignified and profitable jobs. A small corps of perennial police reporters, men who dodged promotion to stay on their uncomfortable but challenging beats, squabbled endlessly among themselves as they struggled for exclusive news. But they stood shoulder to shoulder like musk oxen threatened by encircling wolves when it was whispered that "the office" was making trouble for one of their number. The intoxicating syncopation of fire engines thundering to 5-11 fires, the wail of police sirens hurrying to the scene of the most recent gang killing and the sometimes more than verbal interrogation of robbery suspects in police squad rooms were all strong stuff which some eager young men could not resist.

In the early thirties there were five police beats in Chicago, which corresponded roughly to those laid out in 1899 to correspond with the police divisions of the day: Central, with three shifts covering five police stations, all police offices in police headquarters and the detective bureau; West, with two shifts covering twelve police stations; North, with two shifts covering eight stations; Hyde Park, with two shifts covering fourteen stations and the stockyards; and South, night shift only, covering five police stations as a relief for the Central man. In addition, reporters were expected to cover in these beats various hospitals, orphanages, fires, courts, coroner's inquests and coastguard stations.

The West beat was always the toughest. In the '90's it had fewer police stations than the other beats, but the transportation going west was slower, and communication on the west side was less efficient than in other parts of the city. Before World War I all the evening papers kept reporters on the beat, which meant toil with no let-up for the City Press man, who had to keep one step in front of the newspapermen. He came to the office at 8:30 a.m., ready to work until his last story was finished, which could be ten, twelve or even eighteen hours later. He had to complete his early checks with the police stations by 9 a.m. so that he could turn his attention to the courts, of which there were two at the Maxwell street station, two at Desplaines street, two at West Chicago avenue, and one each at three other stations. In the afternoon the presiding magistrates became "justices' and heard civil suits in the same court.

The day reporter usually made the Maxwell street station his headquarters. The station included, of course, the famous ghetto district. The magistrates there were famous for their wit, and reporters liked to hang out there in search of feature stories. The magistrates did not mind the publicity either.

Some of the smaller stations had no public telephones and had to be checked through the police call board from division headquarters. In addition to police and courts, the assignments included funerals of notables, meetings of civic organizations, women's clubs and other groups, the west side races and Park board activities.

In most cases the courts were on the second floor of the police stations. The weary reporter had to trudge up and down the stairs, worried always by the fear that some competitor was busy in another court working up a story. If a spectacular lumberyard fire broke out on the far southwest side as it did the same day the Will Trax murder case broke in the Cragin district, the reporter had to abandon his police and courts, ride to the fire, wait until it was out, then take a slow street car back to the murder scene. When he was interrupted in this manner, he was expected to get his court news after court closed, from the bailiffs and clerks—if he could find them.

A reporter reminisces:

> I recall one morning when as usual I was expected to be in five places at once. I covered one inquest by phone. I found that the brother of the victim [an Italian blackhand killing] had risen to shoot and kill the chief suspect. It didn't bother me much for had I attended the inquest I would have taken the seat next to the witness chair. And some Italians are such bad shots!

The old Harrison street station, known as the Armory, was in the center of the notorious levee district, near LaSalle and Harrison streets. Chinatown was nearby, with long blocks of opium dens and gambling hells. There was also the red light district, with its barber shops where customers got a variety of "trimmings", at a charge of ten or fifteen dollars, and bathhouses with a variety of rubdowns at a variety of prices. When the police raided disorderly houses they searched the patrons to see how much money they carried. (Many had very little, because of the "panel game" popular at these resorts: the panel was a secret door in the wall that swung open, so that a denizen of the house could creep forward and remove the wallet from the trouser pocket of the patron who was distracted by his pursuit of pleasure.) The bailiffs whispered to the magistrates the amount of money the police had found on the patron. By a strange coincidence, the magistrate almost always imposed a fine that corresponded exactly to that amount of money. The patron left cleaned out, and the politicians did very well financially. Besides being responsible for the very active Harrison street court and station news, the bureau reporter there had to check with other stations: Cottage Grove, Stanton avenue and Brighton Park. While he was busy keeping track of events in court all sorts of things could be happening out in his territory. He was held responsible for everything that happened anywhere there, and if he were scooped on a big story, no excuses were accepted. He might just as well not bother to show up for work the next morning.

In the 90's the City Press man at Harrison street was Al Johnson, who had started at the bureau as a copy boy when he bought his job, the story goes, for fifty cents from a black boy who had grown tired of the boorish prejudices of the other messengers. Leckie noticed Johnson pecking at a typewriter one day and, impressed by his enterprising nature, sent him to substitute for the regular reporter at the 35th and Halsted street station, where he met Larry Coffey, a reporter for the old *Dispatch*, who offered to write the boy's copy for him. If the managers were surprised at the smoothness of young Johnson's style, they made no comment, and eventually the cub learned to write his own stories, and was regularly assigned to Harrison street. It was an important beat, so Johnson was forced to compete with such reporters as Richard Henry Little of the *Tribune*, Ben Atwell, who had been trained by City Press, Billy Phelon who was to become a well-known sports and feature writer and Guy Steely who later became an advance man for the Ringling Brothers Circus.

Captain Charles Koch was in charge of the Harrison street station. He was a large man with curling moustaches and chin whiskers who always wore a wide-brimmed hat, and bore a startling resemblance to Buffalo Bill. Inspector Jack

"Hardboiled" Shea also had his headquarters at Harrison street for a while. It was through his friendship with Koch and Shea that Al Johnson was able to pull off an exclusive scoop, and one on which the newspapers could not enlarge. Which in fact they could not even verify. This is a fact worth noting, since the papers always have dug instantly into any story turned in by a City Press reporter, often to that reporter's deep chagrin.

Chicago at that time was still suffering from a case of anarchist fright. The Haymarket bombing had occurred only a few years before and was still fresh in everyone's memory. Up on the north side, on Sedgwick court (which later became Felton court) Mrs. Charles Beyrels ran a rooming house not far from the old Lane school. One day one of her roomers disappeared, and Mrs. Beyrels entered his room to see what she could find out about him. A large trunk stood in the corner of the room. She opened it and found to her horror that it was packed full of black, scary-looking bombs. There were also some letters written in code. Her roomer was an anarchist who had been communicating with a secret organization!

Mrs. Beyrels, agitated, told one of her sons to dump the trunk and its dangerous contents into the lake. She did not want to notify the police because she was afraid of the ensuing publicity. As it happened, Al Johnson was a neighbor of the Beyrels, and it was to him that the son came for advice. Johnson, not unaware of the news value of the story, told young Beyrels that if the trunk were to be discovered later, the Beyrels family would have a lot of explaining to do: far better to put up with the publicity, and have a clean conscience.

The Chicago avenue police station was the Beyrels' station, but Inspector Schaak of that station was no friend of City Press, which had its deepest roots at Harrison street. If Schaak were told about the Beyrels' discovery, he would undoubtedly go at once to his own newspaper reporter friends with the story. Johnson solved his problem by going at once to Captain Koch at Harrison street, who was only too happy to work with City Press against his Chicago avenue colleagues: there was rivalry in the police department, too. Koch sent a patrol wagon to the Beyrels' house, stopping it half a block away to avert suspicion. Detectives went into the house and got the bombs, carrying them to the wagon in bushel baskets. They were real bombs, of the kind seen in cartoons: round metal balls with fuses protruding from stems, and packed with real explosives.

This loot was carried carefully to the Harrison street station where it was inventoried. Then Johnson went to the City Press offices and wrote his story. When the newspapers received it they began at once to call the police, and naturally they called police in the Beyrels' district. But no one at East Chicago avenue station had heard anything about the bombs. The news bureau copy credited Captain Koch, but there was no Captain Koch at East Chicago. And no one else there had worked on the case. As deadlines neared, the morning papers sent reporters to the Beyrels house. No one was home. Johnson had suggested they visit relatives for a few days. The neighbors said they had seen some men carrying things away, but no one knew anything about any bombs.

The newspaper editors were in a quandary. It was too big a story to ignore, but it could not be verified with the police. They finally decided to carry it in the morning editions under a big headline, protecting themselves with the notation that the information had been furnished by the City Press Association and that they had been "unable to verify".

Johnson read the stories as he rode to work that morning, filled with a smug feeling of a task well done. The usual reward for such work was a raise in pay, and that was what he expected when he was called into Sayler's office as soon as he arrived.

"What happened on that story, Johnson?" Sayler said.

Looking down modestly, Johnson told how he had succeeded in getting the story exclusively for City Press, how he had seen to it that no one reached Captain Koch, the detectives or the Beyrels family...

"I ought to fire you," Sayler said. "Only you aren't old

enough yet to know what you're doing. You have to understand that the newspapers own this organization. You're
working for them, not against them."

Like a yesterday's scare head, the puffed-up reporter collapsed to normal size. He slunk nervously toward the door.
But Sayler called him back.

"It was a good piece of work, Johnson," Sayler said. He did
not smile.

Al Johnson later went to work for the *Journal*, and then
was City Hall man for the *Evening Post*. He made a lot of
friends among the city's officialdom, and eventually when
the *Post* collapsed he became head of publicity for the Chicago headquarters of the Illinois Commerce Commission.
His brother Charles "Elie" Johnson has been immortalized
in the book *Come into my Parlor*, about the times of the
notorious Everleigh sisters, by Charles Washburne, another
City Press alumnus: "Elie" was the reporter who refused to
be bought by the hundred dollar bribes of a drunken millionaire patron of the Everleigh's establishment. A third Johnson brother, Enoch, started with the bureau in 1903 and, like
his brothers, progressed from copy boy to reporter, later joining the staff of the *Daily News*.

It was the "scoop" which could make or break a City Press
reporter. He might have originated a story but the reporters
for the newspapers would pick it up and possibly scoop him
on features of his own story. If he learned, say, that Mrs.
Rufus Goldbags has been robbed of her purse containing
$135 in cash, her diamond wrist-watch—a gift from her third
husband, now divorced—her dinner rings, brooch and
matched-pearl earrings, but failed to discover, as a newspaperman did later, that the purse also contained her false
teeth, he was in trouble with "the desk".

Such feature scoops, and all others, were clipped carefully
from the papers in the office, marked with a large "X" and
placed in his record. Although the management had a good
idea of which reporters were "live ones" who originated stories, it was felt that constant vigilance was necessary to keep
City Press standards up.

Nevertheless it was virtually impossible for even an experienced City Press reporter to keep from being scooped. The best anyone could do was try to keep down the number of scoops, and try also to avoid being scooped on important stories. One beginner was constantly being scooped and being chewed out by the office. Considering that he had been used unfairly, he wrote a story about a streetcar accident on Milwaukee avenue, and put enough gory details in it to fill nearly a column.

A close observer might have detected something odd about that story, but on the surface it read like an ordinary City Press accident yarn: close to deadlines most of the papers print these kind of stories without checking them. In this case that was what happened, and then hysterical mothers began to call hospitals, and the street car company was furious. The reporter was called up before Leckie.

"I wanted to get even with those other reporters for scooping me," the novice said. "I'm sorry about that list of injured. They're all the names of friends of mine."

Leckie's face twitched, but he laid down the law in a manner that left no room for doubt. In a long career on Chicago newspapers that reporter never again committed the cardinal sin of faking a story.

There are other examples of the touching devotion to duty of a City News reporter. Edward Doherty has left this memoir of his devotion to City Press when he was a copy boy there employed to take down reports from the city coroner's office:

> Every morning, Buddy McHugh...called up with the list of those who had died during the night by violence, "under suspicious circumstances" or "without medical assistance".
>
> "Hello, Eddie, here's the stiffs."
>
> Names and addresses followed, the cause of death, perhaps a few details, the disposition of the body... I took notes in pencil, then turned to the typewriter and pounded the wax...

It was on a Monday morning that I wrote my last coroner's cases for the City Press.

Buddy McHugh called.

"Hello, Eddie, here's the stiffs. Got your pencil ready?"

"Shoot, Buddy."

"O.K. Lucy Doherty. Three years old. Daughter of Lieutenant James E. Doherty of the East Chicago avenue police station. Died in St. Elizabeth's hospital. Burns. Body home. Eddie, this little girl was getting up on a chair to light the gas in her home, 1425 North Central Park avenue. The match fell on her little cotton dress. They put out the fire, but I guess the kid swallowed some of the flames. Coroner says her lungs is burnt out."

"O.K., Buddy," I said. What else was there to say?

"That's all this morning."

Just one coroner's case. No bodies found in the river. No one shot or stabbed or poisoned during the night. Only my kid sister on the list. I wrote the story and went home.

P.J. McCarthy and others with whom I worked in those years often remind me of this incident. They regard it as extraordinary that I should have written the story before I went home. It proved to them, they say, that I was a "true newspaperman." But I don't look at it that way. And there are many others who have done the same thing—among them Marty Casey of the *New York American* who wrote the story of his daughter's death under the wheels of a truck before he left the office.

These incidents did not occur only under Leckie's suzerainity. The *Tribune* for October 28, 1934 carried the following item on the front page:

Anthony Sowa is a reporter. To be exact he is a police reporter for the City News Bureau. Last night Sowa walked into the Marquette station and glanced over the teletype message from police headquarters.

One message caught his eye. All police squads were ordered to watch for a hit and run motorist.

The victim was his father, Walenty Sowa, 58 years old, 3343 West Thirty-seventh Street. He was killed as he crossed Crawford Avenue at Forty-fourth Street.

Reporter Sowa called his office with the information. Then he went home.

Victor Lawson

Getting the news of Anton Cermak's death. From Left: Ald. Thomas P. Keane; Edward
Denemark; Commissioner Kaspar; City Treasurer John Cervenka; Ald. John Toman; Ald. John
F. Healy; Ald. Henry Sonnenschein.
(Courtesy Special Collections Division, the Chicago Public Library.)

At the funeral of Mayor Anton Cermak, 1932. From left, Aldermen: Oscar F. Nelson; Thomas
P. Keane; John J. Lagodny; James R. Quinn; James B. Bowler; Louis B. Anderson; John
Toman; Thomas Terrell; Jacob Arvey; Berthold Cronson.
(Courtesy Special Collections Division, the Chicago Public Library.)

Left to right, front row: Marie Davidsen Gehrmann, secretary; Isaac Gershman, general manager; Joseph A. Levandier; night city editor; Gladys Ryan Wherity, secretary-receptionist; Larry Mulay, city editor. Rear row: Frank T. Fitzpatrick, superintendent of City Press; George Deutschle, city hall; Clarence Jensen, rewrite and desk; Arthur F. Kozelka, assistant day city editor; Rocky Wolfe, sports editor; Edward H. Eulenberg, night editor; Anthony Kedzior, superintendent of copy room; Phil Weisman, assistant sports editor; Walter Ryberg, assistant editor and rewrite. 1945. (From *The City Newsletter*.)

City Editor Larry Mulay, 1945.
(From *The City Newsletter*.)

Joe Levandier, night city editor,
without his cigar, 1945.
(From *The City Newsletter*.)

Tom Doherty of the *Chicago American* takes four reporters to Riverview. From left: Shir
Lowry Haas, CNB; Jeanne Beaton Clinnin, *Chicago American*; Selma Friend Hayman, CN
Patricia Leeds, CNB.
(Courtesy Shirley Haas.)

Some of the earliest of the CNB women reporters of the World War II period. From left: Margaret Kirkling Lytle; Arthur F. Kozelka, assistant city editor; Helen Fleming; Larry Mulay, city editor; Dorothy Cook McKnight; Patricia Leeds; Isaac Gershman, general manager; Chester Opal (in background); Maureen Daly; Alene Harris (seated); and Elaine Peterson. (From *The City Newsletter*.)

The same young women in a different grouping, with Gershman and Mulay. (From *The City Newsletter*.)

COPY!

Created especially for the *City Press Bulletin*, October, 1951, by Pulitzer Prize-winning cartoonist Jacob Burck of the *Chicago Sun-Times*.

From left: Fred Thomas, assistant night city editor; Arnold Dornfeld, night city editor; Alex Zelchenko, night radio-TV editor, 1959.
(From *The Trib* magazine.)

Isaac Gershman, managing editor and general manager of CNB, 1959.
(From *The Trib* magazine.)

City Editor Larry Mulay checks out a story with Sy Adelman, County Building reporter, 1959.
(From *The Trib* magazine.)

Walter Ryberg, day city editor, 1959.
(From *The Trib* magazine.)

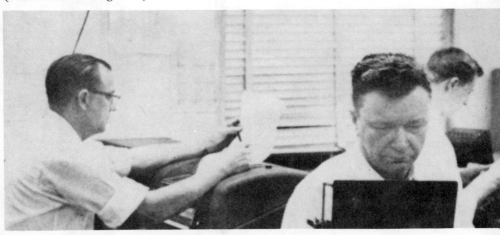

Operating CNB's PR News Service: Clarence Jensen, right, service manager, and Stanley Kedzior, office manager, 1959.
(From *The Trib* magazine.)

Election coverage in the County Building, 1960's.

1.—Terry Mahoney; 2.—Clarence Jensen; 3.—Marie Davidsen; 4.—Larry Mulay; 5.—Paul Zimbrakos; 6.—Norm Rohrsen; 7.—Isaac Gershman. (Photo courtesy CNB.)

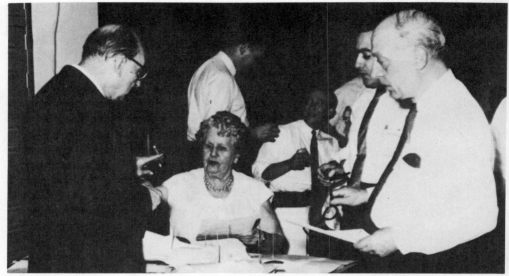

Left to right: Isaac Gershman, "Ruby" Ryan, Paul Zimbrakos, Larry Mulay at election headquarters.
(From CNB files).

Bob Billings (left) and Paul Zimbrakos (center) help publisher Seymour Hersh admire his new weekly newspaper in Evergreen Park, Illinois, 1962.
(Courtesy Paul Zimbrakos.)

Mayor Daley honors City News Bureau's Gladys Ryan Wherity on her selection as Senior Citizen of the Year, 1976.
(Courtesy Shirley Haas.)

Ronald Reagan calms the multitudes after Gera-Lind Kolarik is punched out by a Secret Service agent.
(Courtesy Gera-Lind Kolarik.)

Offices at 188 West Randolph Street.
(Courtesy CNB.)

Left to right: Gary Tucker, Paul Zimbrakos, Stan Romeo, Ron Berquist, Wayne Klatt and Bill Sabo at 188 West Randolph Street.
(Courtesy CNB.)

Frank Fitzpatrick, tube system manager.
(Courtesy CNB.)

Tube system from the basement at 188 West Randolph Street.
(Courtesy CNB.)

Paul Zimbrakos and Roger Torda.
(Courtesy Paul Zimbrakos.)

Barbara Miller, desk assistant at the CNB Morgue.
(Courtesy CNB.)

New CNB headquarters at 35 East Wacker Drive.
(Courtesy CNB.)

Bernie Judge, general manager and managing editor as of 1983. (Courtesy CNB.)

James Peneff, general manager and managing editor from 1974 to 1983. (Courtesy CNB.)

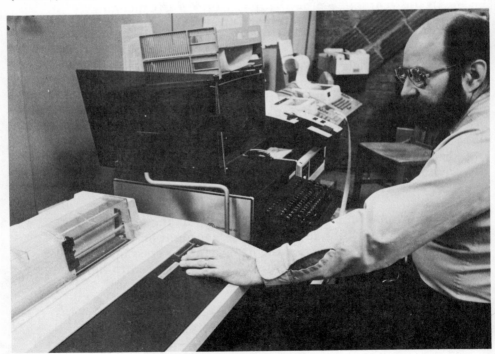

Stan Romeo at teletype system at 35 East Wacker Drive. (Courtesy Ron Berquist.)

10

World War I

In the years preceding the first World War Chicago was rife with change. In 1911 Mayor Carter Harrison, the son of the murdered mayor, closed the Everleigh Club, the most impressive of the sin palaces. The handwriting was on the wall: the brothels were going. The following summer there was a protest march by homeless prostitutes down Michigan avenue: honest women fought off mashers with hatpins. Automobiles were becoming a common sight: Teddy Webb had the distinction of being the first automobile bandit. And there was the new entertainment, the movies, which baffled drama critics at the *Post* and the *Tribune*. Other social conventions were wearing thin. A story in the *Tribune* for June 1, 1913, carried the following lead:

> Women diners smoked cigarettes at the banquet of the Walt Whitman Fellowship last night on the anniversary of the author's birth... During the speeches that followed the meal, several women were seen to light dainty cigarettes and enjoy luxurious inhalations.

Walter Brown, who was known to newsmen all over the country as "Brownie", had come to City Press in 1899, thus missing by one year being the first manager to join the press in the twentieth century. He had been born in Corning, New

York, and had served with the New York regiment in the Spanish-American War. He left the bureau briefly in 1900 to work on the *Tribune*, but returned to the bureau that same year, serving in turn as city editor, day manager and finally general manager upon Sayler's death in 1913. Brown was a capable newsman, but he was something of a stubborn stickler for accuracy and could be explosive when he encountered what he considered to be inefficiency. The reporters who worked for him had mixed attitudes toward him. One who was apparently not broken up at his demise, wrote:

> At Brownie's funeral I nearly laughed out loud in the undertaking rooms as memories of funny things occurred to me... Particularly the time he spent half an hour with me trying to show how I could call on all the police stations on the northwest beat for seven cents and the judicious use of transfers. I couldn't keep that transfer business out of my mind as Snively read a tribute to one who had received a free pass on the longest road in the world...

Another reporter had more respectful memories:

> I was covering the county building for a time and John Boettiger was on the Trib trying to get me fired by three scoops a day because my attitude wasn't sufficiently subservient. Wise old Walter Brown (defying public opinion, I still think he was a great guy) sighed over the scoops but told me to continue getting scooped—not to play ball with John...

A third reporter was less respectful:

> Most of my experiences in the bureau were silly. For example: I was covering the far south side daytime, and living on Eastwood avenue. At 5 p.m., quitting time, one day, I had just checked out from Englewood station at 64th and Wentworth and faced a hell of a long haul

home via street car and El. Just then a call for all wagons on the south side came in, ordering them to proceed to 22nd and State, I believe. I hopped in, figuring it would save me time getting home. We drove to the destination and found that an explosion had killed one or two girls and injured others at Bauer and Black, medical manufacturers.

A cop gave me the names of the dead and injured, and, since there was a phone handy, I phoned it into the office and caught the El at 22nd street and went home.

The next day Walter Brown, manager, called me up and said, 'Young man, you are a real reporter. Any youngster imbued with the spirit of blah blah to go off his beat after working hours for a story... blah blah blah... Brown gave me a three dollar bonus and up until that time I think he had just been waiting for a chance to fire me...

Finally, a fourth reporter evinces signs of irritation:

My most vivid recollection of the CNB is the day of the Drake hotel robbery when large numbers of victims and bandits were shot. The timesheet was as thick as a mattress after thirty minutes of bulletins, sub-bulletins, kills, new leads, sub leads, etc.

Walter Brown left his sanctum and, to make the confusion more complete, insisted on dictating leads which he later destroyed. A stubborn, methodical man myself, I was never able to see the idea of dropping all other news for one big story. So I left my rewrite desk to check a report of a man killed on the far north side and discovered he was the missing bandit. All of which necessitated more kills, subs, new leads, etc...

Closely associated with Brown in the minds of former employees was Emil Hubka, a crusty, gruff efficient man who had started with the bureau in 1903, and had been appointed assistant day editor in 1908, and city editor in 1913 when Brown became general manager. Hubka remained at the bureau until 1926, when he went to the *Daily News* as night city editor.

It was consequently under Brown and Hubka that the legendary reporters of the twenties were trained. The most famous were probably Charles MacArthur, who, with Ben Hecht, wrote *The Front Page*, and Hilding Johnson and Walter Howey, the thinly disguised heroes of that play. MacArthur, Howey and Johnson moved eventually to the *Herald-Examiner*.

Like many another man who later gained prestige as a reporter, Hilding Johnson started his career at the age of fifteen in the back room of the City News Bureau, turning off copy on the Cyclograph. Johnson, whose father was a tailor, had been born in Sweden. He was a natty dresser, considered to be the Beau Brummel of the bureau staff, a title easily within reach. He was promoted to reporter and assigned to Criminal court to replace Enoch Johnson (no relation) who left in 1910 to go to the *News*.

Johnson had not been covering the court beat very long, when he covered himself with glory by getting a series of interviews with Thomas Foulkes, a downstate Illinois farmer who had accused a Chicago attorney of defrauding him of his savings. Hilding exerted his considerable charm to win Foulkes' confidence, and each day was able to produce an exclusive story, much to the chagrin of the other reporters.

Despite Johnson's charm, sartorial elegance, consideration of young reporters, and eminent honesty, he was not known to be gentle, nor was he known willingly to turn down a drink. He had a tendency to carry on feuds, and he did not worry about the slightness of his build when he wanted to score a point or two. George Murray recalls one incident:

> ...he could not have punched his way out of a paper bag, but he had heart... Once Hildy chose C. Wayland Brooks, then a states attorney in Chicago and later a United States senator. Brooks, an ex-Marine, was big and burly and hard as nails. Something Hildy had done

had "Curly" Brooks really aroused. He was whaling the daylights out of the little reporter when half a dozen bailiffs and newspapermen intervened. Hildy picked himself up off the floor and pleaded, 'Turn him loose. I haven't finished with him yet.'

Johnson was a merciless scooper:

On one occasion newspaper readers were treated to an unusual sight on the city's newsstands. The story of the day dealt with the jury's duty in a murder case. The *Herald Examiner*—Hildy's sheet—carried the headline: GUILTY; 14 YEARS, while the *Tribune*—Hildy's rival paper—reported: NOT GUILTY. Hildy had tricked a competitor.

The jury had been instructed to deliver a sealed verdict if it reached agreement during the night, then to remain locked up until morning. Its members thus would get an extra night's bedding and an extra morning's breakfast at county expense. When the jury left its room after reaching a verdict, Hildy Johnson entered and pawed through the room's single wastebasket. He dug out some of the printed forms that had been furnished the jury.

Each of these forms represented a possible verdict. Hildy observed there was no form for manslaughter. He correctly deduced it had been the jury's verdict and that the jury had turned in the form to report its finding in the case. Before leaving the room Hildy set a trap for the *Trib* reporter. He put all the forms back into the wastebasket except one—he pocketed that which read "Not Guilty." As Hildy had calculated, the *Trib* man sneaked into the room, dumped the wastebasket, observed the "Not Guilty" form was missing, and jumped to the wrong conclusion.

There are various legends about Johnson's relationship with a convicted murderer named Carl Wanderer. The

Herald-Examiner, for which Johnson, Walter Howey and Harry Romanoff worked after World War I, took a strong hand in the Wanderer case.

Wanderer, a war hero, had returned to his apartment on the night of June 21, 1920, to find a tattered derelict lurking in the vestibule. When the derelict became threatening, according to Wanderer, he shot him with his handy service automatic. He then discovered the body of his pregnant wife, Ruth, whom he deduced the intruder, dubbed "the Ragged Stranger" by the press, had shot before he got home. The Stranger was clutching a weapon not unlike Wanderer's own.

The police apparently seemed inclined to accept the story from the war hero, but Howey and Romanoff, not satisfied, traced the Stranger's pistol to a cousin of Wanderer's who freely admitted that he had lent that pistol to Wanderer the night of the murders. Eventually, what with one thing and another, including the discovery of other women in Wanderer's life, the ex-hero was led to confess a double murder: he had no desire to settle into family life and had paid the Stranger a small sum to come into the apartment, ostensibly to give Wanderer the opportunity to look like a hero in front of his wife, and rekindle the flames of passion, but in actuality to allow Wanderer to murder his wife and pin the murder on the Stranger who, being dead, would not be in a condition to explain anything.

Wanderer was tried for the murder of his wife and sentenced by a lenient jury to twenty years in the penitentiary at Joliet. But Howey, outraged, began a campaign to have him hanged, and the authorities, under fire from the *Herald-Examiner*, indicted Wanderer for the murder of the Ragged Stranger, tried him, found him guilty, and this time sentenced him to death.

It is at this point that the legends concerning Johnson and Wanderer—and even Johnson, Wanderer and Walter Howey—begin to heat up, thanks largely to George Murray's vivid imagination.

One story has it that the *Herald-Examiner* paid Wanderer

$300 for his life story, a fitting gesture since they had done so much to end it. Wanderer was in the county jail, where reporters had a tendency to hang out. The money supposedly was given to Johnson to deliver to Wanderer on the night of his execution. The upshot was that the reporter got into a rummy game with the condemned man and, shortly before Wanderer went to the gallows, won the $300 away from him. Wanderer's last words, according to Murray, were, "Don't play rummy with Hildy Johnson. I think he cheats."

But Murray supplies another story about Wanderer's end. In that one it was Charles MacArthur of the *Herald-Examiner*, and Ben Hecht of the *Daily News* who, having learned that Wanderer had been a choir boy, requested a song from him, and were touched to hear him render "Old Pal, Why Don't You Answer Me?" Frank Carson, another ex-City News man, was MacArthur's city editor, and he suggested that MacArthur get Wanderer to belt off a couple of choruses of the song on the gallows, which Wanderer did, his melody being interrupted only by the tightening of the rope.

Jack McPhaul supplies yet another segment of the Carl Wanderer story. According to this one, after Johnson won the $300 back from the condemned man, Hecht and Mac-Arthur asked Wanderer to read two statements from the gallows. He agreed, but the reporters forgot that the man's hands would be bound:

> Wanderer couldn't reach the missives in his shirt pocket. He plunged through the trap, the commentaries of the mischievous pair unread. One was an excoriation of MacArthur's managing editor, Walter Howey; the other a similarly vivid denunciation of Hecht's city editor, John Craig.

MacArthur had started off as Oak Park correspondent for the bureau, and even that early in his career he was anxious to pay off old scores. This vindictive streak in his nature was no doubt responsible for his writing a story in which the homeless tramp who had been arrested for begging from door to door in the suburb had been given the same name as MacArthur's high school principal.

One night the chauffeur who worked for John Farson, a wealthy Oak Parker, failed to show up for drill as a member of the National Guard, and a detachment was sent out to round him up. Farson's estate was guarded by a high fence and two vicious dogs who had no respect for uniforms. MacArthur phoned in a story in which the guardsmen were forced to drop their muskets and scramble back over the fence, leaving at least one dog with a mouthful of trouser seat.

The next evening a grim squad of uniformed men marched into the City Press offices. Joe Levandier, who had written the story, saw them coming and slipped quickly out to lunch. George Wharton, who was on the desk, had no idea about what was happening, and could offer no information. The troopers waited a considerable time, growing more and more disgruntled, but Joe seemed to be taking a most leisurely meal that evening, and finally they filed out, frustrated and still enraged.

A more dramatic story involved the capture of the "Albino", after the volatile Oak Park correspondent had been transferred to a city police beat.

The "Albino" was one of those characters who are nurtured by a word in the news columns, seized upon by the headline writers. A man had been found with his throat slashed. Hours later a woman fled screaming from a pale fiend with a razor. The newspapers played it up. Police squads made nightly patrols of the areas where the fiend had been seen. All in vain. Each night brought some new outrage: a woman assaulted, a family roused by a white-haired phantom who bent over them as they slept. It was rumored that the Albino had escaped from an asylum.

Some expressed the belief that he was a black man with his face painted white. There were many false alarms about his whereabouts.

One day city editor Hubka picked up his telephone when it rang and heard a hoarse whisper.

"Hey, Em. It's me, Charlie. I've got a tip on the Albino."

Abruptly the call was cut off. Ten minutes later Hubka's phone rang again. The same voice:

"Em. I've got the Albino cornered."

At the same time a call came into the office from another police reporter, who said police squads had been sent to an apartment building at 21st and Halsted.

Bulletins flashed. The police surrounded the building. The dread Albino was inside, ready to shoot it out. The police held their revolvers, waiting for reinforcements.

The City Press desk phone rang.

"Hey, Em. I'm in the building. I've got the Albino."

"What do you mean?" the exasperated Hubka yelled. "How do you think you're going to get him out of there? They'll shoot the minute you stick your head out the door."

"Don't worry, boss," MacArthur said. "I'll march him out."

Moments afterward watchers at the building saw the ground floor door open cautiously. The police brought up their guns. Suddenly, apparently as a result of a shove from the rear, a man flew out: a palsied, white-haired ill-kempt creature, whose ancient features bore some faint resemblance to the descriptions of the terrifying Albino. After a discreet pause Charles MacArthur emerged, carrying an ancient revolver and a rusty razor. Triumphantly he surrendered his prisoner to police, who somewhat skeptically accepted him as the Albino, and returned him to the institution from which he had escaped.

Later MacArthur recounted his exploit.

>...he slashed at me with a razor. I knocked it out of his hand. He took the gun and pointed it at my head. And what do you think I did?

A ring of reporters were listening in a hushed silence. MacArthur held up a pencil.

>I pushed this pencil down the gun barrel.

On Saturday, July 24, 1915 things were quiet at City News. George Wright, who was on the desk for the last watch, was chatting in the very small hours of the morning with Frank Fleming who was a reporter assigned to the detective bureau.

"There's a Western Electric picnic," Wright said to Fleming. "Why don't you try going up to the boat and see if you can scare up some news?"

Fleming set out and just as he arrived at the Clark street bridge, over the Chicago River where 2,000 employees of the Western Electric company and their families were boarding the excursion steamer, *Eastland*, the ship suddenly began to tip, and amidst screams and shouts, turned over on its port side. In what seemed like a flash the river was dotted with the struggling, drowning forms of the excursionists.

Fleming ran two blocks to find a telephone and give the bureau a bulletin and an eyewitness report. Ten minutes after the bureau flash, the scene was swarming with reporters, photographers, police, firemen, divers, and a growing, horrified mob.

The enormity of the tragedy was unbelievable. A copyboy for the Evening *American*, who was known as "Ginger," was said to have been the first to estimate the true number of victims. He had been aboard and was thrown into the water when the ship capsized, but was able to swim ashore.

"There's a thousand people dead in there," he told reporters. "No one got out except those on the upper deck. They're all dead. Every one of them."

His story was incredible. By nine that morning City News was reporting four hundred dead. Some papers had a larger estimate, but the bureau had to stick to verifiable facts. Walter Brown was nervous about the report of four hundred when he arrived for work that morning.

"Are you sure you're not overestimating it?" he asked.

Hubka, intent on his work, replied without looking up.

"We're raising it now to five hundred."

Before the day was over, it was a thousand. Ginger had been right.

Both Brown and Hubka had worked on the Iroquois theatre fire of 1903, and they knew the long delays in identifications which were common in such enormous disasters. They arranged with Coroner Peter Hoffman to move the bodies, which had been laid out in long rows in South Water street, to the second regiment armory at Washington boulevard and Racine avenue. There they were placed on the floor again in rows, with wide aisles between them. Eleven City News cub reporters and the rest of the staff were sworn in as deputies. To the left leg of each victim was attached a numbered tag, and the City News people wrote a description for each tag:

> No. 1—man, about fifty years old, blue eyes, gray hair, five feet eight, 180 pounds, brown shirt, Masonic ring.
> No. 2—boy, about twelve years old, dark hair, blue suit, scar on left cheek.

At eleven o'clock that night a long, mournful procession began to wind through the armory. Sobs broke out as someone recognized a relative. A wife claimed the body of her husband. But the crowd was orderly. As each body was identified the name was taken by waiting reporters to the front of the hall, where Hubka had improvised a desk from overturned baskets, which had been used for carrying the bodies. From that "desk" the names were bulletined to the papers.

The City News staff did notable work that night, in relieving the anxiety of thousands of people uncertain of the fate of their friends and relatives. By 2:30 in the morning some four hundred bodies had been identified. By Tuesday morning, the third day after the tragedy, only seven of the more than eight hundred bodies recovered, remained unidentified. The *Tribune* commented that nothing like it in the way of speedy identification had ever been achieved.

Accounts differ as to the number of people killed in the *Eastland* sinking. The *Tribune*, on July 27, 1915, gave the number as eight hundred and twenty-one identified dead, seven unidentified and four hundred and thirteen missing. On July 31 the same paper reported eight hundred and thirty-five identified dead, and one not identified. The *Daily News Almanac* put the deaths at eight hundred and twelve.

Another enterprising young City News reporter was John Dienhart, who was something of a celebrity among newsmen because of his friendship with Billy Skidmore, a local hanger-on of political bosses who was a sort of clearing-house for petty criminal activity, and some not so petty. Dienhart got in touch with Skidmore whenever a reporter's pocket was picked or his wallet stolen. So long as the job had not been done by an amateur, Dienhart could retrieve most stolen property for his colleagues.

It was Dienhart who was later to put the immortal words, "I'm glad it was me, instead of you," into the mouth of Chicago Mayor Anton Cermak when he was dying from an assassin's bullet which hit him as he sat in an open car with Franklin D. Roosevelt, who had just been elected President. Dienhart happened to be present at the shooting because he was a friend of Cermak's. Everyone else who was near Cermak that day in Miami swore that Cermak had said, "Where the hell was that goddam bodyguard?"

But it was Dienhart's version that went out over the wires and into the history books. He was not at that time working for City News, of course. However, in connection with that shooting, reporters at police headquarters had an opportunity to demonstrate the truth of a statement they often made, to wit, that police reporters were better at covering a fast-breaking news story than the Washington press corps, a group to whom they often referred as "them striped-pants cookie pushers."

Cermak's bodyguards, all Chicago detectives, quickly phoned the bad news to their headquarters. First they shouted, "The mayor's been shot!" Then they called back, when they were calmer, with more details. Helpful detectives at the bureau handed the phone to City News and other reporters, who speedily put together eyewitness accounts of the shooting. Within minutes. Meanwhile, at the scene of the crime, confusion was rampant. The Washington corres-pondents were all caught with their questions down. By the time they pulled themselves together, Chicago newsrooms had already received a fairly accurate account of the whole affair.

During the first World War, J.L. Maloney, who was to become city editor of the *Tribune*, covered City Hall for the bureau. Harry Romanoff, who was called by *Colliers'* the greatest Chicago telephone reporter, and who was to become city editor of the *Herald-Examiner*, was covering the detective bureau for City News. One of Romanoff's more famous escapades is recounted by Jack McPhaul:

> Sgt. Francis (Jiggs) Donohue, chief investigator for the coroner's office, was frequently impersonated. Telephoning a barroom where a murder had occurred, Harry Romanoff of the *Herald-Examiner* said, 'This is Sgt. Donohue of the Coroner's office.' The voice at the other end said, 'That's funny. So is this.' Jiggs had reached the scene faster than Harry had anticipated.

At other times Romanoff was more successful in his impersonations. One night a group of eager reporters were clustered on the front porch of the house of a policeman who had been killed by a bank robber. They wanted the policemen's picture and the grieving family was not in the mood to cooperate. Romanoff got the widow on the phone, identified himself as the police captain, and told her the *Herald* was the policeman's best friend, and she should give her husband's picture to the *Examiner* man. Which she did.

On another occasion Romanoff, in attempting to find out the conditon of the gambler Tex Rickard, whom the wire services had reported as ill, phoned Mrs. Rickard, identified himself as the Governor of Illinois and asked after his old friend. The gambler's wife burst into tears and told the "governor" that her husband was dying. Romanoff had a scoop.

His most famous impersonation occurred when he heard that the SS *Wisconsin* was foundering in heavy seas in Lake Michigan, and the Coast Guard was attempting to rescue fifty-two people aboard. Romanoff called the RCA marine radio station in Chicago, the only source of news on the *Wisconsin*, identified himself as the owner of the ship, got all details and instructed the operator to refuse any information to the newspapers. The rescue went on for several hours with happy results, but no one knew anything about it until they read Romanoff's story in the *Examiner*.

Edwin J. "Ham" Hamilton, the hotel reporter for the bureau during the World War I years, was known the country over to convention groups whose meetings he covered in Chicago hotels year after year. He was a little hunchbacked man, whom everyone on the staff respected. One of his stories was reprinted in the "Twenty Years Ago" column of the *Tribune* on March 14. 1937:

> Chicago—A young heiress yesterday married a penniless invalid living in a north side lodging house that the terms of her wealthy uncle's will might be fulfilled, according to a story told the City News bureau by the trustee of the wealthy uncle. The bride was Miss Philippa Hartley of New York and the bridegroom John Colfax, who is suffering from a lesion of the heart.

It was a touching tale: the beautiful, lonely girl marrying a dying derelict to make his last days happy and at the same time satisfy the will of her eccentric millionaire uncle who had specified that she marry by a certain date in order to inherit his money. It was one of those yarns which are too good to be true. Investigation proved that Hamilton had, perhaps, been taken in. He left the bureau sometime later, and wrote under his by-line for the *Daily News*.

In 1917 the Contagious Disease hospital opened. A sign of war appeared in the assignment book: "Austrian parade—watch for trouble." Soon the book bristled with war notations:

Bolda flag insult case... First regiment mustered in... Joffre visit... Infantrymen arrested hearings... Labor cases—Dr. Robertson... Aliens register U.S. Marshal's office... Peace

riot arrest hearings... Signal Corps drill, Grant Park...
Recruiting, First Cavalry Engineers... Registration enroll-
ment... Slackers developments... Appel anti-draft... Saloon
cases... The Spy film case... Meatless days... Great Lakes food
thefts... Women mail carriers begin duties... Alien enemies
banned zones... The Ideal Man sermon...

In the midst of its war activities the government took over
the telegraph services and needed additional space in the
Western Union building. On October 1, 1917, therefore, the
news bureau moved with the AP to new quarters on the
seventh floor of the Ashland block, 155 North Clark street. It
was a tremendous task to change the tube systems at a time
when a full crew of able-bodied men could scarcely be held
together for a day. Frank Fitzpatrick, superintendent of the
tubes since 1898, supervised the work and managed somehow to complete it on time. Not one carrier missed its trip.

One later incident stands forth. When the old Western
Union building was torn down, workmen found rolls of
ancient copy stuffed in the wall beneath a hole in the plaster-
ing, where indolent messengers had disposed of it. A less
resourceful boy had at one time unsuccessfully sought to
solve the never-ending task of running wax sheets on the
Cyclograph by simply tossing them out the window.

At the time of the draft, the news bureau took over the
council chambers in City Hall with a special staff of thirty or
more women typists. Every woman had a list of registrants
in one Chicago district. As the draft number, drawn in
Washington, came in over the wire, the editor called it out
from the mayor's chair, the women typing out the corres-
ponding name from their lists. The names were assembled at
the "desk" and bulletined to the papers. Those reading that
their number had been drawn were expected to report at once
to the nearest recruiting station. Thus quickly the work of
mobilization was aided.

The draft and the enlistments made almost daily inroads.
Cipriani went to the navy. Gershman to the Army. Others
joined various divisions of the colors. George Lyman, a copy

boy, had boosted his age to enlist, and went over the top with the first Americans in France, and was one of those killed that day.

In the emergency almost anyone was a reporter. The staff dwindled down to married men and boys. Some of the latter undertook the tasks of full-fledged reporters. One old-timer recalled to Vickerman that he had covered three hangings before he was eighteen, and another wrote:

> I would like to see something said concerning the lack of training given to cubs by the bureau. At least in my day there it seemed to be a case of sink or swim. The theory seemed to be that if a cub had "it in him" he would be a reporter. Looking back it seems to me that there was a terrible cost in labor turnover. A cub was hired and no editor sat down and told him what was expected of him, how the bureau operated or its functions. As a consequence he very often got the wrong slant from the office bum, or had a trick played on him and bang, he was fired. The bureau was the only place I have encountered where it was expected that brains could be hired in the untrained state and overnight become experienced.

Women began to replace men in the industries, and they broke a long-standing tradition now when they became news bureau reporters. This was to happen again during World War II. Kurt Vonnegut, who was at CNB briefly during that war, tells this anecdote in *Slaughterhouse-Five*:

> While I was studying to be an anthropologist, I was also working as a police reporter for the famous Chicago City News Bureau for twenty-eight dollars a week. One time they switched me from the night shift to the day shift, so I worked sixteen hours straight. We were supported by all the newspapers in town, and the AP and the UP and all that. And we would cover the courts and the police stations and the Fire Department and the

Coast Guard out on Lake Michigan and all that. We were connected to the institutions that supported us by means of pneumatic tubes which ran under the streets of Chicago.

Reporters would telephone in stories to writers wearing headphones, and the writers would stencil the stories on mimeograph sheets. The stories were mimeographed and stuffed into the brass and velvet cartridges which the pneumatic tubes ate. The very toughest reporters and writers were women who had taken over the jobs of men who'd gone to war.

And the first story I covered I had to dictate over the telephone to one of those beastly girls. It was about a young veteran who had taken a job running an old-fashioned elevator in an office building. The elevator door on the first floor was ornamental iron lace. Iron ivy snaked in and out of the holes. There was an iron twig with two iron lovebirds perched upon it.

This veteran decided to take his car into the basement, and he closed the door and started down, but his wedding ring was caught in all the ornaments. So he was hoisted into the air and the floor of the car went down, dropped out from under him, and the top of the car squashed him. So it goes.

So I phoned this in, and the woman who was going to cut the stencil asked me, "What did his wife say?"

"She doesn't know yet," I said. "It just happened."

"Call her up and get a statement."

"What?"

"Tell her you're Captain Finn of the Police Department. Say you have some bad news. Give her the news, and see what she says."

So I did. She said about what you would expect her to say. There was a baby. And so on.

When I got back to the office, the woman writer asked me, just for her own information, what the squashed guy had looked like when he was squashed.

I told her.

"Did it bother you?" she said. She was eating a Three Musketeers Candy Bar.

"Heck no, Nancy," I said. "I've seen lots worse than that in the war." *

In the course of the year 1918 Northwestern University opened a shooting gallery, teachers were offered agricultural courses, mail carriers sold war stamps, and Sunday closing arrived. Then on November 11th "not ups" was written on the schedule, "No meetings." Business was cancelled for a city-wide celebration of the Armistice. Like other holidays, this meant no cessation of business for City News employees. They had to keep busy recording the riotous events for newspaper readers.

With the war over, enlisted men began to return home. This meant, of course, the end of the road for women reporters. Many reporters returned to work at the bureau, however briefly: Fort, Hinman, Burnett, Hydenburg, Crieghton, Cipriani. A lad named Larry Mulay was on the Sunday switchboard. Isaac Gershman returned, to cover a grand jury investigation into the race riots which broke out in the summer of 1919.

Already, on June 8, 1919, the assignment book carried a notation for Jim Doherty: "Watch for race riots." July 27 was a hot Sunday afternoon. A black boy named Eugene Williams swam to a raft in a section of Lake Michigan roped off for whites only on a south side beach. A group of whites began to throw stones, and Eugene was hit in the head, fell off the raft, and drowned. Then erupted one of the nation's bloodiest race riots; it lasted four days and was brought under control only with the assistance of the National Guard, and a heavy rainstorm that began Wednesday night and lasted all day Thursday.

Bureau reporters sped to trouble spots during the riots, mounted on motorcycles, an idea that had been suggested to them by dispatch riders during the War. One reporter, after telephoning a report of a disturbance, found himself marooned in a south side drug store, the only white person in sight.

*excerpted from the book *Slaughterhouse Five or The Children's Crusade* by Kurt Vonnegut Jr. Copyright © 1969 by Kurt Vonnegut Jr. Reprinted by permission of Delacorte Press/Seymour Lawrence.

Hesitating to run for it, he decided to telephone an acquaintance of his who worked for the Chicago *Defender*, a black newspaper. The *Defender* reporter sent an escort of black youths to conduct the bureau man to safety.

On a considerably lighter note, one post-war incident was memorialized in a nostalgic City News Newsletter:

> Though only a few days on CNB, Willie Krause was quick with ideas. It happened in 1919 before the Forest Preserves had become petting grounds and the Des Plaines river still rippled through a natural woodland. A tot of two to three years had disappeared from a western suburb.
>
> Getting a couple of bloodhounds, Reporter Krause decided to make a search of his own. He gave the pooches a whiff of the baby's shoe and started to follow them. The following morning, police, attracted by the baying hounds, rescued Willy, high atop a tree. He still had the baby shoe in his pocket. Upon calling his office he learned that the child had been found safe even before he had decided to make a name for himself in journalism.

11

The Front Page Era

The speakeasy era reeled in and with it the beer gangs and sawed-off shotguns. The passing of saloons changed the method of reporting. In an earlier day reporters did not really have to go to the police station for news; they could pop into the saloon next door and find the lieutenant and the station squads. Almost every station had its counterpart of Kehoe's saloon at Desplaines street. Bailiffs and deputies gave out news at their favorite bar after court. O.O. McIntyre, another famous CNB alum, wrote:

> Newspapering somehow seemed a more enchanted calling in those days. Crack men of the profession cared only for life and its excitements. To the world they were models of modesty, but to their fellows they had the bluster of Edmund Kean, setting down tankards with a bang and roaring contempt for city editors. Quick, fluent, moody, they lived hard and dangerously. Few reached fifty.

In truth, the blustering reporter who set his tankard down with a bang was not always a crack man, nor did he seem enchanted to the unfortunate person who was trying to build an organization around him. In August of 1890, when John Ballantyne was struggling with his fledgling bureau, he wrote to his executive committee about a reporter who may have been quick, fluent and moody, but who did not show roaring contempt for his editor:

> On Friday, August 8, Mr F.O. Bennett left his assignment at the city hall without permission. Between four and five o'clock in the afternoon he telephoned me from 37th street and Cottage Grove, and was directed to come into the office, but did not obey. He reported for duty about noon, Saturday, August 9, but I had already engaged another man to take his place.
>
> Mr. Bennett asks to be reinstated. He claims that his dismissal was due to a misunderstanding. He says that he left the city hall because he received information leading him to believe a prize fight was to take place somewhere outside the city. When he telephoned he gave me the facts regarding the conference held in the mayor's office that day, so far as he had been able to obtain them and also he told me about the prize fight.
>
> The telephone was working badly and I could not fully understand him... On his part he says that he did not understand that I wished him to return to the office and so accompanied the men who, he supposed, were on their way to the fight. He went to North Judson. It turned out the men were merely making arrangements for grounds for a fight which is to take place at some future time. Mr. Bennett missed the first train the next morning, but came in on a later one. He admits he had been drinking, but not enough to incapacitate him from doing his work...

Isaac Gershman was one reporter on the staff of the bureau in the twenties who might typify the new, non-saloon professional. He was hardworking and dependable, although he did seem to have a peculiar knack for being where something was just about to happen. When he came back from the War in 1919 he got himself involved in several exciting incidents which brought him recognition as a reporter. Once he was out for a stroll in Lincoln Park when he suddenly found himself witnessing a revolver battle between a policeman and an embittered gunman, who had just served his term in prison. Both combatants were wounded, and Gershman rode to the hospital in the ambulance, where he took down a full background story from the policeman. He was able to telephone a complete report into the office while the first details of the affair were just beginning to trickle into the detective bureau.

On another occasion he found himself in the middle of a stickup in the drugstore that used to be on the ground floor of the Ashland building. Two gunmen lined up the customers while a third man stood at the front door as a look-out. Gershman slipped out the back door and called the detective bureau from the nearest telephone. Then he rushed out toward Clark street and found a uniformed policeman. Together Gershman and the cop rushed back to the drugstore.

The result was a gun battle, in which the policeman was shot. The killer ran north on Clark street, and was shot and killed there by the detectives who were responding to Gershman's call. Gershman took the wounded policeman in a cab to the old Iroquois hospital and was unbuttoning the jacket of his uniform when the policeman died.

It was not long after this that Gershman was promoted to "last watch" editor. Then, in 1920, Robert Hage, who was assistant day city editor, joined William Fort to produce the *Standard*, a paper that was dedicated to carrying all news except crime news. Since there *was* practically no news *except* crime news, the *Standard* was, as would be expected, short-lived, but Gershman was able to move into Hage's place. With the succession coming, as it did in those days, from within the bureau, it was obvious that Gershman was going to take over from Walter Brown, since he was young, energetic and open to new ideas. A letter to Vickerman from an ex-employee testifies to this:

> In those days when the bureau was running at high speed with an insufficient force and a very quick turn-

over, Gershman as assistant city editor functioned as a buffer between the staff and the powers above. He had the confidence of all and was able by tact and persuasion, with nevertheless a firm hand, to guide neophytes and even the more experienced, so that crises were overcome or mitigated. Incidentally, I think he is deserving of considerable credit for the change which has taken place in the bureau, making it a real newspaper organization.

Has the training been of benefit to me? Most emphatically, but that does not mean I relish thinking about it. On the whole it was a hideous experience with killing hours and little money. The only bright spot was Gershman, who was fair and considerate. I've never forgotten him.

Changes of all kinds were of course taking place after the War, and the twenties were thus a time of transition. It was true that the newspapers were dwindling in number, but the demands they made were more exciting and the bureau needed to be tuned up to stay even with the times.

In 1918 the expiring *Herald* was purchased by William Randolph Hearst, who combined it with the *Examiner* to create the *Herald-Examiner*, as we have seen. The *Journal* was in bad shape in 1925 when its publisher John C. Eastman died and left it to his drama critic, O.H. "Doc" Hall, his business manager John Deuter, and his advertising manager, Frank Dunn. In December, 1929, the paper was sold and transformed into the *Times*, the city's first tabloid daily. The *Post*, whose publisher, John C. Schaffer, had anticipated great days, and had moved into a new building at 211 West Wacker drive, was hit by the first wave of the Depression in 1929, and Schaffer was forced to sell it to a syndicate headed by Knowlton Ames Jr. It was moved to new quarters on LaSalle street north of the river, and there it expired in 1932. Hearst bought its Associated Press license for his *American* and the *Daily News* took over its unexpired subscriptions.

Victor Lawson died on August 19, 1925. His passing did indeed mark the end of an era. Leckie wrote a tribute to him:

> Mr. Lawson's genius was conceded, never asserted. The public heard practically nothing of him. From his newspaper one would not know he existed. Yet no good movement in Chicago was without his powerful influence, no bad one but that felt his opposition and felt it keenly. He was a master of detail and organization. His memory was infallible and his every action eminently just. The comparatively few who knew him at all intimately and were aware of his work agreed that he was the greatest and most practical influence for good in Chicago's political history.

Following Lawson's death the *News*, run by a company headed by Walter Strong, Lawson's nephew, moved into a magnificent new building on Madison street, just west of the river, adjoining Union station. Strong himself died of a heart attack on May 10, 1931, and the paper was taken over by Colonel Frank Knox.

There was much moving of newspaper offices. The *Tribune* moved into its Gothic tower on Michigan avenue in 1925. The *Times* prospered and moved into the new Wacker drive building which had been vacated by the *Post*. Then on September 13, 1934, the Associated Press broke a forty-year tradition by leaving the premises it shared with City News and moving to new quarters at 101 North LaSalle street.

Along with its reputation for accuracy and thoroughness, the bureau very early gained a justified reputation for making unreasonable demands on its employees. Typical is August Arnold's story of his covering of the sinking of the excursion boat *Favorite* in the twenties. A dozen lives were lost. Arnold recalls:

> I had been slated to cover the detective bureau that day, on the 4:30 p.m. shift. When I arrived I heard about the disaster and was ordered by the city desk to beat it to

the foot of Schiller street near the scene of the sinking. I managed to scrounge a ride with a reporter who had a car. From the shore the top deck of the sunken craft was just visible. Eugene McDonald, head of the Zenith Radio Company, took us out to the wreck in his yacht and supplied considerable data on the tragedy. He had been on the scene early.

I phoned his stuff in when I returned to shore.

Next I went to a hospital where people were being treated who had been thrown into the water but had escaped drowning. They gave vivid eyewitness details of the panic and horror. There were tearful inquiries about relatives and friends who had not shown up at the hospital.

By order, I returned to the lakeshore from there. I could just make out some men diving and bringing up bodies. When these were all accounted for, the desk sent me to an undertaker to witness the heart-breaking business of identifying the victims. It was midnight before this was over. Other City News men were released from duty, but I was kept on. Some genius in the office had heard that I owned a small sailboat. That made me irreplaceable as a nautical expert.

After that I went to the Navy pier, called the Municipal pier in those days, to watch the raising of the wreck by tug and a wrecking barge. Then to the foot of Randolph street, where the wreck was taken. By this time it was long after dawn. A request for a good night was met with a thunderous negative.

"Hang around," ordered the editor, now a day side editor. "There's bound to be a lot of investigation into this one. We need your expertise on this."

Sure enough, there were a lot of investigations. One by city police. Another by the Park District police, a separate unit in those days. Still another by the United States Steamboat Inspection Service, now part of the Coast Guard. The mayor shouted that he would look into this sinking. So did the state's attorney. While the coroner, not to be left out of the publicity, announced that he personally would direct an inquest into the multiple deaths which would certainly pin the responsibility on the person responsible and sweep all 'rat ships' like the *Favorite* from the lake.

I covered a good deal of this glory-grabbing. The day was nearing its end when I once more called the desk, asking for a good night.

"What are you talking about?" snapped Joe Lavandier, the night desk man. "You want a good night! Why, its only 4:30 in the afternoon; your day is just starting. You must be nuts. Where you at?"

I told him I was at the coroner's office in the county building.

"You're due at the detective bureau right now," Joe said. "The day man there is yelling for his relief. Get over there right away."

I got over there. Joe Lavandier, incidentally, was one of the nicest guys I've ever known. In his private capacity, that is. He got the last watch reporter, my relief, down to the detective bureau at ten o'clock that night instead of midnight, his usual starting hour. So I got home a little early, at that.

Overtime? Don't make me laugh. But I was given what was called 'supper money' to pay for the meals I bought while I was working. I forget whether that was one or two bucks.

Salaries were not princely at the bureau. The starting pay for copyboys was $3.50 a week; cub reporters got $7. The rate of increase for those good enough to be kept on was pretty well standardized at a dollar a week a year. Hector Elwell became something of a legend because he did so outstanding a job one year that he got a raise of $1.50 at Christmas.

As a substitute for money, the cub reporter in the twenties had a feeling of being on the inside of events. He could pick up the telephone at any hour of the day or night and talk to politicians, bankers, industrialists, and be received with attention. However, to most of the young reporters these solid citizens were not half as interesting as the pimps and prostitutes, the madams and the murderers. None of these latter could afford to be abrupt with a reporter because if a newspaper demanded that a joint be closed it did not matter how high or into whose pocket the "fix" went—the joint closed.

One cub who made something of a name for himself investigating murders was Leroy "Buddy" McHugh, who left the bureau in 1915 for the *American*, where Hector Elwell had gone as city editor. McHugh is immortalized in *The Front Page* as "Buddy McCue", a character who askes the question, "Is it true, Madam, that you were the victim of a Peeping Tom?"

Buddy's first murder, in 1909, was a Black Hand killing: as a result he became something of an expert on the Mafia. The first murder that Buddy solved occurred in 1916. Agnes Middleton, who was dubbed by the press "the Merry Widow of Armitage Avenue", was found dead in her bed. Her head had been crushed by a blunt instrument, and her throat had been cut with a razor. The razor was found on the floor near the bed; the blunt instrument, however, was missing. The unfortunate victim had had a host of admirers, all of whom were considered suspect by the police, and all of whom were duly interrogated. It should be noted here that the police used both third and fourth degree tactics to elicit confessions from suspects.

The third degree consisted largely of kidney punches. The fourth degree was a little more complicated: it involved a kindly police officer who had not taken part in the third degree, except to express some concern about it. This officer would remain behind with the battered prisoner when the others had left, and bring him a soothing drink of water or a cigarette. Often the prisoner would break down and confess to his "friend".

None of the widow's followers responded satisfactorily to police investigation. The case had reached a dead end when Buddy McHugh decided to go over the Middleton apartment once more. He went up there with Sgt. John Quinn of the police homicide detail and came across an old hatchet underneath a pile of rags in a small tool closet. The hatchet, carried from door to door in the neighborhood, was finally identified by the owner of a local paint store. The hatchet was the murder weapon, and the paint store owner had a feeble-minded stepson named Eddie Nettinger, who worked as an usher in a movie theater next door to the Middleton apartment building.

Sgt. Quinn put Eddie through the third degree while Buddy was there, with no results. Then Buddy asked casually, "Did she scream when you hit her, Eddie?" "No," Eddie said. And McHugh had solved his first case. Eddie had wanted some money to buy a bicycle, and he had heard that Mrs. Middleton had money.

Another reporter who was doggedly persistent when he was covering a story was Larry Mulay. One day in 1921 when Larry was on the west police beat, he was hanging around the neighborhood of a rooming house where Harvey Church, a deluded youth from a small town in Wisconsin, had lived before being arrested for the slaying of two automobile salesmen. The body of one salesman had been found in the river, but police were still looking for the other one. Mulay knew that the police had been over the rooming house and environs, but he wanted to check for himself. He wandered into the garage of the rooming house and paused there. Something smelled funny. He contacted the police lieutenant in charge of the investigation, who sent out a force. They dug into the dirt floor of the garage—not very far into the floor—and uncovered the body of the second salesman. To a bureau news reporter who had been assigned to the old county morgue, the smell of blood and decomposing bodies was unmistakeable. Mulay had a real "nose for news."

Not long after this, on Sunday, December 11, 1921, Mulay flashed a bulletin from the detective bureau:

"Tommy O'Connor has escaped."

That flash electrified the city and was the beginning of a story that lasted for months and, indeed, was the source for the plot of *The Front Page*. Within an hour extras were on the street. O'Connor was to have been hanged the following Friday for a murder of which some people believed him to be innocent. He had been convicted of murdering Detective Paddy O'Neil. When O'Connor escaped, he vanished completely. For weeks there were false reports of his whereabouts; police and reporters were constantly on the run. But O'Connor, like Willie Tascott, was never found. Mulay's scoop made him famous.

In 1933, during the Capone-Touhy war for beer territory, James "Fur" Sammons disguised himself as a woman and rode in an armored car with a machine gun on his lap, to assassinate Roger Touhy. That reminded some people of the O'Connor disappearance, and speculation was rife that O'Connor too must have disguised himself as a woman and been ignored by the police. But most of the reporters and policemen who worked on the case were convinced that O'Connor had fled the country, possibly emigrating to South America.

Incidentally, the Oak Park police confiscated the armored car used by Sammons, and kept it to use as a station car. Although its tires had been riddled with machine gun bullets by the Touhyites, it was a veritable tank. The suburban police could never afford to buy one like it.

Both Gershman and Mulay grew up in their craft in the hardbitten school of the twenties: the Capone Era, with its bombings, machine-gunnings and mass executions.

As early as August of 1922, Capone—whose name was then Caponi—made an appearance in the City News time-sheet:

Alfred Caponi, 25 years old, living at the notorious Four Deuces, a disorderly house at 2222 South Wabash avenue, will appear in the South Clark street court today to answer to a charge of assault with an automobile. Early this morning his automobile crashed into a Town taxicab driven by Fred Krause, 741 Drake avenue, at North Wabash avenue and East Randolph street, injuring the driver.

Three men and a woman who were with Caponi, fled before the arrival of police.

Caponi is said to have been driving east on Randolph street at a high rate of speed. The taxicab was parked at the curb.

Following the accident, Caponi alighted and, flourishing a revolver, displayed a special deputy sheriff's badge and threatened to shoot Krause...

Capone may well have appeared anonymously before this in the timesheet: on April 11, 1922, the assignment book read, in succession: "O'Callaghan bomb developments... Roger bomb developments... Patti bomb developments.. Abbata bomb developments..."

Capone blamed accumulated publicity for the decline of his power. He owed this publicity to the diligent City News bureau man more than to anyone else. From small police court cases grew the ever lengthening story, constantly tended by bureau reporters, which led finally to the sensational income tax trial of 1931, and his imprisonment and death.

Throughout the twenties reporters and copyboys who were to become well-known to the country, continued to begin their careers at the bureau. One who will be remembered was carried on the bureau records, from his hiring in October of 1921, as "Bottinger". Years later when he married the daughter of President Roosevelt, he was referred to in City News copy more correctly as "Boettiger". Another famous trainee was named Hesselberg then; he is famous now as Melvyn Douglas, the actor.

In 1922 came a school board scandal in which George Wright of City News and Harry Read of the *American* gave details of the supposedly secret discussions of a special grand jury, much to that body's angry embarrassment. Although no one knows precisely how the pair overheard the deliberations, it is generally believed that a stethoscope was pushed against the plaster walls of the Cook County Grand Jury room. Incidentally, the corruption that was disclosed by Wright and Read moved the bureau for once to editorial comment: Thurman Harshman, night manager, wrote a censorious lead that was widely reprinted as the expression of outrage by a neutral organization that had no political affiliation.

One reporter who was the victim of corruption was Fred Lovering, who covered a case so thoroughly for City News that when he moved to the *Journal* he continued his investigation, particularly into the way the convicted criminals were bribing guards at the jail. When the unfortunate reporter came to the jail in the course of his investigations one day he was seized and held by guards in a corridor while the prisoner bashed his face in unmercifully. Lovering's nose was broken, and he developed a permanent speech impediment. In fact, he never recovered from that beating. When the *Journal* folded he went to New York, but could not work there, and returned to City News. The grind was too much for him, however, and he committed suicide quietly one day with sleeping tablets. He left a note thanking Gershman, who had tried to help him get his strength back. His death cast a pall over the office that lasted for months.

George Wright used his stethoscope again during the Grand Jury hearings on the Bobby Franks murder. The walls of the old Criminal Court building were flimsy: Wright heard the state's attorney read the murder confessions of Loeb and Leopold to the Grand Jury. The result were scoop headlines and three columns of factual details.

Loren Carroll and Kenneth Laird were City News reporters who covered the Loeb-Leopold trials with Wright. But it was Wright who stopped Clarence Darrow for questions between court sessions and reported a flash that Darrow would plead the two University of Chicago men guilty. Darrow usually weighed every word, and it was apparently a slip of the tongue that gave Wright his second scoop. The two scoops got Wright a job on the Chicago *Tribune*, where he continued to cover Criminal Courts cases.

In a letter to Vickerman, Loren Carroll, who later became a novelist, reminisced in the thirties about the Loeb-Leopold case:

> The principal thing that emerges after all these years about the *cause célèbre* was the fact that the newspapers took the case of two common perverts and built it up by false emphasis on the education and family background of the boys. Their education was ordinary, their parents were merely wealthy beyond the average. Loeb, far from being an intellectual youth, was really dense. Leopold, in a mechanical sense, had a good mind; his intelligence was mediocre. What they knew about Nietzsche, Freud and company was what any boy could learn by reading an article in the New International Encyclopedia. Aside from their murderous and homosexual activities the pair of them were low characters. I base this on daily interviews with them through the whole period of the trial...

Carroll also recalled an incident connected with his coverage of the trial that shed some light on the working methods of Walter Brown:

> When I had finished the Loeb-Leopold trial, I had written thousands of words and it was generally agreed I had done well, at least for a cub. Brown without a word gave me two raises and then took the entire stack of copy I had written (a huge bale) and referred to a certain page. I saw this sentence: " 'Oh no,' said Darrow, with a denigrating gesture." The word 'denigrating' was ringed and this note followed: "Carroll, a very unfortunate word in an otherwise fine piece of work."

The St. Valentine's day massacre was one of the few times the bureau had been caught napping on an important story.

Walter Spirko heard the news about the murders while he was covering the coroner's office. He immediately phoned it in, but Isaac Gershman, who was on the desk refused to believe it. Instead of accepting the "massacre" story, he sent out the famous bulletin that began, "Six men are reported to have been seriously injured..."

Joe Ator recalled that day:

> I remember in 1929, having my lunch interrupted to chase off on what seemed a silly City Press bulletin which said: "Six men are reported to have been seriously injured in a fight in a pool room at 2122 N. Clark st." It wasn't a pool room, there were seven men, not six, and they weren't seriously injured. They were blown apart with tommy guns and shotgun slugs... But the address of the St. Valentine's day massacre was correct.

Willis O'Rourke, another City Press man, as he wandered across the unattractively littered floor of the garage, made a remark that has become bureau legend: "Some of us guys have got more brains on our shoes than we have under our hats."

Abe Lincoln Mahoney, another bureau reporter, was lurking about the scene of the crime, looking for a story, when he spotted the overcoats of the slain gangsters hanging on a long coatrack on the wall of the garage. No one was paying any attention to him; although the place was swarming with policemen and reporters, most of them were concentrating on interviews with the coroner, Dr. Herman N. Bundesen, a popular pediatrician who had been transferred only recently from the Health Department. Mahoney spied a sheaf of papers in the pocket of one of the overcoats. While everyone was distracted he quickly seized the papers and made off with them, hoping for a scoop. A few minutes later he slunk back into the garage and stuffed the papers into what he hoped was the right pocket. They were a sheaf of notes for one of Dr. Bundesen's articles on baby care.

No finger of scandal ever touched the badly paid young

bureau reporters, although there was much soul-searching in newspapers offices all over the city in the aftermath of the shooting of *Tribune* reporter Jake Lingle, on a June day in 1930 in the middle of the busy Illinois Central station underpass at Randolph street near Michigan. The shooting, the eleventh murder in Chicago in ten days, caused an outraged outcry from the newspaper community not only in Chicago, but throughout the country.

Lingle had been considered a model reporter, who specialized in crime stories. It had been noticed that he spent a great deal of money for a man who earned sixty-five dollars a week. He bet heavily on the horses, owned a summer home and kept a suite at the Stevens hotel, in addition to his family home on the west side. He also wore a diamond-studded belt which it was rumored had been given to him by Al Capone. Lingle explained all this by saying that he had inherited fifty thousand dollars from his father. The *Tribune*, the rival Hearst papers and the Chicago Press club all offered rewards for Lingle's murderer. It was assumed that the reporter had been murdered to punish the press for its agitations against gangsters. Harry Chandler of the *Los Angeles Times* called Lingle a "first-line soldier" who had been felled in the war on crime. Al Capone himself was moved to announce that he had assigned fifty men to find Lingle's killer. As it happened, they were unsuccessful.

When some of the emotion drained away, it was discovered that Lingle had inherited only five hundred dollars, which he had lost in 1929, and that he had worked for the gangs as a middleman between them and the police, arranging transfers of troublesome policemen and carrying favors back and forth. He had received the diamond belt from Al Capone as a mark of the gangster's esteem.

Colonel McCormick's wrath was terrible, and the lives of all his reporters were gone over with a fine-tooth comb. John Boettiger, the City News veteran, had led the probe and later wrote a book about it. Boettiger had found fourteen hundred dollars in Lingle's pocket and had turned it in to the police, an act which produced some amazement in the hardened citizens of the Windy City. But this was typical of honest City News men. There was of course Harry Smith, a bureau reporter who wore expensive clothes and a diamond belt buckle. He was eyed, after the Lingle scandal, with some interest by newcomers. He had a habit of signalling to a cub with a jerk of his head, drawing him aside with a finger in his buttonhole, and then saying in a conspiratorial low voice, "It's a nice day." Smitty came from a well-to-do family.

There were other bureau men who had private means. Phil Chancellor lived at the Sherman hotel and drove the bookkeeper to distraction by forgetting to cash his paychecks for weeks. On one of his first nights, when he was sent out to cover a fire, he drove up to the Hyde Park station in his new Stutz car and hurried inside to ask the desk sergeant for a street direction. The sergeant became suspicious: he was unused to seeing a bureau reporter in such luxury. He attempted to arrest Chancellor for stealing the car, and was only dissuaded by frantic assurances from the office.

Another wealthy reporter was Edward "Pat" Peabody, the son of Stuyvesant Peabody, and the heir to a coal mine fortune. When Louis K. Straub was murdered in the Saddle and Cycle club on February 4, 1935, the police reporters were not allowed in, and stood disconsolately outside the gates, while Peabody drove up in his Pierce Arrow, got out and swept past them to investigate to his heart's content within. He was a member of the club.

Most of the beer gangsters were on friendly terms with bureau reporters. Red Bolton, a bootlegger from the west side, was resting one evening in a Warren avenue police cell, philosophically awaiting the arrival of bail money. When he spied a bureau man, he called out:

"Hey, kid. I left my car up at North avenue and Paulina. Go get it for me, will you?"

He handed the reporter a five dollar bill and his keys. The bureau man set out, found the car and was driving it grandly down the street in twelve-cylinder elegance, when a detective bureau squad car with sirens screaming, bore down on him and forced him to the curb. The sergeant leaped out with his gun in his hand. When he recognized the cowering driver he threw open the door, collared him and dragged him out.

"You little fool," he said. "Don't you know a dozen guys in this district have that car spotted and are all ready to pour lead into it?"

So much for favors to gangsters.

Some people did not get off so easily. There is a tale of a City Press man who was fired, went to Oklahoma, held up a train, shot and wounded several people in his escape, and then committed suicide while a posse was closing in on him.

The Oak Park police once seized a versatile deceiver who was committing robberies in the suburbs and then hurrying into the police station to inquire about them as a reporter. Early in 1937 dark-haired Dick Nolan, one-time altar boy, editor of his church paper, Golden Glove contender, favorite of police officials and one of the most promising of the younger reporters, stole a pistol from the detective bureau and was caught not long afterward attempting a holdup. An investigation revealed that both he and his brother had juvenile crime records, a fact that had not been suspected when he was hired. Curiously, the story had been covered and forgotten. On the assignment book for April, 1929, appears the entry: "Nolan brothers firebugs."

At least some police reporters have always been fascinated by guns. Sayler, who kept bound copies of old newspapers, to which he often referred, in a vault in the Western Union building, opened one of his books one day and was horrified when a mass of flattened lead fell out of it. Some of the police reporters had been using the vault for target practice.

Bureau reporters may well consider turning to a life of crime in desperation: they must compete fully with newspapers on important stories, they must check on a mass of routine deaths, arrests, fires, suit filings, court cases, most of which never develop into a story but all of which have to be investigated nevertheless. Since the newspapers depend on the bureau for this kind of work, their own men are left free to dig up exclusive stories which, when printed, mean further woe for the drudges of City News. John Latimer, a writer for

Collier's, wrote a mystery novel called *The Lady in the Morgue*, in which he describes Jerry Johnson, a City News reporter assigned to the county morgue:

> His face had an unhealthy pallor; his black eyes were set deep in discolored sockets; he was drinking himself to death as fast as he could on a salary of twenty-six dollars a week.

When the news of the murder breaks, Latimer describes the gathering of the clans:

> ...the squad car detailed to rove in the neighborhood of the morgue arrived first, poured out men with revolvers, sawed-off shotguns. Then came the homicide squad from police headquarters, the official police photographer, two special investigators from the coroner's office, an assistant state's attorney, photographers from all the papers and four *Tribune* reporters.

Only an ex-bureau man could have added that last touch.

Sometimes it is no advantage to the bureau man even to be among the first on the scene. In a burglary in the thirties at the Conway building, the battle-scarred bureau veteran was first to arrive and found the building manager determined to admit no reporters. The bureau man argued vehemently as other reporters began to come in, and finally the manager officiously agreed to admit the press—all except the bureau man, who hung around outside but failed to get even a line of information as consolation from the others as they emerged and hurried off to make deadlines.

Some ex-employees of the bureau who wrote to Vickerman in the thirties were rather bitter; some were more light-hearted:

> My own recollections are few and not all pleasant. The idiotic custom of writing reams no paper would use

was then in vogue and life was a miserable round of checking coroner cases and writing inane pieces about meetings which had no use but which had to be represented in the time sheet...

The bureau was a sort of flophouse for newspapermen currently without jobs or out too late to go home. The favorite sleeping place was on a group of old wooden desks spread with papers. Occasionally one's shoes, wrapped in paper, formed a good pillow. And then there were the visits at three or four in the morning when the town was practically asleep to a restaurant on Randolph street. Of course arrangements had to be made with someone to stay at the switchboard or with the Central police reporter not to disturb the office quiet with his calls.

Sunday nights were gala events when the lads used to turn out the lights and turn on binoculars to the Sherman hotel. They sometimes spotted carnalities in various stages of development. They knew how to tick off the numbers by floor and counting from the corner. They they'd call the number of the room and say, "Shame on you!" Down would come the curtains... Sometimes they saw wenches they fancied, and called up and made arrangements...

The depression, crashing down at the end of 1929, brought an end to much of this post-war hilarity.

One thing that every City News reporter wanted was a verbatim reprinting of his story in the newspapers. Walter Ryberg describes it as the thrill of a reporter's life. A few, he says, always got verbatim reprints. Some mediocre ones never got them. Larry Mulay, when he was manager of the bureau, always went out of his way to congratulate reporters on verbatims. One that covered its author with glory was printed verbatim in almost every paper in the country, and in the *Tribune* appeared in a box on the front page, underneath the cartoon. The writer was the usual anonymous City News reporter, but he was actually Joe Ator, who later joined the *Tribune* staff.

Fireman John Cosgrove of Engine Company 39 was toiling with grappling hooks yesterday on the dock at the foot of Iron street on the south branch.

"He's looking for a body," said the first bystander to the second bystander.

"O," said the second bystander, turning to the third bystander. "He's looking for a body. It's a girl."

"O," said the third bystander, and he turned to the fourth bystander and said, "He's looking for a body. It's a girl. Her fellow threw her down. She left a note."

"O," said the fifth bystander. "Who was this dastardly fellow?" he asked Fireman Cosgrove.

"It was fireman Harry Hammergreen," he replied, "and I hope someone pours glue in his boots."

"And who was the beautiful maiden?"

"What do you mean, beautiful maiden?"

"Why, the one you're trying to get out of the river."

"What are you talking about?" asked Fireman Cosgrove. "I'm fishing for my hat. Hammergreen knocked it into the river when we came down here on a fire last night."

"O," said the first, second, third, fourth and fifth bystanders. And they went home.

12

Worm's Eye View

Here is a reconstruction of a day in the life of a City News police reporter back in the alcoholic and explosive twenties.

He leaves his office at six p.m. and heads for the Desplaines street station from which he is expected to watch six police districts on the turbulent west side. He can smell the station before he is actually inside it: cockroach powder, ammonia, and unscrubbed humanity. The only sanitary facility in the old building is a sluggish trickle of polluted water meandering through a shallow groove in the concrete floor, from cell to cell.

There are three Cadillac touring cars standing at the curb outside the station; these are used by squads from the detective bureau, the "smart shop". The reporter pushes aside the celluloid side curtain and addresses a fat squad man lolling in the rear seat, with the standard City News query:

"What's doing, Sarge?"

"Nothing at all, kid. Not a leaf stirring."

"Oh yeah? With three squads from the smart shop here? Nothing on the fire?"

The plainclothesman leans forward and rests his elbows on a box attached to the front seat before him: it houses two sawed-off shotguns. Squads do not carry machine guns as a rule; they check them out of the detective bureau when they need them. He tells the kid that the Big Man, the deputy chief, expects trouble from Communists in Haymarket Square, because Sacco and Vanzetti are due to be hanged soon.

While the reporter is trying to negotiate a ride to Haymarket Square, a window in the station, opaque with dirt, slides open and the desk sergeant bawls out, "Hey, City News. Your office is after you. Called you three times."

The reporter trots upstairs, slides behind a desk and calls State 8100 on one of the three desk phones. He knows he's supposed to use the public wall phone, but that costs a nickel. The police do not object. They know about City News and money.

The switchboard boy answers at the bureau and snarls: it's about time the reporter called in. He's holding two dead ones for him—deceased persons whose deaths require investigation by the coroner's office. One of the dead ones is a west side bum who seems to have succumbed to bad booze. No story there. Too common. The other dead one is more promising: he was killed by a hit and run in Albany Park on the northwest side.

The youth begins to phone Albany Park, but is interrupted by the sounds of Cadillacs revving up outside. He hangs up, rushes outside and they are off to Haymarket Square, with the reporter in the rear seat. The side curtains rattle, and the siren blares, while the fabric top of the car slaps against the steel frame. The squad men check their pistols and blackjacks, ruminating over the superior qualities of large banana stalks. "They don't put a mark on the guy," one says dreamily. The Cadillac lurches to the right to avoid two rats munching offal near a wholesale grocery on Randolph street.

Sirens howl from the left and right. The Big Man is bringing in everything he's got. A medium-sized crowd is standing quietly in the square, listening to a shouting orator. The squad cars screech up accompanied by motorcycle police, and park in a circle round the square. The detectives climb out, pinning their badges to their jackets. They begin to shout "Go home!" at the crowd, and to swing their black-jacks. Panic sets in. The crowd is hemmed in by the police. A few people escape; some fall down and are trampled.

The reporter has been busy taking notes. When everyone has gotten away except for some prone figures on the ground, he returns to the car and asks the squad leader, who has tumbled breathlessly back into his seat, what his name is. There is no reply, so he writes "Sgt. John Murphy" on an old envelope, and adds other notes: "No women in crowd—Guys well dressed—a few bums—No knives or guns—yelling in foreign language—Italian?"

He decides he had better go to the Jefferson Park hospital and check on the wounded, but first he calls his office.

"Where you been?" says the switchboard boy. "Trying to get you for an hour. Sergeant says you're somewhere. Don't you know you're not supposed to leave the station without telling me? Here, the desk wants you."

The man on the desk contents himself with a reproof about leaving the station without notice, and then listens to the story of the riot. The reporter should turn in his stuff to the rewrite man, he says, and go to the hospital, then he should get back to the station and call his beat.

There is no street car to the hospital, so the reporter goes there on foot. Pushed around by interns, rebuffed by nurses, he manages to get the data on the men being treated for cuts and bruises. Then he spends another nickel to report his findings to the office.

"Where you at?" says the switchboard boy. "I been trying to get you for an hour. You got that hit and run in your pocket for two hours now. How about turning in something on it?"

The reporter has learned not to argue with the switchboard boy. He gives his list of injured and adds a quote from the squad leader about the dangerous situation in which the police found themselves. Then he walks back to Desplaines street where he phones Albany Park about the hit and run auto death. He checks the names of the victim's survivors with the telephone book and with the undertaker. He phones a relative to find out about the dead man. He learns that the police are looking for a 1921 Hudson with a smashed left headlight.

In due course he calls these facts in to another rewrite man.

"What's the name of the driver of the death car?" the rewrite man asks.

The reporter responds politely that the Albany Park police are asking that very question. The reporter and the writer hang up simultaneously. The reporter then embarks on a round of phone calls to his dozen stations, inquiring about murders, fires, arsons and rapes. After several rounds he gets only an account of a streetcar smashing into a junkman's wagon. One casualty: the horse lost his tail.

At midnight the reporter knocks off for dinner, after getting permission from the office. He orders chowder into which he pours lots of ketchup to kill the taste, and watery coffee.

When he gets back to the station there have been calls for him.

The switchboard boy, who has been looking for him for an hour, gives him another dead one. And so the night wears on. Quitting time is three a.m.

"Can I have a good night?" he asks the desk in what he hopes is his last call.

"Sure," the desk says cheerfully. And adds, "We did real good on that Haymarket story. The *Trib* and the *Her-Ex* both used a page one column on it."

The next night, however, is a different story. The reporter is assigned to the north side, and told to hang around the Chicago avenue station. There is a rumor that there will be trouble at Washington park, called Bughouse square, because of the Sacco-Vanzetti hangings.

The Chicago avenue station smells much like Desplaines street. There are no Cadillacs in front, but there have been some arrests at a neighboring bawdy house. The desk is not interested in this, unless a former Miss America has been picked up. The reporter should check.

But all the women have been shipped off to the lockup for women in the Racine street station. They are out of reach.

Sadly, the youth reports again. The desk says it doesn't matter, "whorehouse raids are a dime a dozen." But what about Bughouse square?

The reporter rushes over to the park, and wanders around. There are a lot of people listening moodily to three angry orators. No turmoil.

The reporter calls in his negative report, and then returns to the park which is now strangely empty, except for a few policemen, who are noncomittal. They suggest the reporter talk to the lieutenant.

The lieutenant is back in the station. After a lot of arguing, the reporter gets into the lieutenant's office, and then phones the resulting story in. The lieutenant just sent detectives from other districts circulating through the crowd. They all pinned on their badges and suggested quietly that the group disperse. Which it did.

The desk was not enthusiastic about this news.

"No riot? Nothing? Listen, you better check Henrotin hospital. See if anyone got clubbed and ended up there. Call me right back."

"Don't hang up," gasps the reporter. "I did check Henrotin. And Augustana. And County. No dice."

The desk man hangs up, depressed.

The reporter then takes off on a fire alarm. There is a blaze four blocks away at Erie and Michigan. By the time the youth arrives the fire is out. A flivver squad—a Model T roadster mounted on rubber tires—pulls up and two fat patrolmen roll out. Puffing, they mount the stairs. The fire was on the first floor, but it is a three story building.

The larger of the two patrolmen explains to the reporter that they have to make sure no one is trapped on the upper floors. The third floor is fitted out as a speakeasy. No one is there.

The officer places several bottles under his coat, and hands a quart of Scotch cordially to the reporter. "Go ahead," he says. "It's good stuff. Imported. You don't get bathtub gin here."

The reporter, embarrassed, shoves the bottle into the

waistband of his trousers. He thanks the policemen and returns downstairs past the sweating firemen, who are hurling their hose into a hook-and-ladder truck. He hunts up an all-night phone, makes a call, and returns to the fire. The firemen are still there, or at least they are coming downstairs in small groups. Their rubber coats are bulging.

The reporter returns to the station and hides the bottle of Scotch in the flush tank of a toilet. Then he returns to the teletype and reads about a reported robbery. A phone call to the victims elicits a gruff response from a man who doesn't want to talk about it. His wife, however, does want to talk about it and talks about it for a considerable period. The robbers took twenty-seven dollars but they stupidly over-looked the most valuable thing in the house—her Pekinese Fifi, the watchdog, who slept through the burglary.

The reporter finally gets off the line and phones in his report, watchdog and all. Next there is a reported rape from a young woman who has allowed a meter reader for the gas company to come into her apartment at ten o'clock that night. The detective in charge expresses some doubt about this case, and the desk echoes it. The young woman is famil-iar to him. Generally speaking she makes these complaints, the desk says, to get the police department to act as a collec-tion agency for her.

"Forget it, kid," the desk says. "Go home, it's almost three. But first let me tell you that you fell down on that Bughouse thing. No one used a line on it."

So. Yesterday, the reporter thinks, *we* did good on the Haymarket thing. But tonight *I* fall down on Bughouse Square.

Before he leaves he lifts the lid off the toilet flush tank to get the Scotch. It's gone.

13

The Thirties

When Walter Brown retired from the bureau in 1931, a new age was obviously dawning. The Great Depression had hit the country, and newspapers, along with almost everything else, were in trouble. When, four years later, on June 13, 1935, Brown died, in Monrovia California, where he had gone in an attempt to recover his health, the New Deal was in full swing, and the new age was a fact. Probably Brown's most important contribution was his work on the bureau's election-return system. The *Daily News* commented on this in their obituary on him: "He brought to a high point of perfection the system of gathering election returns to fit the present rapid handling of news." The City News bureau report on his death remarked on his wide acquaintance "with the police of all ranks."

When Gershman became general manager there were six newspapers subsidizing City News. In 1932 the *Evening Post* folded, leaving five. Income was down, and Gershman had the headache of trying to effect economies. In 1938 the *Herald-Examiner* bit the dust, making things worse. Departments were contracted. A few beats were eliminated, including the Board of Education and the hotel beats. The police beats were coalesced into four beats.

One of the big stories in Chicago in the early thirties was the Wynekoop murder case:

> A dingy two-story brick building on the southwest corner of Fillmore street and South Crawford avenue was the scene of the greatest drama in the nation today as Earle Wynekoop, widower of the slain girl, and his grim-lipped mother, Dr. Alice Lindsay Wynekoop, were subject to gruelling questions by police. [City News Bureau Timesheet Nov. 24, 1933].

Throughout that hectic November morning Bob Kennedy had sat at his rewrite desk, headphones glued to his ears. A break in the story was due. At the Fillmore street station where Dr. Wynekoop and her philandering son Earle were being questioned in the death of Earle's wife Rheta Gardner Wynekoop, Tom Cahill was camped in a telephone booth, afraid to hang up the receiver for fear someone would take his place. Joe Faye and Charles "Red" Trowbridge relayed him the news. Each rumor earned a flurry on Kennedy's typewriter. Other rewrite men—Jack Thompson, Harold Smith, Don Ownby—were busy on angles of the story. The hours ticked by.

Trowbridge and Faye checked every policeman who emerged from the room where Dr. Wynekoop was being questioned by top police brass. They had no success. Finally Red Trowbridge followed a policeman from the squad room down to his locker, and got the story at last. At 11:35 Cahill gave the flash: "Dr. Wynekoop confessed."

> ...with great difficulty one cartridge was exploded at a distance of some half dozen inches from the patient. The gun was dropped from the hand. The scene was so overwhelming that no action was possible for several minutes. [City News Bureau Timesheet, Excerpt Dr. Wynekoop's confession.]

While the newspapers were arguing about whether Dr. Wynekoop's confession was legitimate, assistant states attorney Charles S. Daugherty secretly obtained another confession. The next week, when Trowbridge and Faye were in the Criminal Court building on the same case, Faye "borrowed" the key to the states attorney's private office from a guard. That night, while Trowbridge acted as lookout, Faye got a copy of the transcript of the second confession. It was unwittingly authenticated by a police captain. The guard, incidentally, never knew that his key had been taken and returned.

But then came one of the great discouragements of news bureau reporting. Just as the story was released by the bureau one paper broke a fictitious scoop purporting to shift new suspicion onto Earle Wynekoop, and the rest of the papers went baying down this false trail. Several days later the *Times* awoke to the second confession and emblazoned the story with a streamer on the front page. But by that time the luster had faded. For consolation the two reporters were given raises. Faye eventually went to the *Sun-Times* and Trowbridge to the *Herald-American*.

As an added note: it was not until three days after the murder of her daughter-in-law in the dark old house at 3406 West Monroe street that Dr. Wynekoop made her confession. However, twelve hours after the murder City News carried a confidential note to city editors that the doctor had been accused of the murder by her brother-in-law, Dr. Gilbert Wynekoop, who was, at the time, in County jail on a sex charge involving a pretty nurse. The charge was unprintable at the time, but when it was printed after the confession it had an embarrassing typo. A psychiatrist said that Gilbert Wynekoop was suffering from megalomania: the word was printed "legalomania".

With the repeal of prohibition the gangs had to find other outlets for their energies than beer and alcohol traffic. Most turned to gambling, vice and labor rackets. The "Terrible Touhys" of the northwest side were vanquished early in 1934 with the sentencing of Roger Touhy, "Polly Nose" Kator and "Gloomy Gus" Schaeffer for the kidnaping of John "Jake the Barber" Factor. "Machine Gun" Kelly and other bank raiders had brief notoriety. But none approached the exploits of the Dillinger gang against whom the G-Men, with Melvin Purvis as the Chicago head, rose to glory.

Purvis was friendly to newspapermen at first, but he turned against them because of a story which he believed gave greater credit to the city police than to his agents. After that he rarely spoke freely for publication. But one occasion on which he did speak freely was the slaying of John Dillinger.

It was on a stiflingly hot evening in July, during the World's Fair summer of 1934, that Dillinger met his end. The Havoline thermometer on the Fair grounds reached ninety that day. Twenty-two people died of the heat. One man drowned. Members of three families became ill from eating corned beef sandwiches. A blonde beauty in a bathing suit was found wandering in a dazed condition on the north side. A tavern keeper shot a robber. The police issued 106 summonses to motorists who did not have their 1934 state licenses. It was a quiet Chicago Sunday.

Elwood Faust, a bureau police reporter, was in the Sheffield avenue station when a call came in from the manager of the Biograph theatre, with a report that several tough-looking men were hanging around the area. Faust rushed to his jalopy to race the squad car to the scene. He envisioned an eyewitness story headlined "Bandits Nabbed in the Act." But Faust got there a little late. There was a dead body in the alley.

There were a lot of plainclothesmen in the crowd, carrying guns. They told Faust that the dead man was just "some Chinaman," and added, "Get lost, kid." That wasn't very interesting. But then the reporter recognized Melvin Purvis from newspaper pictures.

At 10:40 p.m. Faust sent a bulletin:

Department of Justice agents are reported to have

shot and killed John Dillinger in front of the Biograph theatre, 2433 North Lincoln avenue.

At 11:01 p.m. Purvis identified the body as that of Dillinger, and with that flash the story grew swiftly:

John Dillinger, most noted desperado of modern times, was slain tonight by government agents...

Within fifteen minutes after that first City Press bulletin, telephone calls were swamping the detective bureau, newspaper and radio offices. Fifteen minutes more and a crowd of one thousand had gathered near the theater, tying up traffic and troubling police. By that time the news bureau story was well under way with the entire night staff and part of the day crew at work. Harshman had been summoned from his Sunday night off.

Imaginative reporters who scooped the world on the Dillinger shooting are as numerous as survivors of Custer's Last Stand. The real story is less thrilling—only a lucky break for a six-months cub, E.R. Faust, who happened to be on the job. The *Tribune* man, incidentally, was still sitting in the Sheffield avenue station when Faust rushed out.

As in most big stories it was some time before conflicting versions could be reconciled. Argument still exists as to whether Dillinger was shot from behind without a show of resistance. The bureau copy quotes Mrs. Esther Gusino, 2427 Lincoln avenue, who was looking out her bedroom window and saw the shooting:

...I saw a man come out of the theatre with two young women and start walking down the street. There were two men, government men I guess, standing a little south of the theatre... The man and the women with him passed the two agents and started across the alley. Suddenly one of the agents pulled out a gun and fired. The man fell and the women disappeared... All the other agents came running and bent over the body. The man who fired was a tall man with a light gray suit and a Panama hat. I thought it was peculiar they asked no questions and suddenly I realized it must have been Dillinger...

Another account was given by another eyewitness, Edward Garbel, who lived at the same address as Mrs. Gusino:

I saw the government men bend over the body and examine it. They took a pistol out of one of his back pockets.

At the same time Purvis had gathered newspapermen in his office and was telling them:

Dillinger gave one hunted look and attempted to run up an alley where several of my men were waiting. As he ran he drew an automatic pistol from his pocket, although I have always been told he carried his weapons in his waistband. As his hand came up with the gun in it, several shots were fired by my men...

The "Manhattan Melodrama"* had ended. Dillinger's body was taken to the county morgue while a crowd of the curious remained in the alley fighting to dip handkerchiefs in his blood or soak it up in newspapers as a momento. By 12:50 p.m. the news bureau, still in feverish activity, had returned some attention to routine news:

Twenty-five tickets for parking in dead end streets were issued by police tonight in a drive against lovers' lane motorists...

---

* The name of the movie showing at the Biograph that night.

14

Labor Problems

In 1907 Sayler was defending expenditures in one of the endless financial crises that the bureau has faced:

> An examination of our payroll will show that the men are the poorest paid and the hardest worked in Chicago...

Practically nobody would dispute that statement. In 1894 the hours for reporters on the day shift were 8 and 8:30 a.m. to "until their work is finished. This may be 5:45 or midnight. It is generally between 6 and 7 o'clock." [Committee report to Medill McCormick, president. Feb. 26, 1907.]

In those early years many reporters worked twelve to sixteen hours a day for ten, fifteen and eighteen dollars a week, and overtime pay was unheard of. Those who got twenty-six dollars were considered high-salaried. Copyboys got as little as two dollars a week, although some did earn as much as six.

These low wages and long hours did not last only through the early years of the century. It was not until the twenties that employees got one day a week off instead of one day every two weeks.

Walter Ryberg, who started at the bureau in 1926, was told he could have every other Sunday off. After two weeks, he took his second Sunday off, only to be greeted harshly when he came into the office on Monday morning to get his paycheck: "Where were you yesterday?" It was true that the reporters had a day off every other week, but they were supposed to call first to make sure that they were not needed.

Ryberg was covering Oak Park his first few months with the bureau. The Oak Park man was responsible for all the western suburbs of Cook County. Ryberg lost a pleasant room in Oak Park because the landlord disapproved of midnight calls from the bureau. Since the telephone was in the downstairs hall, the ringing woke up the whole house. The call that brought down the landlord's wrath was about a scoop in the *Daily News*, concerning a shooting in Cicero. The editor wanted to know whether Ryberg had the story.

If he did not have the story, Ryberg would have had to get dressed and go to Cicero immediately, midnight or not. On several occasions he did work all night, but the desk did not necessarily know about it. Often he would phone in and report to Joe Levandier, who would respond, "Okay. Don't come in today."

Ryberg was relieved to move back to Chicago after a few months, and work an eight hour day, with a day off every week. The suburban men worked more hours. There were police news and accidents, but otherwise it was pretty quiet in the suburbs. The news was largely official suburban news. The bureau did not cover business news—nothing commercial, no publicity. Business was covered only when there was an investigation by a regulatory body, like the Illinois Commerce Commission.

Another reporter who covered a suburban beat for CNB was Bob Kennedy, who started working for the bureau a few weeks after the St. Valentine day's massacre in 1929:

> I was assigned to the Evanston beat because they needed somebody that lived in or near Evanston and I qualified because I lived in Rogers Park. The territory was from Evanston to and including Glencoe, the county line, and west to include the Morton Grove county highway police station. There wasn't much out west anyway. Niles Center (now Skokie) was a little village, noted mostly for speakeasies.
>
> The hours on the suburban beat at that time were from 9 a.m. to 10 p.m. with every other Sunday off. Of

course, you were on call between 10 p.m. and 9 a.m. anyway, so it was a 24 hour job. The pay was eighteen dollars a week. There was a "generous" expense account for telephones. Two or three times a day you were supposed to call the other police stations on the beat (Wilmette, Winnetka, Kenilworth, Glencoe and Morton Grove... I don't remember if Glenview and Niles Center were included, but nothing happened there anyway) from the public phone booth in the Evanston station. The total cost was sixty cents per round and it was standard practice, undoubtedly known in the CNB office, for the reporters stationed at Evanston (*Daily News, Herald Examiner, Trib* and *American*) to take turns making the calls, if there, and everyone put in for the sixty cents.

Chicago papers were not popular in the Evanston station because most of the "news" out of Evanston was feature stuff, some of which made sort of fun of suburban life. Gino DeServi, the dog catcher, was always good for a story on a slow day. I did get a rather important story one day and as I recall I had it "exclusive". (It was common practice to pass stories around among the reporters because they were so unimportant.) A motorcycle cop named Franklin D. Kreml, who was also a law student at Northwestern, told me he was working on something, and if it was okayed by Chief William Freeman when he came back from vacation, it would be a story. I asked for an inkling. He said it had to do with an idea for an accident prevention department that he was working on. I said, "Why, accidents just happen, how can you prevent them?" My ignorance reflected the general ignorance of the subject at that time. The chief did approve Kreml's idea, I got my story, and the first accident prevention department in the world was created in Evanston. Kreml later went to great fame in teaching the idea around the world, and NU to this day has a course on it...

One of the reporters at the Evanston station was

Harold P. Smith, who worked for the *Evanston News-Index*. Later he went to work for the CNB and in 1932 or thereabouts he and I started the first clipping morgue arrangement for the CNB. Up to that time the only reference for back stories was a listing of stories in the *Chicago Tribune* in a student's composition book. Tony Kedzior, who ran the hectograph machine at 155 N. Clark, made bound copies of each day's file of hectograph copies and you could look up a story in that file if you could remember the date and the time of day.

Larry Jacobs and Kirk Earnshaw were on rewrite when I started. They were stern taskmasters... It was really a teaching school. Kids didn't have to have a journalism degree in those days. In fact, I had only a high school diploma. But I had been an editor of the Senn *News* high school paper (working along with the cartoonist, Herb Block) and I was publishing a monthly paper for a high school fraternity, which impressed Gersh when I showed him a copy one day. Kirk Earnshaw had gone to Senn too, but I had not known him.

Rewritemen made you go back for fact after fact, sometimes, it seemed to me, in a sort of hazing process. Once I took a street car out to look into a report of a death in a poor family's house. I think it was routine. But after I had made my way some distance to get to a phone, Jacobs made me go all the way back to get a middle initial. (The family was too poor to have a phone.) Most of the time, of course, we could cover a story by phone.

After six months in Evanston, I was brought into Chicago and covered the various police beats. Cops were friendly with reporters in those days before the "new journalism". One police captain even took me into his office in the Racine street station one day, and we had a long conversation in which he taught me quite a few things a young reporter should know about covering police. He had a good nose for news and public relations. In fact, he became one of the most newsmaking cops of his time: he was Dan Gilbert, the "world's richest cop", the target of the Kefauver congressional investigation a generation or so later.

I guess Gersh remembered I could run a typewriter because I was not on the police beats too long. I was brought into the office for general assignments or a spell at rewrite. Early on during this period, Larry Mulay told me to go cover a meeting of the school board in their old headquarters on South Dearborn street. I had not the slightest idea how to cover a school board meeting. I didn't even know about the press table. I listened to it all and at the conclusion went up and asked the secretary what happened. He handed me a dossier about two inches thick with the agenda on it. I took it back and handed it to Mulay and said hopelessly, "This is what happened."

I fully expected to be fired on the spot as an incompetent. Larry looked at it, and of course he couldn't figure out anything from it either. He looked at me with contempt or pity, or both, and said, "You go right back down there and *find out* what happened." He tossed the agenda back at me. Back I went, by street car all the way to the board room. Luckily, this time I met other reporters from the papers who had covered the meeting. They felt sorry for me and filled me in with comprehensible information. They saved my career.

I had almost gotten fired on an earlier occasion, when I was in Evanston. I turned in a story about the president of the Hertz rental car company being involved in a minor traffic accident: that was "news" in those days. A few days later I was called into Mr. Brown's office. Gersh had hired me; this was my first meeting with Walter Brown. He said that the Hertz story, which had been carried by the *Daily News*, had an error. I had listed a Negro woman as a passenger in Hertz's car, but she had actually not been in the car at all. Very bad reporting, Mr. Brown said, how could I have made such an error?

Fortunately, I decided to tell Brown the truth: I had not gotten the story from the desk sergeant's report myself. I had taken it down from Charles Finklestein, the Evanston reporter for the *Daily News*. Brown said, very seriously, that this should be a good lesson for me. I should get my own stories. He said he had intended to fire me but since I had been honest with him he would give me another chance. In the back of my mind I realized that he was gloating inwardly: the complaint had come to him from the *Daily News*, and now he could tell the *News* that their reporter had made the mistake. As I turned to leave, I asked, "Who complained? Mr. Hertz?" "No," Brown said. "The Negro lady."

In 1932 Gersh assigned me to cover the Democratic National Convention at which Franklin Roosevelt was nominated. My job was feature stuff and police. Gersh always had an eye out for having CNB do things that gave it access to important events. It worked out; one day the *Post* or the *Journal*, I forget which, ran a full column of my feature stuff verbatim. Like how many people bought popcorn or how many cops did what. One day I scooped the national press because I was the only reporter in the Chicago Stadium who knew where its temporary police station was. Some guy created some kind of disturbance and was arrested and hustled off the floor. Because I knew where the station was, I got there and got his name and the story. The national guys got call-backs from their offices when the AP picked up the CNB copy. (In 1940 I scooped the national guys again by identifying the "voice of the sewers" but I worked for the *Times* by that time.)

In 1933 and again in 1934 Gersh assigned me to cover the Century of Progress. Again it was features and police stuff but it kept me quite busy, day and night. I also had a car to get around the grounds in. I remember interviewing Sally Rand in her dressing room but I don't remember if CNB carried my story. I was always a nut on statistics. Once I figured out how high a pile the popcorn would make that was sold in a month at the fair. In the office, in that same connection, I once figured out how many tons of snow fell on Chicago during a big blizzard. Mulay made me check my figures with the weather bureau—or rather, he told me to ask the weather bureau to figure out the problem. When their result came within .0001 of my figure, he never again questioned any of my screwy statistics.

One of Gersh's enterprising ideas was to cover a multiple execution in 1931 or 1932 by having a phone in the death room in County jail. The papers liked the idea because the execution was scheduled for midnight, a bad time for their deadlines. Such stories were big news in those days. Five guys were due to go. The phone idea paid off at the very beginning: as we were walking into the death room, one of the guys got a reprieve. That was the first thing I dictated into the phone.

The telephone company had equipped that phone with a very sensitive mouthpiece. We'd call it a microphone now. But they goofed because, since the phone was at the rear wall of the viewing room, I had to stand up to get a good view of what was going on. But the phone cord was not long enough, so I had to look, then duck down and dictate a sentence or two, and then stand up to look again. Joe Levandier was on the other end of the phone and he had a hard time understanding me. It probably was my fault. I remember spelling the word "visage" out for him. I don't know why I just didn't say that the mask got pulled off by mistake revealing a twisted *face*.

Gersh said he picked me for the job because I could dictate and because I had seen two or three other executions and "had not gotten sick". A couple of years later there was another multiple execution, also covered by phone. Art Summerfield, our Criminal Courts reporter, covered that. I think he is under the impression that he was the first reporter to telephone a report that way, but he wasn't.

I got my share of criminal courts after being on re-write also because I could dictate. The Alice Wynekoop trial, and the John "Jake the Barber" Factor kidnaping of Touhy were two. I covered the Sam Insull trial in Federal court. On the Capone trial I was in the office taking the dictation. By the way, the CNB coverage of a trial was all questions and answers. I don't think any of us who took the q. and a. knew shorthand. In fact, it would have handicapped us because we would have taken too much. It was a very good experience for me later, when I covered political speeches and White House press conferences.

A funny thing happened one day when I was on re-write. I was sitting on the desk temporarily while Larry Mulay was on vacation. Tom Morrow was on rewrite. I found an error in his copy. After the postmortem I was put back on rewrite and Tom Morrow took the desk in my place! Who could explain the reasoning there? Later I worked at the *Times* with Tom. He was a jolly fellow with a weird sense of humor that got him the assignment to conduct the Line o' Type column at the *Trib*.

I was making thirty-four dollars a week when I got married in October of 1933. Gersh said he would give me a two dollar raise. I asked him whether it was because I deserved it or because I was getting married. He assured me it was the former. In 1935 I was making forty-five dollars a week working the day desk. Al Rose of the *Times* offered me forty dollars a week to be assistant city editor there and then night city editor. Taking a five dollar cut was a big decision, which I talked over with my wife. But the *Times* could not pay as much as its own subsidiary, the CNB. I took the job as an investment in the future. It eventually paid off, and I wound up as associate editor when I retired in 1975.

Another reporter, now a free-lance, who remembers 1929 and 1930 at the City News is Frank Walsh:

My training period was brief to the point of non-existence. Earl Mullen dropped me off at East Chicago station one summer night in '29, gave me ten nickels, and told me to call the office every half hour. But a couple of street-wise Irish cops were more helpful. They told me about the police teletype. There you learned that more than half the wanted criminals in the city were "dark complected" and equipped with "a Charlie Chaplin moustache". The friendly cops also said it was okay to use the desk sergeant's phone to save a few nickels. "But," they added, "don't get caught at it."

After you learned the ropes you might con your way into a ride to "the scene" in one of those enormous yellow Cadillac touring cars with a great gong upfront and shotguns in the trunk. Sources, connections, were everything. It didn't hurt to have a name like Walsh.

There were a lot of funny tricks played in the press room at 11th and State, aside from those pulled off in the non-stop hearts games. I used to relish listening to the canny old-timers trying to find out what building might be burning at, say, Madison and Kedzie. In that stone age most reporters worked afoot and you didn't make a move until you knew where you were going and what might be at the end of the line. The fire alarm office could tell you whether the blaze was a "two-bagger" or a "four-bagger" but nobody knew in those first minutes what was burning. Could be an orphanage, bank or speakeasy. Here was one case where the mutually distrustful reporters would pool their knowledge. Quite soundly street-wise, they would remember among them that the corner in question held Little Jack's restaurant, a theater, a bank, and, inevitably a United Cigar store. The cigar store always got the call as they were most likely to be open and willing to get into the act. A high percentage of fire stories started with a query to the night clerks at United. There were a few niceties in all this grubby newsgathering! Among other things, four guys with a quarter apiece could get a quart of decent dago red wine from Marcel's, a speak-easy over on Wabash avenue.

The night trick was called "working the middle". It could last to 2 a.m. with spells of no news. With luck you could catch a little nap. In an anteroom off the old press room was an eight-foot long sturdy mahogany table, likely a cast-off from some courtroom. Perfect for sleeping. The big city directory, spread open, was a reasonable pillow. The rules of the game required that after you woke up, you turn the page to give the next guy a clean pillow slip. Even the crypto front pagers observed that rule.

And there was the thrill of authorship. If you called in for a "good night" about midnight, and to offer details on a closing story the night man might say, "Bring it in and write it up." So you went in and banged out your immortal litany of who, what, where, why, when, on the ribbonless Underwoods (#5). Ribbonless because you wanted the bare keys to bite through a "book" of ten carboned flimsies, one each for the night city editors of the newspapers served by City Press. You went home and dreamed that maybe Harry Canfield at the *Examiner* might see your copy and call up Dornfeld and say, "Who did that thing about 'Mother of three fights off rapist'?"

I never got that kind of call but Mose Lamson, one-time circulation slugger turned reporter for the *Tribune* did hire me for his paper. Basis for his decision? A non-reader (and non-writer) he was impressed by the fact that I carried a book to work, stayed out of the hearts game and drank red wine instead of gin. The book I carried was, I believe, by Proust. To this day a sip of dago red will set me to remembering things past, just as nibbling on a madeleine inspired the masterpiece by the French master.

As the twenties waned, newspaper staffs tended to become more permanent. Reporters no longer shifted from paper to paper with ease, working "on every sheet in town." Consequently there were fewer opportunities for City News men to advance to the newspapers. Many family men were trying to live on the inadequate bureau salaries.

Gershman was caught between the legitimate demands of his employees for higher wages and better conditions, and the tight-fisted attitude of the newspaper publishers, whom he represented. Change was certainly in the air in the thirties: Roosevelt's NRA, which was later outlawed, brought a five day week to some of the papers and to the police reporters at the bureau. The most important factor in the demand for more money was probably the Newspaper Guild, which had made very slow progress in Chicago. It was fought successfully by the publishers. Employees were threatened with dismissal or other reprisals if they joined the Guild. This situation was true, too, at City News, where Gershman retaliated against people who leaned toward the union: some were demoted, some fired, and others were threatened. There were stool pigeons who attended organization meetings, reported to Gershman, and were rewarded with promotion. Bureau men, leaving their meetings, clearly heard Gershman's man on the phone, giving his report.

Gershman was, as we have said, under the gun at this time. He was answerable to the publishers for every penny he spent, since the bureau was completely dependent on weekly assessments of the newspapers for its existence. As an example of the continuing strain under which the bureau managers were forced to live, here are a series of letters sent to Gershman in February of 1937.

The first, forwarded to Gershman by S.E. Thomason, publisher of the *Times*, was a letter to Colonel McCormick from R.M. Lee, managing editor of the *Tribune*, dated February 8, which McCormick had forwarded to Thomason:

Dear Colonel:

Several times during the past ten years or more the subject of City News Bureau has been discussed. I think some of the memoranda may be found in your files.

Inasmuch as we have made several news surveys since the last discussion I thought you would like to be reminded that our regular assessment now has grown to $660 a week. In addition the cost for rental of telephones and special assessments amount to approximately $42 a week, making the grand total cost $702 per week. The following table shows how the City News Bureau costs have been mounting since 1930:

```
1930...$29479.00
1931... 30004.00
1932... 29814.95
1933... 30717.35
1934... 36632.57
1935... 36575.51
1936 .. 36504.00
```

You may recall that in 1925 I spoke of this to you and suggested that we could readily carry our own City news reports, but that we would incur some unusual expense in covering elections.

If you think the subject should be explored further I can submit a detailed survey.

Colonel McCormick forwarded this letter to Thomason who was chairman of the publishers board at that time, with a letter of his own dated February 9:

Dear Emory:

Enclosed please find letter from Bob Lee.

Lee was of this opinion all the time that he was City Editor. Now that he is Managing Editor with full responsibility, I am not disposed to override him.

However, I do not want to do anything that is not friendly to other newspapers, and I certainly do not want to turn men out on the street suddenly.

> Suggest that when the editors are all in town, we hold a meeting for the initial purpose of cutting the cost of the City News Bureau in two....and further consider whether it is of any substantial value to us.
>
> I am sending copies of this letter to the other members.

Thomason replied to McCormick on February 11:

> Dear Bert:
>
> I have yours of the 9th enclosing Bob Lee's letter of the 8th, in which he expresses the opinion that you could carry your own City News reports at some saving in expense. I agree with you that as soon as Col. Knox and Babe Meigs have returned we should have a meeting to consider the expense of the News Bureau and its value to the several members.
>
> Personally I cannot conceive that it is possible that expense can be saved by discontinuing an organization that has functioned efficiently for 46 years, and has had sound and careful administration both under Mr. Gershman and his predecessor, Walter Brown. As you know, I have always felt that the City News Bureau is one of the few non-competitive activities that we have done particularly well.
>
> As the titular head of the City News Bureau I am asking Mr. Gershman to prepare a report that will present all the data that we will want to consider at the meeting you suggest, so that each of us may have a copy in hand when we foregather when Col. Knox and Babe Meigs return.

On the same day Thomason forwarded this material to Gershman with a note asking for the necessary data as soon as it was available.

As might be expected, Gershman responded quickly to this correspondence, and sent Thomason a thorough report on the bureau, its history and its coverage, along with a breakdown of assessment charges from 1928 to 1937. The newspapers still with the bureau in 1937 were the *Tribune*, the *Herald-Examiner*, the *News*, the *Times-Journal* and the *American*. The *Post* was eliminated on November 5, 1932, when it ceased publication, and the newspapers took over the assessment of the AP on December 9, 1933, so that AP received the service without charge from that date.

Enclosed with the report was a private letter to Thomason from Gershman:

Dear Mr. Thomason:

Enclosed please find the City News Bureau report on costs and coverage. If you have any suggestions for changes or additions I shall be glad to revise it before you send it to the other publishers.

As you suggested during our talk last week I am listing in this letter for your personal use several points which could not be made in my report.

The *Tribune* has the largest staff of reporters in Chicago and if the City News Bureau staff were partially reduced, it is not likely that the *Tribune* would have to increase their group. The other four papers, however, would be forced to cover the open territories. For example: dropping ten men on the City News Bureau, with an average $32 salary and $8 expenses, would reduce our assessment $400 a week. This would save the Tribune $100 a week in their assessment, and while the *Herald-Examiner* would also cut off $100 and the afternoon papers $68, these four papers would have to replace these men on their own staffs at a cost to each of $400. In other words, in order that the *Tribune* might save $5,000 a year, the other four papers would each have to spend $20,000 a year or a combined total of $80,000.

There is the possibility that the *Tribune*'s action may be a wedge in asking for a revision of present assessment methods so that all five papers would pay an equal amount. This would shift about $200 from the two morning papers to the three afternoon papers.

Four years ago I went through this same situation with the *Tribune* after Mr. Beck, at Lee's request, had written a letter to Jim Shryock. I discussed the entire matter in Beck's office with Lee present. Lee finally declared that the *Tribune* ought to pay less than the other members and I pointed out that assessment matters were not in my province and should be taken up directly with the other publishers. At that time, however, the matter was dropped.

The complaint of the *Tribune* that they get less value out of the City News Bureau than do the other members because they use less of our news, is always true with a paper whose policy requires special coverage. A press association must remain neutral. The case of the City News is similar to that of the Associated Press. The *Tribune* pays a full assessment for the Associated Press report, but uses very little, preferring the extra cost for special correspondents to get their stories slanted as they want them.

Among the advantages of the Bureau is the training of reporters, and the *Tribune* has taken more City News Bureau men than all other papers combined. Their staff from Pat Maloney down through city desk, rewrite and reporters are mostly City News men.

In his letter to Col. McCormick, Mr. Lee's figures for the City News Bureau also include the cost of the City News Press tube system. While the City Press cost of $40 a week may be regarded as part of our general expense, I doubt whether the *Tribune* would be willing to give up the tube system were the City News abandoned. The *Tribune* in addition to its regular service obtains further benefit in that we operate two private tubes for their sole use; their Dearborn office tube for advertising copy and a second line to their attorney's office on Washington street. Their value alone would offset the cost of the regular news service.

The Newspaper Guild operating as a union will soon adopt union tactics.

Once the papers establish more news beats, the Guild will demand a manning table as does the pressmen and the additional expense will become fixed.

Under the five day week, costs for reporters have increased some 25%, as for every two men working, four days relief a week are necessary. I think it reasonable to assume that the trend, under present conditions, is to save money by expanding press associations rather than to add more men and expense to individual staffs.

If the *Tribune* succeeds in crippling the City News Bureau by cutting the staff, they would have a news monopoly that would bring on a scoop war and create additional friction among the papers just at a time when all efforts are being directed toward harmony and better co-operation.

Apparently Gershman and Thomason were able to contain the *Tribune*'s unrest, because there are no further letters to this point in the files.

Following the presidential election of 1936 the labor movement had gained momentum and the Newspaper Guild prosecuted successful strikes against Hearst papers in Milwaukee, Wisconsin, and in Seattle. When these strikes were settled favorably to the Guild—and especially in Seattle, where John Boettiger, the former City News cub, was appointed publisher of the *Post-Intelligencer* as a peace move—the Guild began to make swift headway in Chicago.

Strong units were formed on the *Times*, which supported Roosevelt's policies, on the *Herald-Examiner* and the *American*. Organization lagged on the *News*, the *Tribune* and the Associated Press, where wages as a rule were already high and employment conditions more stable than on the other papers. At the *Tribune*, especially, wages were high: Colonel McCormick was not enamored of unions, and he chose to fight a union on his newspaper by bettering union demands.

The news bureau staff unit, almost one hundred percent

strong, elected Charles B. Johnson its first chairman and
meetings were held, despite managerial intimidation, to
draw up a proposed contract. There were persistent rumors
that the publishers would abolish the bureau if negotiations
were pressed. It would appear from his correspondence with
Thomason that Gershman knew that this would not be the
case, but he may have considered it in the best interest of the
bureau that these rumors not be put to rest. In any case before
a crisis was reached, a new working agreement was posted
by the management. The bureau Guild unit no longer exists.

TO THE STAFF OF THE CITY NEWS BUREAU:

Beginning April 5, 1937, and continuing thereafter
until 90 days posted notice of change, the following
conditions of employment should be in effect.

(1) *NATURE OF EMPLOYMENT*
The Bureau shall remain the sole judge of the qualifi-
cations of any employee to perform the duties to which
he shall be assigned, of his fitness to work in the office,
and of his ability to progress in general reportorial
work.

The City News Bureau is a corporation organized
under the laws of Illinois as a "corporation not for
profit". One of the major purposes for which it is organized, as provided in its charter, is to provide a school for
apprentice reporters, where, under actual working conditions, an apprentice may obtain training and education in newspaper work. In pursuance of this charter
provision, the period of apprenticeship shall hereafter
be fixed at 3 years.

The provisions of apprenticeship as covered by this
notice shall not apply to those employed as copyboys,
unless and until a copyboy shall be employed as an
apprentice member of the staff.

(2) *HOURS*

5 days of 8 hours each, within 7 days, shall constitute a working week for all employees of the Bureau with the exception of the General Manager, his Confidential Secretary, Day City Editor, Night City Editor, and Sports Editor.

(3) *RATES OF MINIMUM PAY*

Apprentice Reporters—First year $20. per week; second year $25. per week; third year $35. per week.

Note: When an apprentice reporter shall have been assigned to "substitute rewrite work", and shall have accumulated 60 days at "training rewrite work", he shall be paid the minimum rewrite scale as provided below.

Reporters—(Retained after 3 years employment as apprentices) $45. per week.

Rewrite Men:
(a) Rewrite men who have had 60 days of "training rewrite" experience; 1 year of "substitute rewrite" experience and 1 year of "relief rewrite" experience—$50. per week.
(b) Rewrite men who have had 60 days of "training rewrite" experience; and 1 year of "substitute rewrite" experience—$42.50 per week.
(c) Rewrite men who have had 60 days of "training rewrite" experience—$35. per week.

Copyboys—First year $12.50 per week; second year $15. per week; third year $17.50 per week.

Note: The term "experience" when used in this statement shall refer exclusively to experience in the employ of the City News Bureau.

(4) *OVERTIME*

All employees shall be paid for overtime by either equal time-off or, pro-rata pay, provided

(a) No employee shall be entitled to overtime pay until his overtime work shall exceed 1 hour in any day, or a total of 3 hours in any week. No 8 hours of time-off payment shall be split into shorter periods of time-off. Having once been released from regular or overtime duty, no employee shall be called back to duty before his next regular shift begins without payment to him for the actual overtime worked on return to duty.

(5) *VACATIONS*

Paid vacations of 1 week shall be given to all employees employed more than 6 months and less than 1 year before May 1st in any year. Paid vacations of 2 weeks each year shall be given to employees employed more than 1 year before May 1st.

Vacations, except by agreement with the individual employee, shall be given only during the months of May, June, July and August.

(6) *DISMISSAL PAYMENTS*

No employee shall be dismissed or discharged unless said employee be given written notice thereof, and be paid 1 week's pay for each year of his employment up to 5 years. The weekly rate to be paid on dismissal shall be the employee's average weekly pay during the previous 26 weeks of his employment.

Dismissal pay shall not be paid in the case of any employee discharged for willful breach of duty or misconduct.

The Bureau recognizes the right of members of the staff to join any organization of their own choosing, or to refuse to join, and therefore, no employee shall be discharged for exercising such prerogatives.

(7) *ILLNESS*
The Bureau's policy of payments to sick employees will be continued. The duration of the period of such payments shall be determined by the management in each case.

(8) *EXPENSES*
Necessary expenses of employees in their daily work shall be paid by the Bureau in accordance with the table of expense allowances now in force.

(9) *CORRESPONDENTS*
Staff members employed in suburbs outside the city limits of Chicago are employed as correspondents and are not covered by the terms of this notice. Terms of pay and working conditions shall be concluded by individual arrangement in the case of all correspondents.

This agreement was signed in the midst of a wide-spread wave of "sitdown strikes" that swept the country that spring, centering chiefly in Detroit where automobile workers of the CIO, headed by John L. Lewis, made spectacular headlines.

Chicago did not escape this labor unrest. A tear gas battle ousted strikers from the Fansteel plant in North Chicago, and early in March a taxi cab strike brought rioting to the Loop, where taxicabs were overturned and there was much violence. On May 30, 1937, there was a Memorial day riot at the Republic Steel plant in which ten pickets were killed by the police. The bureau's neutral account of the affair was strikingly dissimilar to the accounts which appeared in most of the Chicago papers. Yet even bureau news was based on "official" sources and was apt to contain only what the police, coroner or states attorney saw fit to release.

15

Gershman

When Gershman took over the bureau from Brown in 1932, the changes which he began to institute were not major. Probably the most important thing Brown had done was to refine by 1926 the bureau's election coverage, which had been firmed up to some degree in 1897. Gershman pointed with pride to this election coverage in his 1937 report to the publishers' committee:

> Coverage of elections is probably the outstanding service of the City News Bureau, and despite large increases in number of candidates in primaries, total votes cast and precincts (which now number 4136 against 3090 in 1928) costs have been reduced and service speeded up by seven hours.
>
> Were the City News Bureau abandoned, the importance of costs in covering elections would be outweighed by the question of the method by which they could be covered. For a major county or national election more than 5,700 people are used. It is necessary to organize, train and direct 4,000 police in a three-part recording, delivery and telephone system; 275 paid country town correspondents; 300 county election employees; 25 county auto messengers; 18 country town police departments; 50 telephone men, and a headquarters personnel for tabulation and distribution totaling 400...

Election coverage usually is thought of only in connection with the national and state campaigns which occur every two years. However, the election department operates almost continuously. Since 1932 there have been 9 major elections (national, state, county, city, judicial, and aldermanic) and 20 minor elections, including townships, cities, country towns and schools. This year we will handle 5 minor elections, three of mass handling such as townships with 30 different slates, schools with 55 sets of candidates, and 88 village elections, which are scattered throughout the 48 mile area of Cook county, and includes such cities as Evanston, Cicero, Oak Park and Chicago Heights.

Granted that Gershman here was fighting to save his bureau, he was not exaggerating the importance, nor the complication, of City News election coverage. Preparation for election night vote counting always started at least three months before election night. Through long-standing arrangement with county officials, the bureau took over, and still takes over, almost an entire floor of the County building. An outside accounting firm supplied auditors, calculating machine operators, file clerks, messengers and supervisors for the vote tally. The phone company installed sixty special telephones with headsets to handle incoming calls. The phones were manned by bureau staffers and former CNB employees.

Stanley L. Kedzior, who began at the bureau as a copy boy in the early 1930's, later became director of election coverage. He ran the whole works, which was divided into election new desk, suburban supervision, congressional and legislative desk, delivered intake desk and county clerk-delivered intake. Because all the voting in the county is by no means under the sole supervision of the Chicago Board of Election Commissioners, a seventh of the voting arrangement is directed by the clerk of Cook county, whose returns have to be fed into the general stream of data pulled together by the calculating crews.

A policeman was assigned to each polling place, and a special tally form was given to him, to be filled out when the judges took the tally from the backs of the voting machines. The policeman then phoned the results into the headquarters at the County building, where the workers there—off-duty policemen, students, and other selected extra staff—fed the information to the statistical people. The count was then flashed to all the news media by reporters.

At a few minutes after seven o'clock when the polls closed the first returns began to be phoned in. Everyone was already in place at headquarters straining, as one copywriter put it, like "hound dogs waiting to be released." The first figures were sent out instantly by teletype. Within half an hour returns were coming in steadily and all incoming lines were busy. The tension turned into frantic activity. The single sending teletype was surrounded by politicians and others eager for a first glance at the latest information.

As the returns flowed in steadily, noises in the huge room settled down to a low buzz of conversation against the clatter of machines. Politicians bustled about, demanding returns from certain critical wards—and they wanted them immediately. Columnists, news analysts and other seers walked around, dropping names and cigarette ash. Copy people danced through the throng, distributing copy and offering coffee: "Last coffee until eight o'clock. Anyone like coffee?"

As the hours went by the cigarette smoke thickened into smog. Toward midnight most contests were settled. Although the final, complete returns would not be in for hours, there was enough information for trend-spotters to do their stuff. The precinct captains and ward committeemen departed to congratulate or console one another at party headquarters. A few diehards lingered for the last return of close races, but sometime after midnight the tumult and the shouting died.

Dedicated CNB executives stayed on to mop up the last details. The installation of voting machines brought an improvement in methods that allowed the bureau bosses to call a halt before dawn, with only a few precincts missing. In the old days, when paper ballots were used, activity lasted

much longer. Gershman used to mark the names of key executives with the word "stays" on the working schedule he
made out, which included his own name. And stay they did,
until the last return was counted—in those days, often well
into Wednesday afternoon.

Strange difficulties were encountered in cleaning up the
last returns. "Cleaning" was in fact not a misnomer: some of
the returns sheets turned up at City News election headquarters with large black shoe prints all over them. This was
because polling place officials sometimes spread them out on
the floor to check them before sending them in, and then
absentmindedly walked all over them. In other cases election
judges or clerks wadded the returns into their pockets and
went home with them in the small hours—or took them with
them to a handy all-night saloon. It was useless to phone the
polling places. Sometimes the district police station was
asked to send a policeman to the official's house in order to
get the delinquent return routed to the County building.

Carol Stevenson, once a copy girl, recalls that the rented
machinery and huge volumes of records used in the counting
process were loaded onto a large four-wheel flatbed hand
truck when the closing whistle blew, usually around morning rush hour. Exhausted copy writers trundled the truck
back to bureau headquarters. They formed a procession
down the sidewalk, and did a sort of snake dance across the
streets, disregarding oncoming traffic. Brave writers shoved
the truck; the weaker ones rested on top of the cargo, singing
drinking songs, although their only intoxicant was lack of
sleep. Traffic cops never interfered with the procession. Most
of them, too, had been working extra election duty.

All this has been changed to some extent by the introduction of punch-card voting. Computers have entered the scene,
and in 1980 the Board of Election Commissioners took over
city and county tabulation. City News still does suburban
tallies, though, and still takes over a floor of the County
building staffed with five hundred hand-picked people who
receive the special ballots filled out for the bureau in the 2,453
suburban precincts. These ballots are sent to collection sta-

tions around the suburbs, from which fleets of autos bring them to the County building. Larry Mulay thinks fondly of the days when the results of most local elections were in before midnight, while in presidential and state elections the bureau usually had everything wrapped up by two a.m. He notes that the new system takes much longer.

Gershman had his share of peculiar experiences on election night. One found its way into the *Daily News*. A Cook county sheriff, described as "thick of tongue and unsteady of gait", and accompanied by ten dull-eyed hangers-on, pushed his way past two city policemen and invaded the bureau election headquarters in the early hours of Wednesday morning.

"I want to find out about the vote finagling that's going on here," the sheriff shouted.

There were about 150 employees still working at desks and tabulating machines. A deathly stillness descended upon them.

The sheriff demanded to see Gershman. He fingered the bone-handled revolver he wore on his hip, and turned to his posse. "I'm going to find out what's going on here," he shouted.

At this point Larry Mulay addressed the sheriff from his desk. "Please be quiet," he said. "You're interrupting our work."

The sheriff pointed his finger at Mulay. "Hey you," he said. "Come here."

Mulay remained seated. The sheriff became abusive. "You guys are only here because of our sufferance," he said. "I'm the building custodian and I want to find out what's going on."

Gershman finally appeared. The sheriff began to shout at him. "What's happening to Phil Mitchell?" he said loudly.

Philip Mitchell, the Republican candidate for County recorder of deeds, was one of the group accompanying the sheriff.

"Yeah," he said, "what's happening to me, Gershman? I've lost 25,000 votes in 100 precincts in an hour."

"There's something wrong here, Gershman, awful wrong," the sheriff boomed.

Gershman explained as quietly as he could that the vote-gathering operation was an entirely neutral public service operated by the city's daily newspapers.

"You will have to go now," he said to the sheriff. "You are interfering with our work."

Eventually the sheriff's more sober followers prevailed upon him to leave without bloodshed.

It is possible that Gershman enjoyed talking to the enraged sheriff, since he prided himself on his ability to deal with disturbed people. He was something of an amateur psychologist, and was fascinated with mental illness.

Among the changes which Gershman wrought when he took over in 1931 were a sports department added in 1933 at a cost, he told the publishers, of $79 a week. In 1933 the tube service was expanded to go round the clock, twenty-four hours a day. Under Brown the tubes were shut down between 2:30 a.m. and 7 a.m. and only flash telephone service was maintained.

One thing that Gershman did that had a lasting impact was to abolish the distinction between "night manager" and "day manager" that undoubtedly stemmed from the days of Saylor and Leckie. Under Brown, too, this was the system. Brown was day manager, and Thurman Harshman was night manager: the two shared equal auhority, just as Saylor and Leckie did. Under Harshman was Joe Levandier and next to Joe was Edward Eulenberg.

Gershman took the title "General Manager" and demoted Harshman to "Night City Editor". Thus Gershman gathered the reins into his hands, and made Harshman, along with everybody else, subordinate to him. Harshman was not happy about this, nor were his lieutenants, Levandier and Eulenberg. One of the things that was most upsetting about it was that the change was put into operation while Harshman was away from the office mourning the death of his daughter. Harshman was a gentle, knowledgeable man who inspired deep loyalty.

One reporter who remembers Harshman is Jim Mundis who was fired from his first job, on a Hearst newspaper in 1937, and was hired at City News despite the fact that Ruby Ryan, the switchboard operator, told him there was a waiting list of 400 names. He had various adventures on the night beat:

> ...what a learning experience. I went through the usual break-in for three days—one on each of the police beats. The first day the reporter (I think his name was Arnow) took me to the hardware store which was on the first floor of the Ashland block where CNB had offices on the seventh floor. There he introduced me to the means for cheap pay-phone calls—the slug. Seems like I bought something like fifty for a quarter. When I asked 'Isn't this illegal?' he gave me a glance of disbelief and said, 'How in the hell do you think you're going to make it on a dollar-a-day expense money?'
>
> That was lesson no. 1. The *Her-Ex* had paid me twenty-five dollars a week but CNB paid twenty dollars with the promise of a raise after one year to twenty-five dollars. I did get that raise since I worked at CNB for nineteen months.
>
> It didn't take me long on night police to learn that the name of the game was the veteran *Tribune* police reporters—Clem Manning, north; Moose Krause, west; and Shadow Brown, south. You were always "the City Press kid" and if you worked the routine, nitty-gritty stuff—keeping them informed, of course—then you were assured of a ride in their car when the big story broke. . .
>
> It was between Christmas and New Years right after I went to work for CNB that I met Shadow Brown. A quiet, pleasant, likeable man with a warm smile. I met him that night at Grand Crossing. A call came in that "two were dead in a house" and Shadow said, "We go in my car."
>
> It was a modest, well-kept bungalow. The husband

had killed his wife as she was ironing. The shotgun sprayed half of her head across the wall. Then he killed himself. Everything else in the house was in order, including a stack of presents, unopened, under the Christmas tree. One of the detectives squatted down, and began tossing the presents to the other officers. Suddenly he was aware of my presence. He tossed me a carton of cigarettes. My stomach did flipflops: two dead people in the cold house; presents meant for them. . . I looked at Shadow. He just smiled. I tossed the carton back with the feeble excuse that the cigarettes weren't my brand. Another lesson.

More lessons. I was in the office one day when the police radio reported a robbery in progress at a suit rental firm on Randolph between Dearborn and Clark. Larry Mulay said go. I ran all the way, including three or four flights of stairs. The door to the place was open and I saw no one but the owner, staring in a trance-like manner. "What happened?" I asked. He looked at me blankly. Then a voice from behind said, 'Freeze!' After that I waited for the cops when I heard about a burglary.

It was when he was promoted from the night to the day side that Mundis met Harshman.

All I knew about the night side in the office was that it consisted of Joe Levandier and a couple of rewrite men. Also a copy boy who seemed to spend most of his time scanning windows where the shades were up in the Sherman hotel across the street. When he found a titillating view he summoned others to the darkened back room to use the binoculars.

I was doing west one night when Joe called and said that when I finished at three a.m. I was to come to the office and talk to Mr. H. Joe always spoke softly and I rarely heard him enunciate. This plus the fact that he liked to talk with the cigar in his mouth made it difficult for me to understand him. So I asked, "Mr. Who?" He repeated "Mr. H" a couple of times and then became impatient and said, "Mr. Harshman." I said, "You mean Mr. Gershman?" He ended it. "Harshman. Be sure you get here."

I had never heard of Mr. H. Perplexed, I called the man doing north that night, Tom McLaughlin. A great guy. He listened to my story and then whistled softly. After a moment of silence he said, "What have you been up to?" I told him, "Nothing." Tom said he couldn't figure it out but generally when a reporter was summoned to see Mr. H there was a problem.

There was a problem, I discovered when I met Mr. H. We sat in his office for more than an hour and a half. As the red from the rising sun reflected from the windows of the Sherman hotel, Mr. H talked on and on. His theme was that not everyone was cut out for newspaper work. He named Melvyn Douglas and a score (or so it seemed to me) of other people who became successful in other fields who hadn't made it at CNB. It seemed clear to me that I was getting the bounce. I couldn't understand why he dragged it out. Finally he announced his decision. I was being transferred to the day side.

Gersh didn't say why the transfer was made but said he wanted me to do some rewrite. He also asked that daily I provide him with a copy of everything I wrote. I did. A week later I was back on the street doing the County building.

16

The War...And Women

City News scooped the world on the bombing of Pearl
Harbor. Larry Mulay cannot recall now whether it was J.
Edward Peabody or Phil Chancellor—both bureau reporters
with large private incomes—who heard the news over his
expensive short-wave radio and called the office. Mulay, who
was city editor at the time believed the report. Everyone else
thought it was an Orson Welles kind of hoax, or misinterpre-
tation of some naval manoevers in Hawaii. As a precaution
Mulay phoned to check with AP. They had nothing on the
story. Nevertheless Mulay decided to go ahead with the
report and bulletined all the papers that the Japanese had
bombed Pearl Harbor. There were fifteen very tense minutes
before there was any official verification of the story. Then
Roosevelt made his announcement.

The second World War caused a manpower shortage at the
bureau, as the first World War had done. Once more it was
necessary for management to hire women to fill the gap.

There had been women working at the bureau before 1917.
Leckie had hired a woman named Marion Heath; she was the
first woman reporter to work for City Press, and her assignments were general. She was joined later by Katherine
Leckie, about whom Leckie wrote to Vickerman:

Katherine Leckie was my cousin, brilliant, magnetic,

187

and a social thoroughbred. I tried to dissuade her from newspaper work, but as always she had her way and I sent her to the County building as a cub. Her success was amazing. She was a bundle of energy and turned up one story after another. She was seized by the *American*, then went to New York and soon established a publicity office in which she and a fine staff handled big stuff, mainly semi-society functions launched by women. She handled the Ford peace ship during the pre-war months, but this I believe was her only failure and anyway, nothing would have saved it. She made a financial success but worked herself to death five years ago. . .

About Marion Heath Leckie was less enthusiastic:

Marion Heath was a bright, dependable, fairly competent and eminently faithful and industrious girl. We called her "General". She did the County building until she married a newspaperman in, I think, Hammond, Indiana.

These two women may have been exceptional, since Vickerman says that after women replaced men in industry during World War I, they "broke a long-standing tradition by becoming newspaper reporters." One of the first women to be hired to replace men who had gone to war was Dorothy Berezniak, who had graduated from the University of Wisconsin. She was the daughter of a Chicago attorney, and later married a City News reporter with whom she went to the Orient, where they started an English language newspaper. She began at the bureau on hotels, helping Hamilton, but soon she was covering Oak Park police beats, courts, and other heavier assignments.

Another woman who came, soon after Dorothy Berezniak, was Eleanor Doty, a graduate of the University of Chicago. The women hired by the bureau then were all college women, although many of the men hired had never gone to college.

Eleanor Doty was assigned to cover the school board. Rose Caylor, another female replacement, who later married Ben Hecht, was so proficient at her job that she was given desk duty. Still another wartime woman employee in 1917 was Dorothy Day, the daughter of an old time Chicago newsman, and the sister of Donald Day, who was a foreign correspondent for the *Tribune*. Day and Caylor were day rewrites for a time. They were a capable team, and did excellent work. Women were not given night assignments.

Vickerman in the thirties gave what was obviously the official line on women:

> As a rule women reporters have not been successful on the City Press, although these wartime workers rose gallantly to the occasion. On the newspapers the women reporters ordinarily have bylines and when visiting a police station the captain or lieutenant personally escorts them around, seeing that they get information. In the rough-and-tumble life of an every day news bureau reporter no such amenities exist. For butting into suicides, arguing with desk sergeants, annoying clerks, bailiffs and prosecutors, for a multitude of trivial details, men have been found more durable. Any sensitiveness to rebuff is quickly blunted.

One woman who was hired at City News in 1928 became an institution in herself. This was Gladys Ryan, later Wherity, who was the switchboard operator for fifty years. Gladys had a strategic post at the nerve center of the agency and she was as closely involved in the relationship between employees and management as anyone could be. She taught all the cubs how to work the switchboard, since this was a skill that might be necessary at any time, and William Dillman said that she "knew the number of every public telephone in Chicago and vicinity. There was no place you could hide if she was looking for you."

But you could hide behind Gladys's skirts if you wanted to, or needed to. The story behind her nickname of "Ruby" demonstrates this. George Deutschle called in one morning from his beat at City Hall in a state of agitation. He told Gladys that he had to leave his post and get some shoes. He had been out celebrating something the night before and in his world-weariness that morning he had left home wearing a black shoe on one foot and a brown shoe on the other. Gladys was soothing: she told George to go ahead; she would cover for him. George Schreiber, who was sitting near Deutschle and overheard this conversation, was impressed by Gladys's kindness. "Gosh," he said, "she's a regular Ruby Taylor." Ruby Taylor was the name of a character on the *Amos n' Andy Show* who supplied alibis for the erring protagonists. So Gladys became known as "Ruby" Ryan.

Although women were not considered, as Vickerman says, to be "durable", it was necessary for the bureau to begin to hire them two months after Pearl Harbor. By December 7, 1942, Larry Mulay was writing in a *Newsletter* designed for "the Men on the War Beat":

> Naturally our boys are thinking of back home and what's happening on the City Press. Well, we have our war coverage and our women reporters. At the start we began with Rockwood, Nunn, Rubins and Hoskins, and at last count we had sixteen of the ladies, three of them already having gone to the papers.

And Ed Eulenberg, who edited the *Newsletter*, which was intended to be a monthly, gave a brief introduction to the contributors:

> Some of the contributors are old-timers who hope you'll get a moment of pleasant nostalgia when you read their message; others are newcomers who remember only a few of you; while others are the newest of the new, boys and girls (yes, we've got 'em—blondes, brunettes, lovelies and loveliers) who don't know any of you, but who want to help bring you a picture of Chicago to make you want to return to us when you've won the war.

The City Newsletter contained contributions by some of the newly hired women. One of these, Virginia Nunn, described some of the reaction at the bureau to the new arrivals:

It was a day of bitter anticipation for employees of the City News Bureau. Feet came clattering from desktops; vocal outbursts were strangled with a blush and a guilty look or wasted in a string of substitute utterances; clean shaven faces and slicked-back hair were the rule, and not the exception; in short, everyone was uncomfortable. Into the sanctified stag circle of City Press reporters was to come a new, unthought of wartime discomfort—the women.

On that January day two young women, the first to be hired by City Press in some twenty years, confronted a barrage of hostile and curious glances. As pioneers in the police stations they faced jibes and fatherly reminders that "the woman's place is in the home." As telephone hounds they braved amazed guffaws at the other end of the wire, frustrated the query, "Say, is this a GIRrul?" with the reply, "Why, my voice hasn't changed yet."

Sixteen girls passed through the CNB filter during that first nine months. Ten survived; three went to the newspapers, and three others left for various reasons. In that period the "woman's touch" reached all the police districts in town, the Circuit, Superior, County, Criminal and Federal courts, the war beat, the City Hall, and the County building. Several have broken into the copy room; several more have been put on rewrite; four landed on the night watch, two of whom have worked on the late shift.

Fame snatched at the CNB girl reporter who went to a beauty shop and was given a facial and an exclusive interview by the sweetheart of Bruno Haupt, exposed Nazi spy; at the twenty-year-old novelist, whose writing was quoted in newspapers and magazines over the country; at the three CNB graduates who received by-lines in Chicago newspapers.

Meanwhile, composure was gradually reinstated in the City Press office. Feet ascended again to desktops; shouting and profanity again automatically accompanied reporters' blunders; office environs resumed that unkempt, uncomfortable look. Lost was the girl reporter's unwanted glamor; but steadily on the upgrade was her desired status as a good fellow who could dig for news as well and take as much abuse as anyone else.

Walter Ryberg contributed a witty and intelligent comment on the new order:

> The difference between the stories turned in by men reporters and women reporters is that the former say "I don't know," more often in A flat, while the women reporters more often use C sharp. A more important difference innovated by the girls is the use of English. Several of the papers are now subsidizing rewrite men who have expressed a desire to learn this strange tongue in order that they might understand what is being said. It is sad that the old lingo is doomed, that sweet nostalgic patois, whose principal locale is Taylor and Blue Island, three doors from the corner two flights up and say Joe sent you, and the only argot that escaped inclusion in *Finnegan's Wake*.
>
> But Time is not to be denied. The editorial room atmosphere changes under the impact of new trends, new concepts of veracity, and examples of daring that have the eyes of old-timers popping out on long stems.

"Gersh," a note in the Newsletter says, "is littering the floor with great tufts of his hair as the draft digs deeper and deeper—with every reduction in age limit making it worse and worse. Even the copy boys are leaving in platoons." This explains Kedzior's note:

The "Fair Sex" is now being called up to replace you boys.... Thus far we have four copy girls (some say they are Hollywood beauties). They really don't mind getting ink on their fingernails while printing copy, hoping eventually to become police reporters; and in the future—who knows—maybe famous writers.

Shebs, Brown and Pugner, the only remaining boys in the copy department, are awaiting their U.S. induction call.

Mary Holsinger, who had worked for City News for seven weeks the previous summer and had then gotten a job on the "Metropolitan" section of the *Tribune*, contributed some memories:

...I'll never forget some of the experiences I had while on the police beat, such as getting lost twice on my first day out and taking the wrong IC train, ending up south of Hyde Park one morning. Another time I wanted to listen to the police question a Hindu robber but being a girl, I was forbidden in the jail. However there was so much excitement around the Town Hall police station that I just walked right in with the police and they never noticed me there until it was too late.

I was the fifth girl hired by the CNB, so the police weren't accustomed to having female newshounds sniffing around the place. Some of the coppers resented it, and others got a terrific bang out of it. I got a lot of bids to free lunches, but never an invitation to play cards with them, so we're probably even on that score.

Finally Frances Bush, one of the copy girls, contributed her impressions in the form of poetry:

> I'm a female.
> I'm the newest of the backhouse gang.
> Excuse me,
> I mean back-room gang.

I don't know where I get off
                writing this
I'm not supposed to be able to
                read yet.
I'm not at all original.

My impressions of the CNB are:
I hang copy.
I sat in two council meetings.
Mayor Kelly presided.
The aldermen were there.
I kept thinking of penguins
                and pirates.
When I got home I took a bath.
I hang copy.

If Mr. Kozelka's tie looked
                like Mr. Eulenberg's
I'd straighten it.
I hang copy.
Have you seen Mr. Jensen smile?
I haven't.
I hang copy.

Sometimes I do creative work.
Nobody knows it.
I make up squad numbers on
                police reports.
I hang copy.
I smile at everybody.
They think I'm friendly.
I'm not.
I'm flirting.
I hang copy.

If I don't quit hanging copy soon
Somebody will be hanging crepe...

The strongest objection to having women work as cubs for the bureau—apart from their famous delicacy and inability to cope with harsh words—was based on the absence of women's restrooms in police stations. This, as might be expected, was the cause of much hilarity among male newsmen and police officers, one of the latter of whom suggested marking the room in question for ladies on alternate hours.

Someone may also have foreseen the kind of incident in which Mary Faith Wilson was embroiled when a fire broke out at the Illinois Athletic Club. Mary Faith went to the club, which was filled with busy firemen, but she didn't see the fire, and she did not know where it was. No one had time to tell her. She decided to follow the fire hoses which were snaking across the floor. She followed them through an unmarked door, and came upon several club members who were sitting nude around the swimming pool. At the sight of Mary Faith they sprang to attention and into the water.

Unfazed, Mary Faith explained that she was looking for the fire. "Not here," the members cried, cowering in the water. "Try downstairs." This story of Mary Faith and the Clubmen was written by Walter Ryberg. The *Tribune* ran it and gave Walter a byline, a most unusual event.

Jack McPhaul tells another Mary Faith story:

> It was Mary Faith who innocently solved a courtroom mystery that had intrigued her colleagues. A judge went on the bench mornings cold sober and managed, without leaving his chair, to be half-stiff by noon. Reporting a trial, a thirsty Mary Faith at noon recess poured herself a drink from the jurist's carafe and choked on straight gin.

It was another female City News reporter, Beata Mueller, who was called at dawn one Sunday morning to get over to the elevated station at Willow street, where a man had reportedly been crucified. The "sunrise editor"—in charge from midnight on—had no one he could spare and he knew that Beata had a car and a B gas ration book.

Beata went to the scene of the crucifixion and then to Augustana hospital where the participant was being treated. This bizarre story had come about at the man's request: he and a few other idealists had decided that his sacrifice would end the war. Fortunately, although his friends had nailed his hands to the cross-arms, nothing vital had been damaged and the man's physical condition was pronounced good. No one was taking any bets on his mental condition. Since his helpful friends had scattered when the police arrived, the latter contented themselves with impounding the cross.

It was nearly ten a.m. when Beata finished gathering the facts of this unappetizing event. On her way home, she toyed with the idea of mentioning to her pastor that she had not been able to get to church that morning because she had had to attend a crucifixion.

Terry Colangelo was one of the first girls hired by City News. One thing she envied her male colleagues was their ability to imitate important people over the telephone in order to get scoops. She hit on the idea of identifying herself as secretary to the district police captain, and got her news that way.

It was Terry who, when she came to the *Times* from the bureau, put Jack McPhaul onto the story that was later filmed as *Call Northside 777*. While she was waiting for a phone call, Terry read the newspaper through and through as she had been instructed to do in her training and noted a classified ad in the personal column that offered a reward for information concerning a murder that had occurred on December 9, 1932, twelve years earlier.

McPhaul took up the story and discovered a web of intrigue: the police, in their zeal to convict someone for the murder of a policeman, had concocted a case against an innocent man. Joe Majczek had served twelve years in prison. His mother had taken a job as a scrubwoman in order to save money to appeal his sentence, and it was she who ran the ad. Majczek was pardoned and released as a result of McPhaul's research and given $42,000 by the Illinois legislature as compensation for his ordeal. McPhaul says:

When Joe came around to the paper to express his thanks to all concerned he had special words of gratitude for Terry Colangelo. If she. . . hadn't been sharp eyed. . . the chances are he would still be in Stateville. . . Terry retired from the newspaper business after marrying Hub Logan, first assistant city editor of the *Sun-Times*.

Shirley Lowry Haas began her career at City News during the war, when she was fresh out of the University of Chicago. During her second week at the bureau she was sent to Maxwell street station on a story big enough to attract reporters and photographers from five dailies. Her father, Sgt. Loftus T. Lowry, was behind the desk at the station, but he refused to answer any of her questions. A convicted murderer and prison escapee that day was being returned to serve out the rest of his sentence after years of having lived a model life as a family man in the community. No one would say who had turned him in.

His wife was beside herself. She was a full-figured Italian matron in the throes of a tragic bereavement. Her voice rang through the streets, her long black hair flowed about her face as she tore it from its knot. She tried to hang onto her husband's arm as he was being led to the wagon for the ride back to Stateville and, frustrated, she pounded her head on the pavement and sobbed as they rode off.

She finally allowed herself to be helped to her feet and led away, still weeping, by sympathetic relatives. Reporters raced to their cars to take the story back to their papers.

Shirley, feeling that she had to get the whole story, gave up on Dad, and wandered into the office of the station captain to ask her question.

"Who turned him in?"

The captain gestured toward the door with his thumb.

"She did," he said.

"Who did?"

"The wife," the captain said.

Stunned, Shirley stammered out a few questions. It was a fight they had, the captain said. The wife got mad at him. Shirley raced back to Dad and asked him if she could use the free desk phone. But Sgt. Lowry stuck by his guns. He was not going to show any partiality just because she was his daughter. So Shirley was forced to use the paid medium of last resort for hard-pressed bureau cubs whose expense accounts rarely exceeded one dollar a day.

She began to give the facts from a phone booth, when Ruby Ryan interrupted her. Hang on, Ruby said. She flashed a bulletin to all the city desks in town. Their reaction convinced Shirley's editor she had scored a scoop and she basked in the limelight for at least two days, and especially after one of the newspaper columnists told the story of how Shirley had to go over her father's head to get her scoop.

In less than a month, Shirley was back in the Maxwell district again—but with far different results. She was sent to cover the wake of an Italian gangster who had been gunned down in what the papers called true 1920's syndicate style. Shirley, who wouldn't have recognized a gangland personality if she had been introduced to one, was assigned to mingle with the mourners and find out what members of the Mafia were present.

She did the best she could. There were as many elaborate floral tributes as there were shady-looking characters. She walked stealthily from one huge wreath to another, studying the cards, trying to memorize names, and now and then scribbling notes on a tiny pad when she thought no one was looking. She did this until a dark handsome "heavy", straight out of an Edward G. Robinson movie, appeared at her elbow.

"Get out of here," he said. "Now."

Shirley did not wait for him to add "Or else". She left Maxwell street, this time without a story.

In all, Larry Mulay says that some thirty-five women were on the staff of City News during the war. Among these were Maureen Daly, who had written a best-seller called *Seventeenth Summer*. She went on to become a top magazine editor. There was also Anne Douglas, who became the *Tribune*'s home furnishings editor, and Jean Kennedy, the sister of the future president, who went back to Boston and married Stephen Smith.

Mulay recalls that a "let-up" in the hiring of women occurred from 1945 to 1952 or so. Some City News women went on to jobs with the wire services and the newspapers; some went into public relations work and some got married and retired.

Selma Friend was one woman who stayed until February of 1950 before going into public relations work.

Another woman who stayed on from 1944 to 1954 was Marjorie Minsk Kriz, who covered the County morgue and County hospital for the bureau. She was put into medical slots, as it were, because her father was head of pediatrics at St. Francis hospital, and she says, both Isaac Gershman and Larry Mulay were fascinated by doctors.

On her first day at City News Marjorie saw her first "floater"—a drowned corpse fished out of the lake. Since she was assigned to the morgue, her work was hardly downhill all the way from there. She covered inquests, and there was only one pay phone at the morgue. Everybody fought for the phone; the women were at a disadvantage in this fight possibly because of some reluctance to jab veteran male reporters in sensitive places. Marjorie discovered a somewhat kinky morgue employee—if that is not redundant—who offered to let her use his private phone if she would agree to look at his "stiffs". For some reason watching Marjorie look at corpses was a thing that turned him on. In order to get at a phone, she obliged him. All the women chewed gum when they went to the morgue, in order to cope with the strong smell of formaldehyde and other things.

Marjorie also covered the forest preserves. In the course of this beat she met conservationists and biologists and took friends on a canoe trip from the county line south to Maywood. In the course of her travels she noted that many wrecks clogged the Des Plaines river: in her spare time she wrote a story on this which resulted eventually in the appointment of the Clean Stream commission. Like some other City News reporters, Marjorie wrote stories in her spare time: on Chicago theatres which were torn down and their histories, for instance. If the newspapers accepted these feature stories the reporters who wrote them got small bonuses.

Marjorie and Art Kozelka worked together in the forties to survey TV stations—to find out what their special needs were, so that the bureau could service them, a service which was to become an important and lucrative aspect of the bureau's work.

In 1954 Marjorie retired to stay home in Evanston and have two children. In 1966 the daughter of Senator Charles Percy was murdered in her bedroom in the Percy home in Kenilworth: Larry Mulay called Marjorie early on that Sunday morning and asked her if she would cover that story for him, for just one day. He had no one else out in the north suburbs. Marjorie obliged, and stayed with the bureau for five more years. Mulay told her he wanted someone to cover all the suburbs or else to cover O'Hare airport, which was not a regular City News beat. Marjorie chose O'Hare, and was able to develop it into a beat by reading columns to see what celebrities were a good source of information. Marjorie occupied the press room at O'Hare and alerted the media when someone important in government or the arts was passing through town.

When she left in 1972 it was not because she had tired of the job, but because her feet and back had given out in the struggle with the hard O'Hare floors. It developed that no one could take her place: the cubs were so young that they had not heard of famous people like Frederic March and Jimmy Durante and were consequently at sea about deciding who was worth noting. The general education of the cubs left something to be desired, too, Marjorie says; she remembers a young reporter telling her that there was no such place as New Zealand; she had never heard of it. People who had never heard of New Zealand would never recognize Gary Merrill, either, so the bureau reluctantly dumped the O'Hare beat, and Marjorie went on to become assistant public relations officer for the Federal Aviation administration, Great Lakes region.

When the fifties ended, perhaps with the advent of John Kennedy, there was a feeling that the time had come to be a little adventuresome at the bureau. Walter Ryberg recalls interviewing Liza Smith, about 1966: she was thirty-five years old, and the newspapers had turned her down because of her age. Ryberg felt that it was time the bureau hired an older woman, and sent her in to see Larry Mulay, who, to Ryberg's satisfaction, hired her.

She did well at the bureau and became the first woman day editor. Eventually she went back to her home turf, Los Angeles, for family reasons.

The female contingent at City News expanded again in the sixties, as it had in the early forties, and this time the flow was not to be shut off, as it had been after both World Wars, despite the fact that as late as 1976 there were those who maintained that although "a few" women reporters had been hired in the sixties, "leg work at City News is largely still a man's job." Among the few women reporters hired in the sixties was Anne Keegan, who went to UPI with Larry Mulay's recommendation and then to the *Tribune*, where she became a star columnist. There is also "Mike" Sneed, who is half of a well-known gossip column for the *Tribune* and Pam Zekman, who was first an investigative reporter for the Chicago *Tribune*, then the *Sun-Times*, and is now an investigative reporter for WBBM-TV, an owned and operated CBS station.

Hiring of women went on apace at the bureau throughout the seventies, and now, in 1983, there are nearly as many women there as men. The women were trained in exactly the same way as men, but conditions in the city apparently deteriorated to the point that James Peneff, general manager after Larry Mulay retired in 1974, has for the last few years been reluctant to allow women to roam between police stations at night. If they go out, they go in cabs. Patricia Leeds remembers working for Gershman and taking her chances in public transportation and police cars. But according to Peneff, even the men complain about the hidden dangers on the el platforms and in dark alleys late at night.

One young woman who came to the bureau in the seventies was not daunted by the dangers of the streets. This was Gera-Lind Kolarik, who went from the bureau to the news assignment desk at WBBM-TV and is now an assignment editor at WLS-TV, ABC's local owned and operated outlet. Gera-Lind, whose adolescent dream was to become a reporter, went from Rosary College to a public relations job with the County, and then heard about the bureau. She immediately applied for a job, but Jim Peneff, who was manager then, told her he had a huge waiting list, and she did not stand a chance, since none of her relatives were in the newspaper field. But Gera-Lind was not one to give up easily: she called Peneff every week, and finally threatened to chain herself to his office door and call photographers if he did not relent. "All I want is a chance," said Gera-Lind. Peneff relented, saying that if she wanted the job that badly she might as well have it.

Gera-Lind immediately bought a car, learned to drive it, and came to work, in that order. She was assigned to police, on the night shift, five p.m. to two a.m. She followed the flashing red lights wherever she could, dressed neatly in skirts and stockings, and wearing perfume at all times. Pat Leeds, whom she admired, told her the police would respect her more if she acted like a lady, did not swear and did not smoke much. One of her most memorable stories evolved when she disguised herself as a prostitute and went out with similarly disguised policewomen from the vice squad in Joliet. Peneff had refused to allow her to do that story; he felt it was too dangerous. So Gera-Lind did it on her own time, and the resulting story, with her name on it, went out over the wires and was printed in the newspapers. She became a minor celebrity and a frequent guest on talk shows as a result of this publicity. Her parents in Berwyn were aghast.

Peneff decided to revive the O'Hare beat to which Gera-Lind was assigned in 1976, a political year. It did not matter that Gera-Lind might not recognize Gary Merrill; there were other things in airports then. Hare Krishna, for instance. Gera-Lind encountered a sad little old man who was in the

airport every day carrying a large sign asking for his grand-
son back from the Hare Krishna people, who had absorbed
him along with his mother some time in the past. The little
old man, whose name was Morris Yanoff, later wrote a book
in which he immortalized Gera-Lind:

> When Gera-Lind Kolarik. . . introduced herself as air-
> port reporter for the City News Bureau, I agreed to meet
> her later in the USO lounge. She wanted to do a story on
> our vigil and explained that the City News Bureau
> reported Chicago events which otherwise might not
> reach the news media. Her story might be picked up as
> written or it might prompt an editor to dispatch a fea-
> ture writer to do a fuller write-up. It sounded like a
> possible news breakthrough for us, and it was.
>
> Though I didn't actually see Kolarik's final story, it
> created interest. The following morning Bob Faw of
> Channel 2, CBS, came out with his TV crew. . . I briefly
> told Faw what we were doing and pointed out the devo-
> tees. . .

Gera-Lind's story generated so much publicity that the
Hare Krishnas decided to return the child to his grandfather,
and there was a happy reunion.

When Ronald Reagan came to Chicago to meet with
uncommitted Republican delegates before the 1976 convention, his aides called a picture-taking session and announced
that no questions would be taken from the press. But Gera-
Lind was concerned about the state of Mrs. Nixon's health;
the former First Lady had had a recent stroke. Consequently
she called out a question about Mrs. Nixon to Mr. Reagan.
"No questions are allowed," an aide barked. But Gera-Lind
asked again, loudly, and was punched in the stomach for her
pains by a Secret Service agent. This unchivalrous action
enraged Ed Rooney of the *Daily News*, who sprang forward
and gave the agent a vigorous shove. A lively altercation
with shuffling amd grunting was in progress when the candidate decided that he could answer that one question. He
came forward as the peacemaker and informed Kolarik that

Mrs. Nixon's condition was stable. Once again Gera-Lind made the papers.

As might be expected, it took much longer for City News to hire black reporters than it had for them to begin hiring women on a regular basis. The city of Chicago, like most northern cities, was racially segregated. Walter Ryberg recalls that it was during the second World War that the city hired its first black motormen: everyone braced for a storm, but to their surprise there was no outcry. The newspapers were not interested in black news. If a bureau police reporter received information about an event from the police, the reporter would ask, if he wasn't sure, "Is that a blue area, Sergeant?" A "blue area" was a black neighborhood. If the sergeant said it was, the item was not used.

But apart from this, there were no applications from black aspirants that anyone living can remember. There is nothing underhanded or defensive about this. It is the simple truth.

Walter Ryberg remembers that the *Daily News* was the first Chicago newspaper to hire a black reporter, and he himself recalls the bureau hiring Luther Jackson about 1961—the bureau's first black reporter, who did not apply in the usual way, but came in by someone's recommendation. Everyone was nervous that the police would harass black reporters, but fortunately this concern proved to be unfounded.

Larry Mulay points out that City News had hired black teletype operators for years before Luther Jackson. These were mostly women. One black reporter who was also a woman, and who went on to become a national TV reporter, was Carole Simpson.

Paul Zimbrakos says that a black reporter was at City News before he himself started at the bureau in 1958: Ben Holman, who was already at the *Daily News* as a reporter. Another black who was there in the '60's was Sam Brown, who went to the *Sun-Times* and then tragically committed suicide. Two notable blacks of the '70's were Michele Stevens, who went to the *Sun-Times* and Michael J. Harrington who later ran unsuccessfully for alderman in the 44th ward and is now executive director of the Citizens Schools Committee.

17

Legendary Dividends

In 1940 when the bureau celebrated its fiftieth anniversary, the *Daily News* ran a story:

> The City News Bureau of Chicago, pioneer news-gathering agency owned by the four major Chicago dailies, today observed the 50th anniversary of its founding. It is the world's first co-operative agency for metropolitan news-gathering...it has served as a training school for more well-known reporters, editors, publishers and foreign correspondents, as well as for men who became famous in other fields, than any other agency of its kind in the country.

Obviously, after fifty years, the bureau was becoming the stuff out of which legends are made.

Some of these legends surfaced in print when, in the fall of 1951, the bureau was honored by the Chicago Press Veterans Association. There were four Chicago dailies at that time: in 1941 Marshall Field had introduced the Chicago *Sun*; by 1951 the Sun had absorbed the old tabloid *Times*, to become the *Sun-Times*. Both *Time* and *Newsweek* ran stories on the bureau. *Newsweek* estimated that it cost the papers $200,000 a year to operate the bureau, but mentioned "legendary dividends" the bureau paid, like the Dillinger scoop and the garbled first report on the St. Valentine's Day massacre. *Newsweek* reported:

> This week for the first time in all those 61 years, CNB called for a reunion of its 1,800 "graduates". On Nov. 3 their hot and hectic alma mater would be honored at the annual dinner of the Chicago Press Veterans Association. A few of the old grads: Phil Reed, managing editor of International News Service, who worked a seven-day beat (12 hours per day) at CNB in 1936; Clifton Utley, radio commentator; Melvyn Douglas and Lyle Talbot, actors now; Walter Howey...now an executive of the Hearst chain; Joel Wolfsohn, assistant to the Secretary of the Interior.
>
> Daily recipients of CNB's output are the four dailies in Chicago, the *Sun-Times*, *Tribune*, *News*, and *Herald-American*, which use and support it as a "backstop" for their own coverage. About 100 former CNB men are now on the staffs of the papers. The Associated Press, by its contracts with the four dailies, also has CNB's 44-man staff to supplement and protect its local coverage.
>
> Running the show at CNB is Isaac Gershman, a quick-acting, 57 year old veteran of 35 years at the bureau. Around him, as top editors and mentors for the cubs, are a half-dozen other men who have chosen to resist the organization's almost monthly turnover.

One of these men was Edward H. Eulenberg, the editor who has been credited with coining the bureau's slogan: "If your mother tells you she loves you, check on it."

Some cubs disliked this tall, bespectacled scholar—at first, at any rate. A few hated him. But most rookies came to believe that Eulenberg's only serious flaw had been pointed out by a *Daily News* reporter in the days when Eulenberg was covering the detective bureau:

> "Aw...Eulie acts like he thinks this job is on the level."

Eulenberg did indeed take news-gathering and writing with deadly seriousness. The casual, even flippant, attitude to be found among most experienced reporters, was not for him. He held that you didn't have to take yourself seriously; you didn't even have to take the boss all that seriously—but you had better take the job seriously. That was the only way to do it properly. You had to be your own disciplinarian because you worked basically on the street, or away from the eyes of your supervisors.

Eulenberg's tireless goading and bottomless patience helped transform many a youth into a consummate newspaperman or woman. The only time he ran out of patience was when someone tried to pass off skimpy work with a smile and an airy phrase. At one point he was heard talking through gritted teeth to a reporter on the other end of the phone. She had neglected to interview a fire department official after a big fire, and had attempted to explain this omission on her part by informing Eulenberg that he really did not understand the way the south side fire brigade operated.

Eulenberg put the phone down momentarily to kick a large hole in the side of the wastebasket. Then he picked up the phone to resume his conversation in a calm, but trembling voice.

"In Chicago, Esther," he said, "a fire fighting boss is never called a director. It may be different in Toronto, but that is the way it is here. And there are no fire brigades in this city. The whole thing is called the fire department. The units are companies, battalions and divisions. Unit designations are by number, never by compass direction. We do not say 'south side'. . ."

After he hung up, Eulenberg offered, knowing the penny-pinching ways of the bureau, to replace the wastebasket at his own expense. But Larry Mulay assured him that that would not be necessary. It was cheaper, Larry said, to replace a wastebasket than to stand the costs of a long rest in a home for Eulenberg if he had not found an immediate outlet for some of his tension.

One thing Eulenberg believed in passionately was the telephone directory. He insisted that reporters verify there all names that cropped up in the news. Usually he asked also that the possessor of the name be telephoned to see if he had anything to add to the story in which he figured. Of equal importance with the directory to Eulenberg was the big Webster's Unabridged Dictionary which rested on a stand near the weather bureau teletype machine. When Eulenberg had become a deskman in the thirties the Dictionary was already there, and already an antique. As soon as he felt sufficiently secure in his job, Eulenberg began to agitate for a new dictionary. He pointed, to bolster his case, to the Webster's definition of the word "galley". It was defined, as would be expected, as the kitchen of a ship, and a tray in which type was placed. But the illustration for the word was a small oar-propelled ship. Underneath the picture were the words: "A Modern Galley."

Eulenberg told the front office that that caption should give an idea of when that book was put together. Eventually he had his way, and the bureau invested in a new dictionary. Which is probably still there.

Eulenberg is remembered with fondness by Jim Mundis:

> Ed Eulenberg was the favorite with the young reporters. He was a fountain of sage advice and encouragement. And he was our banker on short-money weekends. That meant almost every weekend since payday was on Monday. If we could justify our need for the two or three dollars we wanted to borrow, it was always given with advice about not living from paycheck to paycheck.

With seven days a week to cover, twenty-four hours a day, there were at least a half dozen editors and deskmen on the bureau's roster at all times. An editor was the boss of a shift: days, middle watch up to midnight, and last watch from midnight to dawn. Desk men sat in at the city desk when the editor took a day off or was out to lunch or otherwise unavailable. There were also specialists on the roster: radio and sports editors and so on.

Eulenberg started at the bureau in 1927, and stayed there for thirty years. When he went on the desk he was on the middle watch most of the time. He had succeeded Joe Levandier, who had succeeded Harshman. Toward the end of his span he was growing very tired of night work. He told Larry Mulay about this, and said he was going in to Gershman and tell him that it was no more night work, or nothing. Mulay, who was a student of Gershman, uttered some words of caution. "Don't go in without me," Mulay said. "I think I can handle this."

Accordingly Eulenberg and Mulay went in to beard Gershman in his den. As Mulay had foreseen, and as Eulenberg was not unaware, Gershman immediately became excited. "But you can't go on days," he said. "You can't. What will we do? There's nobody else. Who else is there? There isn't anybody else."

"There's Dornfeld," Mulay said soothingly. "Dornfeld is at the Federal building. We can take Dornfeld off the Federal building, put someone else there, and give Dornfeld the middle watch."

This suggestion stopped Gershman cold. He could not think of any objection to it, and Dornfeld went on that watch, which he was to keep until his retirement in 1972. Eulenberg became a rewrite man and fill-in city editor for a period of time, but the magic had gone out of the bureau for him, what with one thing and another, and in 1957 he moved to the *Daily News* where he stayed until his retirement.

Gershman tended to get excited very easily, and his reactions were not always logical. One discouraging aspect of City News work lay in the fact that a tough day or night's work on a big story always ended up the next day as mere "timesheet"—a bound stack of dull copy. A feeling of being let down was inevitable. The staff always wanted their stories with headlines and pictures. It was human nature. Gershman felt this way as much as anybody did.

On one occasion he stormed out of his private office, pointing an evening paper at the city desk like an accusing wand.

"Look at all the stuff they got that we missed," he said, in a low, tense voice. He never shouted, but it was easy to tell when he was upset.

Walter Ryberg, who was not easily upset, took the paper from Gershman's hands and began to scan the column with a pencil. He drew a line every time he recognized a City News story. When he handed the paper back to Gershman, the newspaper was filled with lines.

"That's our stuff," Ryberg said. "They seem to have carried the same stuff we found."

"But they've got headlines," Gershman said. "Look, there's a four inch headline."

This comment was met with silence, and after awhile he went sadly back to his office.

One of Gershman's strong interests was psychology. He was in fact an amateur psychologist, and he was most interested in job applicants who had had psychological problems in their backgrounds. His penchant for hiring these people caused some problems in the bureau, especially since communication with his staff was not his strong point.

One case that interested Gershman for its psychological implications was the William Heirens case, the biggest story in Chicago after the second World War. Beginning in June, 1945, there were a series of murders and shootings in the city: three women were murdered in their apartments, and two more were shot through their windows as they sat quietly at home. The police noted similarities in the crimes which pointed to a single perpetrator.

On the morning of January 7, 1946, James Degnan went to wake his six-year-old daughter Suzanne for school and found her bed empty. There was evidence of kidnapping, and her room had been carefully cleaned and straightened—a peculiarity the police had noted in the other crimes against women. The first person Degnan called was Larry Mulay, who by an odd chance served on a ration board with him. Degnan wanted advice, but he was hesitant to call the police because of the usual warnings in the ransom note. Mulay was able to convince Degnan that the police should be called; there was just no other reasonable course. Thus City News heard about the missing Degnan girl even before the police did.

Later that day the child's head was discovered in a manhole and a grisly search ensued. Shirley Lowry Haas remembers being sent out by the bureau to cover that story, which centered on the city's sewers: reporters haunted the coroner's office as portions of the child's anatomy were retrieved from the sewers. It was an appalling crime. The city's tension was relieved when the murderer, William Heirens, was almost accidentally caught when he began to shoot at the police during a routine call about a burglary.

Something was obviously the matter with Heirens, who was a student at the University of Chicago. Gershman was fascinated by the young man's mental condition. He called a leading Chicago psychiatrist into his office to discuss the case.

They were closeted for half an hour or so. Eventually the psychiatrist emerged, looking rather dazed and wandered down the aisle of the city room toward the door. He paused momentarily at Walter Ryberg's desk. Ryberg looked up.

The psychiatrist gestured with his thumb toward Gershman's office.

"That guy's nuts," he said.

Ryberg remained calm in the face of this assertion. Ryberg was almost always calm, cool and scholarly. His mind was incredibly agile beneath his quiet exterior. He too had started at the bureau in 1926, had come and left three times to work on Chicago dailies and had finally come for good in 1941. He was to remain until his retirement in 1968.

Another unflappable desk man was William E. Garrett who had started at the bureau in 1967 when he was seventeen. He became desk man in his twenties; his youth enabled him to relate to cubs. In 1967 Garrett went to Hearst's *American*, which later became *Chicago Today*, and was bought by the *Tribune*. In 1974 *Chicago Today* died, and Garrett joined the *Tribune* as an assistant editor. He later became city editor.

Clarence Jensen was one of the smoothest writers at the

bureau. He was an assistant city editor and rewrite man on days. He preferred rewrite, because he liked to help reporters. He was gentle and kindly, and gave guidance in the least offensive way. Over the telephone he seemed almost as if he were at the reporter's side. "Why don't you try this...?" he would say tactfully. He was greatly missed when he died suddenly in 1970. He was a strong contrast to a rewrite man like Joe Ator who was often nasty to reporters and who, when he went to the *Tribune*, left a good many dry eyes behind him.

Jensen was much given to culinary images. On one occasion when someone asked him for a formula for the production of flowing prose, he replied, "It's simple. It's like mixing up a batch of oatmeal. You just keep going around and around until all the lumps are beaten out."

On another occasion he explained how to avoid long-winded repetitiousness in copy. "You've seen a butcher with a sharp knife, working on a steak, haven't you? He slices all the fat from it. Try that in your copy. Trim off all the fat. It may take two or three attempts, but try it."

In reply, one bureau employee is said to have asked, "What's a steak?"

Rewrites were also denizens of the city room. A rewrite, also known as a rewriter, rewrite man or rewrite woman, has been described as an individual burdened with a bulging sense of self-importance and an unlimited capacity for asking questions, while sitting behind a typewriter in a news room. Fairminded reporters have been known to concede that occasionally a rewrite will demonstrate a rudimentary grasp of English usage.

Tony Sowa was one reporter who gave rewrites very little trouble. There was never any reason to ask Tony questions; he was a finished workman who thought of everything before he told rewrite, "That's all." There was one rewrite, however, whom we shall call Oswald, who was rarely satisfied with anyone's report. One day Tony gave Oswald a complete account of the wounding of a thirteen-year-old girl by a stray bullet.

"That is," Tony said, "by a bullet whose source could not be determined. No one saw a weapon or heard the sound of a gun when this child was shot as she was walking to church. She was dressed in white for this occasion, which was her first communion. With her were her parents and her brothers and sisters."

Tony provided their names, gave the child's nickname, and the chances for her recovery as estimated by the attending physicians. He finished up:

"She was walking toward the Church of the Seven Holy Martyrs when she was hit by the bullet. That's all."

"Hey," Oswald said. "Wait a minute. What are the names of the seven holy martyrs?"

Tony hung up abruptly and counted to ten. A few days later he gave Oswald the facts about a fire which had caused several injuries in a Polish neighborhood.

"Now I've got some names," Tony said. "Listen carefully and take 'em down the way I give 'em to you. They're kind of tricky. First, Jean de la Lande. J as in jerk, E as in empty, A as in ass, N as in nitwit..."

After he spelled out the name, Tony asked Oswald to spell it back to him.

He went on, painfully slowly, to Isaac Jogues, Antoine Daniel, Jean de Brebeuf, Gabriel Lalement, Charles Garnier and Noel Chabanal. It took a long time.

"Hey," Oswald said. "What is this? What are all these Frenchmen doing in a Polish neighborhood?"

"Well, you asked for them," Tony said. "Those are seven French missionaries who were killed by Indians in colonial days. They are the seven holy martyrs."

Some reporters actually learned something from grilling by rewrites. Tom Abbott, who is now with the Xerox Corporation in Stamford, Connecticut, worked for the bureau in the late forties and early fifties before joining the *Tribune*. He says that he learned the most his third day on the job at the bureau, and from a rewrite woman:

It was a city bus accident in which about 25 passengers were injured. They were being taken to a small, probably no longer existing hospital on Irving Park boulevard.

I don't remember where I was when Gladys "Ruby" Ryan called and said whoever was on the desk, Larry [Mulay] or Walter [Ryberg] or Art [Kozelka] or Clarence [Jensen], wanted me to go to the hospital and get the story. I do remember that I guessed it would take about 40 minutes to get there if I followed the S.O.P. streetcar and bus route. Wanting to make a good initial impression, and having a few bucks in my pocket, I took a cab.

At the sticky-hot, overflowing hospital emergency room, I talked to the cops, the bus driver and *all* of the injured passengers as they were being examined, or waiting, some sitting on the floor in the hall. I got every name, age, address, occupation and actual or complained-of injury. I even found a guy who had been on his way to visit his dying wife in the hospital where he was now nursing a broken arm. And all of that in about half an hour.

I rushed to the phone booth near the emergency room entrance, my supply of nickels and dimes weighing down the pocket of my trousers. I already was sweating through my suit-coat on that hot day in mid-June.

"Give it to Ann," the desk said. Ann, I found out, was Anna Tamarri, one of several females who had carried on at City Press while many of us were fighting World War II and who now was on rewrite.

"What have you got?" A bus accident on Irving Park, no fatalities, many injured and I have all of their names, etc.

"Irving Park what?" Being a native Chicagoan I knew that one without looking it up in my brand new *Leonard's Street Guide*. Irving Park boulevard.

"Are you sure it's a boulevard at that address? Some place it changes to Irving Park road. Better look it up." I did: boulevard.

On to the passenger list. I'd even put it into alphabetical order.

"John Adams, 37, 1237 North Cicero, dishwasher, lacerated little finger on left hand."

"Cicero what? Street, avenue, what? Look it up." I knew: avenue.

And so it went, through the 25. "Hermitage what? Look it up. Western what? Look it up. Seeley what? Look it up."

Juggling my notes taken on a quarter-folded piece of copy paper, trying to cradle the phone receiver between my ear and my shoulder, frantically paging through *Leonard's*, dropping my notes, dropping the receiver, dropping *Leonard's*. Keeping the phone booth door closed (no light and no fan working) to keep out the noise from the emergency room, I soon felt as though I had been soaked by water from a broken fire hose. (I found out how that really felt the following week).

Forty minutes and dozens of "...what? Look it ups" later, I stumbled out of the booth, with my rumpled notes and my damaged *Leonard's* in my hands.

A sympathetic nurse approached me.

"Were you in the bus crash?" she asked.

I mumbled that it might have been less painful if I had been. There were to be more important, sensational and exciting stories to cover in my several separate stints at City Press, but none that made such a lasting impression or that taught me such an important lesson. Look it up!

Jim Mundis also had his problems with rewrite men:

I enjoyed day-side except when I was assigned west. With as many as 12-24 inquests a day—with three going similtaneously—plus the activities in the police stations, it seemed there never was time to do the job. This was complicated sometimes by jokesters called rewrite men. Example: A youngster died while playing with a revolver found in a dresser. The fatal shot had caused gunshot wounds to the victim's eyes. The rewrite man's question on the inquest story was: "What color were the youngster's eyes?" The inquest was over and I couldn't find out. I still don't see the import of the questions. But from then on, he would insist periodically that I get answers to similarly unimportant questions on different stories.

But Art Kozelka (a wonderful guy when he was not barking on a rewrite phone) finally drove me to the brink. It was the usual harried day at the morgue. On No. 3 story I was giving Art, he asked the question that pushed me over the brink. A cigar store owner had been shot and killed in a holdup. The question was: did he fall inside or outside the door?

At that point I selected a large number of words to explain to Art what I thought of him and his stupid, inane, inconsequential etc. questions. I announced that I would take no more of his verbal excrement—that I quit.

I had made this call on a wall phone adjacent to the desk at the morgue. After I hung up, I stood there for a few minutes and thought about the future. I hoped I could collect the three-days' pay I had coming. At that point the phone rang and, absently, I answered. It was Art, apologetic that I had misunderstood him and could he please have the rest of the stories. I couldn't believe it. I gave him the other info mechanically and he didn't ask another question. From that day forward I had no problem with rewrite men. After all, it was great sport to "break in" the young guys.

Some City News copy came from the rewrites in a striking manner, and became legendary. One such was posted on the bulletin board. It was an account of a woman who had been described as the brains behind her boyfriend, a freshly murdered hoodlum. The woman, the bureau copy said, was the motivating force in the beer peddling operation. The hoodlum himself was just a figurehead.

"Intimates knew," the copy said, "that O'Berta was merely a tool in the hands of his mistress."

18

The Fifties

Big events were supposedly outside the bureau's regular run, but the bureau was nevertheless able to take them in its stride. When General MacArthur came to Chicago in April of 1951 he said that he would make only a few off-the-cuff remarks in response to the official welcome. One editor at least, however, expected a lot of comment from the general, and asked the bureau to cover the event.

Two court reporters were stationed in the offices to take the speech off the radio. A wire recorder was cut in and another court reporter was assigned to the speaker's platform in the evening in Soldier Field. Less than five minutes after MacArthur began speaking the verbatim started coming into the newspaper offices. The off-the-cuff remarks ran to 1200 words.

The bureau also covered the Kefauver hearings in Chicago in 1951. Eight court reporters and relays of messengers were assigned to the hearings. Every two minutes a boy ran with a waxed sheet from the Federal building to the nearest tube inlet. The report averaged 70,000 words daily and 389 pages on the most talkative days.

When Queen Elizabeth came to Chicago in 1959 the bureau tried something new: there was a reporter in a helicopter circling overhead, with reporters on the ground communicating back and forth through walkie-talkies. The competition was scooped. This was the same visit by the Queen in which Buddy McHugh, then working for the *American*, is said to have pulled up in his own car beside Prince Philip's open convertible, yelled, "Hey, Prince!" and fired off a few innocuous questions, to which the Prince responded, as he was responding anyway, with nods and smiles. Buddy then filed an "exclusive" interview.

The '50's were not all pleasant visits and sensational inquiries. On August 11, 1953, the first Negro families moved into the Trumbull Park low-rent housing project on Chicago's far south side, and riots ensued. As many as 1,353 policemen were sent on occasion to the 426 family development. An average of 300 policemen were kept on duty, and nearly 250 arrests were made.

To Gershman the press had a role to play in this racial unrest. It was the bureau which fed information to the radio stations in the city, and minutes after there were spot newscasts of the troubles, hundreds of people drove to Trumbull Park: sightseers, hoodlums and passionately engaged partisans—a dangerous mob psychology was ignited.

Accordingly by the summer of 1955 Gershman had worked out what was called "the Chicago plan" for damping down riot potential. The news directors of nine Chicago radio stations, all clients of the bureau, agreed to implement Gershman's suggestions; these were first drawn up in the form of instructions to his own staff:

Race or gang fight stories will be filed as advisory notes during the active stage of trouble in order to help prevent a minor disturbance from exploding into a major conflict. . .

It is hoped that this method of treatment by both broadcasting stations and the City News Bureau Radio-TV News Department will prevent hundreds of racists from concentrating at the trouble scene, and yet provide the assurance that the basic news is reported to the public. . .

Brevity is of special importance.

Do not use superlatives or adjectives that might incite or enlarge a conflict, or—in cases where police have quelled the disorder—might cause renewal of trouble.

Avoid use of the word "riot." If trouble becomes a major conflict, then use of the "riot" label may become unavoidable.

When the first reports of a fight or trouble are received by the police, check and verify situation before filing advisory.

Advisory data to stations should be written in calm, matter-of-fact sentences, and in such a tone that, should the announcer tear it off and read it by mistake, it would not be inflammatory.

If story is of a minor nature it is to be judged in news value on same basis as any other routine story.

"We are obligated to keep the radio and television stations informed when such mob disorders occur," Gershman said. "We do this so that they can send cameramen, reporters and tape recorders to the scene. Our entire radio-TV news handling (as well as press copy) will be a matter of record, and if riots actually occur we should be in a position that no charge of riot incitement can be placed against us."

This was the basic form which Gershman provided to his radio-TV editors and his news desk, to be used for early reports when there was a possibility of violence:

Attention editors and station managers—not for broadcast—note serious nature of this information. Broadcast may heighten tension and draw crowds. This is not for broadcast.

After the information was given, there was another statement:

This is one of those conditions that could become worse if broadcast. We will keep you advised of developments. Meanwhile, this information is not for broadcast.

When the police commander who was on the scene said everything was under control, an all clear for broadcast was given.

Mayor Daley gave the plan his imprimatur, and, after the nine news directors agreed to it, the plan was turned by Gershman over to Francis W. McPeek, the executive director of the Commission on Human Relations of the city. In all, eighteen stations agreed to accept Gershman's "Chicago plan." Newspapers and magazines across the country praised it.

Another Gershman plan was implemented in the '50s. This was not so wide-ranging nor so long-lasting as the "Chicago plan" but it demonstrated Gershman's interest in taking the agency into new paths. It was a cooperative plan between the bureau, with the consent of course of its participating newspapers, and the Northwestern University Medill School of Journalism to set up a professional internship for graduate students in journalism, beginning in the fall of 1958. Sixteen selected graduate students enrolled for a six-credit, two-quarter course called "Professional Reporting." They spent three days a week as members of the CNB staff, covering bureau newsbeats in Chicago.

Walter Ryberg was put in charge of this program. He was at that time assistant city editor for the bureau and a part-time member of the Medill faculty. Once a week there was a nightly session with Ryberg and Prof. Jacob Scher of Medill going over the week's work with the students and answering questions. Guests were brought in, like Jay McMullen of the *Daily News*, Harry F. Reutlinger of the *American* and Karin Walsh of the *Sun-Times*. Lectures were given on technique and strategy in newsgathering and writing. The internship plan only lasted, unfortunately, two semesters and then it had to be disbanded because of lack of interest on the part of the students. Walter Ryberg says, "We couldn't get people to do it. It was too tough. Nobody wanted to work that hard."

The association with TV and radio stations was Gershman's idea. This involved setting up in 1958 a radio department for the stations, which employed the services of a radio editor, a night editor, a day editor, and a teletype man. When the radio editor went to lunch, the news desk took over the radio work. Radio editors wrote their copy especially to be read aloud, so that it would sound conversational, and not stilted.

Gershman also instituted the public relations service when the tubes were no longer used at the end of the fifties and the beginning of the sixties. It had been the bureau's custom to send news releases for public relations people free of charge over the tubes. But without the tubes this kind of service was more expensive and it was thought right to charge for it. It was under Larry Mulay, however, that this PR service of the bureau's was made into a lucrative endeavor.

Another thing which marked the fifties off for the bureau was the move in 1950 to the 188 W. Randolph street tower, on the twelfth floor. The AP moved to the second floor of the same building.

One big story of the late fifties—Dec. 1, 1958—was the holocaust at the Our Lady of Angels school on the near northwest side in which 92 children and three nuns perished. Walter Oleksy covered that fire:

> I had been asleep in my three-room furnished apartment near Belmont harbor after working the overnight rewrite shift. Gladys called from the switchboard and I got the call out in the hall because I had no phone in my room. She said there was a bad fire out west at the school and I was to get there as fast as I could. Before I left the house she called again, instructing me to skip the school and go directly to St. Anne's hospital where dead and injured from the fire were being brought. I was to get the latest figure on deaths when I arrived, and call the city desk.
>
> As soon as I reached the hospital (by cab) I saw that it was a nightmare. A press room had been set up near the entrance and a room I looked into on my way to the

press room contained black bodies. I thought these were Negro children, but later I discovered they were badly burned white children. I got my number of dead and was on my way to calling in the figure to the city desk when in the hall I heard some nuns talking. One said, "Isn't it fantastic what Sister. . .did?"

I stopped in my tracks, went over, and asked what it was that was so fantastic. The nuns didn't identify the heroic nun of their story, because she had insisted upon remaining anonymous, but they told me what she had done when the fire broke out.

The nun had been teaching seventh grade on the second floor of the school when smoke began pouring in under the door. Next, she heard cries outside in the hall that there was a fire. She instructed her students not to panic and not to open the door, fearing it would bring in smoke and flames. Instead she went to the windows and saw neighbors had gathered beneath them, arriving ahead of firemen, and were calling to the children to jump. The nun encouraged the braver children to leap from the windows into the waiting arms of the people below. While some leaped, another student panicked and opened the door. Children began rushing into the hall, and the nun headed them off. Unable to get them to go back into their room, she told them to get on their hands and knees, as close to the floor as possible, and led them to the foot of the stairs by having them link their arms in a human chain. At the top of the stairs she lay her black-habited form over a hole through which flames were leaping, and rolled about a dozen or more students over her with their arms close to their bodies as if they were logs. More people below caught the children as they rolled down the stairs. When the last of them was safely downstairs, the nun went back into the hall-way three times to do the same for dozens of other children.

She was a slight woman, about thirty, and weighed only about 115 pounds. She saved the lives of about forty children.

I called the story in to the office and Howie Ziff said it was just what the afternoon papers were crying for, a strong human interest feature. He wrote it up and did a rare thing for the City News. While the bureau rarely or never gave a byline, Ziff wrote: "At the St. Anne's hospital the night of the fire the nun told a newspaper reporter (Walter Oleksy of the City News Bureau) that 'I felt untold strength.' "

The story ran as the banner headline on both the next day's *Daily News* and *American* front pages and the *American* ran a staff artist's drawing of the nun leading the children to the stairway. It later ran in national magazines.

The nun later agreed to talk to reporters and give her name. Sister Mary Adrienne became a hero of the fire, but insisted her sister nuns had done as much. Three nuns had perished in the fire.

At the hospital I saw seasoned reporters crying, the tragedy was so overwhelming. I didn't feel the full weight of it until after about ten hours covering the story and riding a bus back to my apartment at about three in the morning. I picked up a copy of the *Tribune* someone had left on the bus and looked at the front page stories about the fire and cried. The next afternoon, riding another bus to the City News office, I noticed that no one was reading a paper. Later, fellow reporters said they thought the Our Lady of Angels fire was the best-covered fire in recent memory, and the least read. People just couldn't bear to read about it.

I think more than 100 children died in that fire.

A footnote: a week after turning in my story I was invited to work for the *Tribune*. I figured what got me the nod was that fire story. I'd worked on a weekly in Michigan, had edited an army weekly for two years including a year in Germany; had then worked on daily papers in Indiana and Michigan, and worked for UP in Detroit, but that night covering the Our Lady of the Angels fire, I became a reporter and I think it's stuck.

Ray Bendig was another City News reporter who covered the fire:

> ...nothing could top the school fire. The threat of bodily harm always follows a City News kid and it was bound to happen on this one.
>
> Reporters were ringing doorbells along West Chicago avenue in droves.
>
> "Why don't you guys get together and send one person up to bother us?" asked an irate uncle of one of the dead students. "You're the third (deleted) to ring the bell. . . Now get the hell out of here before I knock you down the stairs. . .!"
>
> One dutiful City News kid called his boss, Bob Billings, to report on the lack of respect by the friends and relatives of the deceased.
>
> "Do you want to work or don't you?" Billings barked. "Get out there and talk to the rest of the families on your list. Do it!"
>
> Sure. Do it. Let 'em take aim on your chin.
>
> The next family on the list had lost a son and a daughter. And they weren't about to get feisty. They were numb. In shock. The boy, only twelve, had just completed a beautiful drawing of The Last Supper. And his younger sister was just as talented.
>
> Mom and Dad were quick to show the City News kid examples of their gifts. And even he began to feel the magnitude of their loss.
>
> But the most poignant scene of all came in a second-floor walkup above an old-fashioned meat market. There must have been fifty mourners in this Italian family and they were all sitting around and no one was talking. The silence was soul deep.
>
> The City News kid sat down too, and experienced the total depth of the moment. It left an indelible mark on his apprenticeship as a reporter.

Another big Chicago story of the time was the Summerdale

police scandal of 1959. Eight or nine policemen were discovered to have been in a burglary ring. It was Walter Spirko a CNB graduate then with the *Sun-Times* who broke that story, as he had broken the St. Valentine's Day massacre story. The suspected policemen were taken for questioning by the Police Burglary Unit to the Union League club, a place that was supposed to have been sufficiently off the beaten track to avoid publicity. But Spirko received a tip.

Ray Bendig remembers the Summerdale scandal too, but as one that got away:

> The City News kid will never forget the effect that "Babbling Burglar" Richard Morrison had on the Chicago Police department, Commissioner Tim O'Connor and the reporter's favorite uncle, Capt. Mike Ahern, chief of traffic. Orlando Wilson flew in from San Francisco with a big broom to sweep out everything from 11th and State to Navy pier.
>
> The City News kid had been in the Summerdale station the day before the whole thing broke. The desk sergeant unceremoniously booted him out from behind the counter as Buddy McHugh went about his business of helping put the finishing touches on the Police department's biggest black-eye ever.

Musing over the Our Lady of Angels fire and the Summerdale scandal, Bendig says:

> The kid learned more than just how to ring doorbells, dial phones and approach deputy coroners. He discovered what it's like to lose a loved one in a disaster and what it's like to witness the fall of a close relative from one of the city's top public public service posts. . . Looking back it was worth it. . .every minute of it.

City News kids were often "unceremoniously booted" around. In 1951 John Murphy wrote this sketch of the kid's first day:

I'm the new City Press man.

I walk into the Skaty-eighth district station.

Here's how it goes:

"Could I use your phone, Sarge?" I quaver, pages of notes fluttering in my hand.

"Who're you?" shouts the mastodon in blue clothing.

"I'm the new City Press man—you know—City Press? I got a story I gotta phone in—OK?"

God Almighty's first assistant gives me the eye, but nods sidewise at one of the phones clustered on the desk.

"Hurry up," he grunts. I grab one.

"That's the PAX, for cripes sake! Use the other one— THE OTHER ONE!"

I finally get the city editor.

"Uh, y'know that Mopery you gave me...?"

"What Mopery?" snaps the desk.

"The one you gave me about..."

"Whaddaya got on it?"

"Well, this guy got caught by two cops..."

"Wait a minute. Here's a rewrite..."

The resulting buzzes and clicks are punctuated by a roar from the desk sergeant.

"Whaddaya got there—a broad or somethin'? Get off the phone."

"OK, let's go?" comes over the phone from rewrite.

The notes flutter to the floor just as the switchboard breaks in: "There's a robbery at 6232 Unameit street, a 2-11 fire at Mobregon and Muskellunge, and hold on, I got some coroner's cases for you."

"Whaddaya got on that Mopery?"

"Get off that phone!"

"Drowned in his bathtub..."

"Calling car two-thirty. A demented man at your station—230, go into your station for a demented man—KSA944."

19

Folklore

In 1959 Mike Royko wrote an article for the Chicago Newspaper Reporters Association *Behind the News* magazine, about bureau legends:

> The legends are many of the brash City Press kids who have scooped the town. Armed only with their wits and a handful of dimes, these embryonic newspapermen are credited with having bugged grand jury hearings, dug up bodies, pilfered hot documents, cornered the telephone market at disasters and gone on, so the stories go, to great fame and fortune.
>
> Told and retold by the eager young copy boys as they crowd around the City Press' pneumatic tubes, these stories are wonderful. They must be or so many CNB alumni wouldn't lay claim to them.
>
> But what of the other stories, related only by sadeyed deskmen as they mark up lost opportunities? The stories of City Press kids who never got to the scene, who ran out of dimes, who forfeited the chance for fame and fortune?
>
> Here are three such instances as they happened in 1958:
>
> A City Press kid was working the north police beat one summer night when three pranksters built a bomb and blew themselves all over the Montrose Harbor parking lot.

"Go to the scene," the reporter was told, "and call us quick."

Seconds stretched to minutes, minutes into an hour and the hour into curses of rage. Finally, long after the story had been gathered by phone, the reporter called in. He explained:

"I couldn't find the parking lot and I was wandering around. Then I saw a guy carrying a big metal box. I figured he was from the crime lab so I followed him. He walked about two miles. Then he set the box down on the rocks. He opened it and took out a fishing rod. . ."

Then there was the quiet night on dog watch when a copy boy, hopefully known as an apprentice reporter, went down for papers and coffee from the bus depot.

He didn't return for more than an hour.

After receiving a lecture on the importance of getting on the team, he crept into the back room.

About an hour later, the editor overheard the copy boy, or apprentice reporter, explain his delay to a rewriteman:

"Gosh, I hope he's not mad at me. I would have got back faster but when I saw a man and a woman fighting with a guy who had a knife, and all those people in the bus depot screaming and running, I had to get the cop. And he hit that guy. It was something the way that couple tracked down the guy who raped their daughter..."

On still another occasion, things were quiet on the dog watch. A copy boy sat in the back room, reading a tale by Ben Hecht and dreaming of glory.

His chance came as the fire box ticked off a four-bagger a mile west of the Loop.

The only available reporter on the shift was tied up on another story, so the copy boy was sent out with explicit instructions to "take a cab and call us with a description."

He did just that. And he called the office every ten minutes during the hour it took him to clean up the fire, which was a smoky, but dull, incident.

Back in the office, swelling with pride over his fine execution of the job, he dropped an expense slip on the desk.

It looked like the national debt. When called to account, he related:

"There were no telephones nearby, so I chartered a cab to stand by and drive me back and forth to an all-night restaurant on Madison street. . ."

(EDITOR'S NOTE: The lad involved in this last anecdote has an inherited talent for making out expense accounts. However, we will not divulge the identity of his sire).

It is certainly true that the bureau has its share of legends. We have retold a good many already, but there are always more. Here is another tale that has kicked around newspaper offices for many years; it was written by August Arnold and printed in the yearbook of the Chicago Newspaper Reporters Association:

I never belonged to any choir or any sort of choral group. But once—many decades ago—I was the object of attention of such an aggregation.

Montrose harbor was at that time only a rock-strewn expanse of lake water. Just a dream in the minds of city planners who later created the pleasant boatman's and fisherman's retreat we know today. . .the rocks lay invisible just below the water, waiting for some heedless boat to run into them. And, one pleasant night, that is exactly what the motor cruiser *Bud* managed to do.

When [the desk man] learned that a boat was stuck about a mile east of Montrose avenue, and was burning distress flares, he. . .detached me from the detective bureau beat with the directive: Get out there. Get out some way. Any way.

I went to the closest spot on the shoreline and by sheer good luck found a kid in a rowboat who was willing to make a buck. . .

He rowed me to the motionless but undamaged vessel. I stepped aboard, into the comfortably fitted-out cabin. Much of the fitting was bonded stuff, back in the doleful days when good booze was not. Quickly I learned the names of the boat, the people on board and other relevant matters. Then I stepped back topside to climb back into the rowboat.

But my ferry boat was gone! I was marooned! With a borrowed megaphone I shoved my data ashore.

"Johnnie! This is the motor cruiser *Bud...*" When I finished I hoped to hear a response from shore but there was none. No one hollered back, "I read you loud and clear." So I consoled myself with drafts of good booze, muttering complacently, "Johnnie must have heard me. I guess he couldn't find a megaphone to answer me with."

Suddenly the sound of a score of well-drilled voices crashed into my happy daze. With admirably precise timing, the voices intoned, to the tune of Handel's *Hallelujah Chorus*:

"*Call* the office. *Call* the office. *Ca-a-wal* the office..." Etc.

I responded, via megaphone:

"Can't do it. I'm marooned out here until the Coast Guard gets here to pull the boat off."

There was a long pause on shore. I put the time to use with a bottle. When the voices on the shore resumed, they were using the tune of *Three Blind Mice*:

"Arnold call the desk! Arnold call the desk! See you call it now."

They repeated the message several times...

It was many hours later, after the Coast Guard had hauled the boat to a harbor. I called the desk. When I explained about being stranded, the desk man was very understanding.

"Why didn't you wade ashore to call?" he demanded sternly. "The water isn't much over six feet deep in the worst places over those rocks... You could have tried to scramble ashore. Maybe you wouldn't have drowned. If you got your pants ruined the office would have paid for—well, anyway, the office would have paid for getting them pressed... Okay... But don't expect overtime pay."

I didn't. But later I learned that Johnnie Clark, [on the northside bureau beat] had met up with a church group strolling to cool off in the lake breeze and had impressed the choir into service as a makeshift public address system.

Far from expecting overtime pay, Arnold was worried that the office might deduct the value of the free booze he had imbibed, while on duty, from his regular paycheck. This fear proved groundless.

Minor misadventures befell practically all reporters who stayed on police beats long enough to get the feel of the job. John Stevenson was sent to look into a rumor that police were closing in on burglars trapped in a south side flat. Shots were exchanged. When the police finally stormed the place they found that the burglars had fled through a bedroom window which gave onto a porch roof. On the bedroom floor was a pile of furs and valuable bric-a-brac which the miscreants had had to abandon in their rush for freedom. Stevenson turned in this information from a phone in the living room of the apartment. When he returned to the bedroom, a policeman was just opening the closet door. There was a sudden burst of pistol fire: a burglar, who had been hiding in the closet, sprayed the place with bullets. Fortunately his aim was bad, and no one was hurt. After the man was overpowered and safely manacled, Stevenson picked himself up off the floor. When he regained the power of speech, he called the office.

Phone booths in police stations were a reliable source of trouble for Walter Ganz, who later joined the state department. Once, when he was in a police station phone booth calling in an account of a shooting affray where police had arrested the gunman, Walter suddenly stopped talking.

There was a silence and then the sound of shots. Rewrite man Morrie Rotman suspected the worst.

"Sounds like they're shooting Walter," he shouted, sitting with the receiver glued to his ear in the office.

He was almost right. A loyal friend had burst into the New City police station to liberate his incarcerated pal. His eye fell on Walter in the telephone booth; he seized the hapless reporter, who left the receiver dangling, and shoved him up against the wall with two other people. A policeman, shooting from concealment on a stairway, finally killed the invader but in the uproar the two people standing with Walter against the wall were wounded. Walter himself was unscathed. He returned to the booth and picked up the receiver again. "Now," he said to the unnerved Rotman, "as I was saying before the interruption. . ."

Walter Ganz had peculiar luck in phone booths. On another occasion he was reporting in from a booth in the old DesPlaines street station when a disturbed woman who had been brought in and was being questioned by a desk sergeant suddenly tore off all her clothes and rushed into the phone booth—to call the police, she said. Walter fended her off until three policemen could assist him and then he finished giving the desk his robbery report—on the original nickel.

Odd things could happen to people in their own offices. One late New Year's Eve, when all the drunks were safely home, Wayne Klatt, night editor, was studying copy at the bureau when a very belated boozer stepped into the office and whipped out a .38 caliber police positive revolver. Klatt recognized the visitor as a policeman who had once worked for the bureau. It flashed through the editor's mind that this worker, like many others who had worked the night shift, might at one time have been reproved by Klatt.

The cop, who was out of uniform, steadied himself and pointed his weapon at Klatt's head. His right forefinger could be seen tightening on the trigger. The hammer fell. Then nothing. Only a harmless metallic click.

"Ha!" the fuddled cop said jovially, as he put his gun away. "I bet you thought it was loaded."

Klatt later denied rumors that he had left for home immediately after this episode for sartorial and sanitary reasons.

"I went home at my usual quitting time, four hours later," Klatt said. When he was told that police who had faced revolvers often said that the hole in the barrel looked to them to be about as big as the entrance to Hubbard's cave, he murmured, "There's something in that."

Klatt figured in another episode some years later when several armed men held up an elevated car full of passengers, wild-west fashion. Klatt surrendered his pocket money and his watch. (The police later recovered the watch.) Klatt found himself in an odd position for a newsman: he was the subject of intense questioning by reporters who wanted details of the crime.

> "What were you doing when the bad guys came into the car?"
>
> "I was reading a book," Klatt said. "A novel by Dostoievski."
>
> "A novel. . . *Crime and Punishment!*" cried the pleased reporter.
>
> "No," Klatt said. "It was *Raw Youth.*"
>
> "Aw, come on, Klatt," pleaded one reporter who was an ex-City News man. "Be a good guy. Forget you're an editor. Make it *Crime and Punishment.*"
>
> Klatt relented. After all, he wasn't in the office.
>
> "Okay," he said. "It was *Crime and Punishment.*

The hours after midnight—called "the last watch"—were often dull. To break up the monotony bureau men found the old-fashioned switchboard with its eleven incoming lines a useful tool. They plugged in an open outgoing line and dialed all but the last digit of the phone number of a police station. Then they closed the key on that wire and plugged in another line, dialed the complete number of another police station, closed the key on that second call, opened the key on the first call and dialed the last digit of that number. Then they opened both keys, as phones rang in both police stations.

If things went as they hoped, two desk sergeants would answer similtaneously and, irritated at being awakened, would accuse each other of making an unnecessary call. A heated conversation would follow, while the people listening in at the bureau switchboard shook with suppressed laughter. On one occasion Sgt. Joseph Whitelaw, at a west side station, answered the phone, as was his custom, with, "Warren avenue police. Whitelaw."

He was answered by a sergeant at a south side station, in the heart of the ghetto, "Stanton avenue police. Black law."

In the early 30s, when George Cardinal Mundelein headed the Chicago Catholic archdiocese, the beloved pastor of a large south side congregation in the heart of the steel mill district was transferred to another church. His parishioners were upset. They announced that they would not permit the pastor's successor to enter the church, and on the Saturday night before the new priest's arrival they threw a solid line of protestors—mostly muscular steel workers who believed in direct action—around the church.

The East Side police district commander detailed a sizeable force to the church to keep the peace. City News dispatched Meyer "Mike" Kramer to the scene. Mike was a little man, but he had a lot of spunk.

The new pastor was expected to arrive shortly before dawn on Sunday, in order to avoid the picketers. Mike stayed close to the police as he had been told to do. By the time the sky was reddening in the east everyone was tired and yawning. Mike grew careless and wandered away from the police. Suddenly he was seized roughly from behind and shoved into a large open car: Mike remembers it as a Paige touring car with a torn side curtain. As they rode along the kidnappers debated about what to do with Mike; they appeared to be under the impression that he was some kind of spy. The mildest suggestion was that they "kick him around good." Another suggestion, from an inebriated parishioner with a pistol, was that he be shot in the foot.

"Listen," Mike said urgently. "I'm a reporter. I'm here to hear your side of things." It was the immemorial statement of a reporter caught in a tight place. "Everyone knows what Cardinal Mundelein is saying. Let's get your side into print too."

His eloquence appeared to have an effect upon them. One burly individual suggested tying a lump of slag to his ankle and tossing him into the Calumet river. He was voted down. Eventually Mike was shoved out of the car on Stony Island avenue, and told to get on a streetcar and not to get off until it turned around.

Mike boarded the next car and lingered on the rear platform where he could keep an eye on the Paige which was following it. When the street car passed the Woodlawn police station, Mike leapt frantically off the steps. The movement of the car gave him enough momentum to sprint in through the station doors.

Panting, he explained the situation to the desk sergeant, and then called the bureau. He gave his story to the last watch desk man, who saw Mike's duty clearly.

"You get back there," the desk man said. "This is a good story. We'll show 'em they can't intimidate us."

Mike took a cab to the East Side station, from whence he returned to the church in a squad car. He remained at the side of the police until the new pastor arrived, and walked into the church past the suddenly paralyzed parishioners.

The whole thing was an anti-climax. When Mike phoned in the story the desk man said, "Oh, go on home. What a lousy story."

John "Nicky" Diehl had earned a Phi Beta Kappa key at Yale, but when he went to work at City News right after the second World War, he was given a job running copy on the Cyclograph. The management liked to say, "We've got an honors man from Yale cranking out copy in the back room."

Nicky's big chance came when the police radio in the bureau newsroom announced a robbery taking place at a cigar store less than two blocks from the office. No one else was available, so Nicky was sent to cover the story. He was thin and moved fast; consequently he beat the squads to the scene by several minutes.

The store was surprisingly quiet when he walked in. He did not see any evidence of a hold-up. "Gosh," he said to the people there, who were busy on the phone and off, "We heard a radio call about a robbery here. I guess it's a mistake, but the cops are coming."

Instantly the place came alive. Scratch sheets and racing forms disappeared; people got off the phone immediately. When the law arrived the cigar store gave no sign of being a handbook. Some disgruntled loser, who had obviously hoped to inspire a raid by a false robbery report, had been foiled. Nicky had not learned at Yale that cigar stores in Chicago often do a brisk business in off-track betting.

Eventually Nicky went back east and became an academic.

Difficulties developed inevitably when reporters rushed to the scene. A football hero once achieved fame by scoring a touchdown between the wrong goal posts: Tom Hall, in the same tradition, hurried in a cab to a 4-11 fire on the 6400 block of North Western avenue to find that the blaze was at 6400 South Western avenue. The result was a three hour delay in coverage, and a whale of a cab bill. Bill Juneau driving to another fire in his own car, arrived four hours late. He explained that he had had a small collision with a police car. It was one of those mystery cars, he said. No markings. No siren.

A classic case of an overly conscientious novice was the case of Ed Britt, who came to the bureau fresh from a country weekly newspaper. On his first day at Hyde Park police station the desk gave him a list of coroner's cases of deaths from heart disease and other catastrophes, so that he could make a cursory check on the victims. That was at three p.m. Shortly after that the desk lost touch with him. At three a.m., when he had almost been assigned as a catastrophe himself, he phoned the desk. He had called personally at every home on his list, collected a full obituary, and extended the condolences of the City News Bureau to the bereaved families.

There is a classic Joe Levandier story. Joe was taking a report over the phone from a newsman covering a foundry fire on the west side. Over the reporter's voice Joe could hear the shouts of firemen and the roar and crackle of the flames.

"Joe, I gotta get out of here—the walls are cracking," the reporter shouted.

"Talk fast and finish," Joe said. "You may not find another phone."

Just as the reporter finished, a loud crash echoed through the earpiece, and the phone went dead. Joe, filled with dread and the pangs of conscience, could not concentrate on writing the story.

Half an hour later the reporter called back. Nervously, Joe asked him, "Is it hot where you're calling from now?"

Another fire story centered about Larry Mulay. A three year old girl, the daughter of a Chicago Park District policeman, had disappeared under mysterious circumstances. A neighbor, the mother of two small children, had admitted seeing the tot shortly before she disappeared.

Mulay had been assigned to the case. The next day he called the office and said he was trying to talk to the neighbor but no one appeared to be home. Neighbors had told him they had seen no one leave the house—not even the two children going to school—but she did not answer the door.

The city editor was adamant: "Get into the house if you have to burn the place down," he said.

Shortly after the reporter hung up, a fire alarm sounded in the neighborhood. A bundle of newspapers was burning on the steps before the woman's door. When the firemen smashed down the door, Larry Mulay followed right behind them into the house.

The missing child was found dead in the basement with her throat slashed. Upstairs were the bodies of the two children, killed in the same way, and the mother herself, who had committed suicide.

Larry turned in the grisly story, but he said he didn't know who had turned in the fire alarm.

20

Larry Mulay

In 1964 Isaac Gershman retired, and the sceptre passed to Larry Mulay, who has himself become the stuff of legend. For one thing, he had a germ phobia—an agonizing thing to have in a place like City News. According to William Dillman, someone once described Larry as "the pinnacle of hygiene on the tower of filth." Dillman said he remembered "pouring benzine on Larry's desk and then dropping a match on it. Instant hygiene." If, said Dillman, "you wanted a day off while working for Mulay, all you had to do was sneeze in his face, or pick your nose. If you were really rotten, he would assign you to nights and A.A. Dornfeld."

Michael Garrett reminisced about Larry:

> I was barely past the age of 19 when I first walked into the city room, when it was in the old Ashland block building at Clark and Randolph streets.
>
> If Larry gave it any thought, and if he looked back on his own start in the business, he may have said to himself, 'Copy boys are getting older.'
>
> He would be right, of course, because when Larry was hired on as a copy boy, he was just 14—and, I'm told, he barely reached the top of the city desk.
>
> Over the years Larry probably has trained more young reporters than any other person I have known in my lifetime.
>
> He would not tolerate shoddy reporting or careless writing, and from this many future newspaper executives emerged.

But even more, he was, and still is, a bug on cleanliness. If more were like him, it might eliminate some of the pollution this country faces today.

It was because of this germ phobia of his that I got in trouble with Larry for the one and only time I worked with him in my twenty-two years at City News.

I was only months in my career as a copy boy when it happened. I was on the midnight shift and one of my last tasks was to clean his desk before he walked in.

I had been well instructed about this duty. The top of the desk had to be scrubbed down and I had to make sure the glass plate was free of any particle of lint.

That glass plate, with clear sides and black-coated center, was probably the only one he had ever used.

Needless to say, I was butterfingers that morning and as I picked up the glass to set it in its place it fell out of my hands.

Larry didn't talk to me for a year after that.

Over the years I felt that he had forgotten the incident, but I could never be sure. We never discussed it.

Still, many years later, before I left City News Bureau and joined the *American*, I discovered another side of Larry's makeup.

At eleven one morning I was on rewrite and got stuck with the story of the day—a multiple alarm fire near the Loop where a number of firemen were killed by collapsing walls.

With four reporters at the scene, it was virtually impossible to take notes from them and transcribe them to a running story.

Almost without letup the reporters at the scene kept a phone open and took turns reporting. I didn't leave my typewriter for four hours—and didn't take a single note from them, just kept writing what they reported.

When the cobwebs lifted, I suddenly began to recall little things happening as I kept grinding out the pages.

I kept drinking coffee throughout the entire ordeal. I didn't know where it came from.

I probably ran out of cigarettes several times, but there was a steady supply of my favorite brand. Even my ashtray was kept empty—as I filled it.

Larry never said a word. It wasn't his nature. I learned later that he saw to it that whatever I needed was supplied. I never even thanked him for this—coffee and cigarettes, the lifeline of the newspaperman.

But I do thank Larry now. . .

Larry himself wrote stories which would have been scoops if City News did not have to tell everything to everyone as soon as they found out about it. In 1943 *Editor and Publisher* recounted one of Larry's exploits:

Larry Mulay. . .was supposed to have had last Saturday and Sunday off, but a tip from a friendly public official sent him on the trail of a sensational story, involving the altering of Cook County hospital records to make the apparent suicide of the secretary of a prominent Chicago doctor appear a natural death.

Mulay worked on the story single-handed from Saturday morning until midnight before he was able to bulletin Chicago Sunday papers and follow through with a complete story, which made the late editions of the Chicago *Tribune, Times* and *Herald-American* and also furnished the AP with a clean beat. Mulay doubled in brass in cracking the story, doing a thorough investigative job before notifying Coroner A.L. Brodie, and then covering every possible angle of the involved story concerning the mysterious death of Miss Marjorie Tyler, 28 year old secretary to Dr. Raymond W. McNealy, chief surgeon at Wesley Memorial hospital and chief of the County hospital staff.

The city editor of the City News Bureau started with a vague tip that "a Miss Tyler, connected with a prominent doctor, had died and the cause given was that of heart disease." After getting the inside history of the case, Mulay learned that the girl's body had been embalmed and was about to be shipped to Plano, Ill., the girl's hometown. He also learned by telephoning her father that her mother was in Chicago. He later learned that Dr. Victor G. Lands, resident physician at Wesley Memorial hospital, had taken the girl to County hospital, although the girl's apartment, where she was found, was just across the street from Wesley Memorial. Mulay also discovered that the intern's records at County hospital had been forged, changing the report from gas poisoning to heart disease.

Mulay was endeavoring to reach Coroner Brodie Saturday afternoon. He finally located the coroner, who was taking a steam bath. After giving him the highlights of the case, Mulay went to the girl's apartment and found that the lock on the door had been forced open and that a padlock had been placed on the outside. He questioned occupants of the building and learned they were not aware of Miss Tyler's absence.

Although unable to delay shipment of the body to Plano, Mulay and Coroner Brodie arranged with the coroner in Kendall county to have two Chicago physicians go to Plano for a post-mortem examination of the body.

Mulay broke the story in time for three Chicago Sunday papers to replate and carry two column front page stories in their late editions. The story was also furnished the AP as an exclusive. Mulay finished the story about 3:30 a.m. Sunday. His feat in breaking the story duplicated his scoop while a police reporter for the City News Bureau 18 years ago when he cracked the story on the escape of "Terrible Tommy" O'Connor from the County jail on the eve of his execution. That story also broke on a Sunday morning and Mulay handled all the details by phone and later went to the office and wrote a sixty-four page recap of the story. Mulay has been with the City News Bureau for twenty-four years, the last twelve as city editor.

Today [Nov. 16] the *Herald-American* begins publication of Miss Tyler's diary, entitled "Me", . . .which she wrote as a school thesis while attending Northwestern University. . .

In 1951 *Editor and Publisher* again featured a Mulay story:

A seven-day-old baby's life was saved. . .last week largely through the efforts of Larry Mulay, city editor of the Chicago City News Bureau.

The dramatic story shared front-page honors with the MacArthur welcome when the CNB broke the story about the parents of the baby refusing to allow a blood transfusion. The infant was suffering from an RH blood factor condition. The parents of Cheryl Lynn Labrenz are Jehovah's Witnesses and had objected to transfusions on religious grounds.

Mr. Mulay learned of the baby's critical condition earlier in the week and set in motion a chain of events which eventually led to the judge who ruled the interest of the state in the child's welfare is greater than that of the parents. Judge Robert F. Dunne appointed a guardian to carry out the court order. The baby was removed to another hospital and given a blood transfusion.

From Monday to Wednesday Mulay worked with Dr. Herman Bundesen, city health commissioner, seeking to find a way to save the child's life despite the parents' staunch refusal to permit a blood transfusion.

Mr. Mulay also alerted the state's attorney's office to the situation which led to the assistant state's attorney evoking an old Illinois statute concerning guardianship. The baby's blood count had dropped to a critically dangerous level before the court order was carried out Wednesday afternoon. Milton Golin, CNB assistant city editor, wrote the story furnished Chicago papers.

John Stevenson, who became a copy editor at the *Tribune*, was the legman on the Labrenz story and spent time on it before Larry took it over and carried it to Dr. Bundesen for action. Stevenson always said that it was because Larry was highly respected by the city's medical community that action was taken quickly enough to save the child's life.

Walter Oleksy tells a Larry Mulay story that involves Mike Royko:

> Every morning Larry would have the backroom boy benzine his desk and light a match to it, to burn off any germs that had accumulated from the night man's occupation of it. Then the boy would wash and clean the desk before Mulay arrived.
>
> One morning when Mike Royko was sleepy-eyed, finishing up his stint on the overnight editor shift, he watched while the copy boy performed his strange morning ritual. It was about ten minutes before Mulay was due to arrive. After the boy poured benzine over the desk and set it on fire, then washed and dried it, Royko somehow managed to cut his finger. Possibly it occurred to Mike that nothing is ever wasted at CNB. Whatever his reason, he walked over to Larry's desk, leaned over it and bled on Larry's telephone.
>
> When Mulay arrived he spotted the blood at once and lost his temper immediately. "What kind of people do we have working here?" he cried, in a rage, staring at Royko's innocent face. The copy boy and some cub reporters stood around watching. No one answered. Grumbling, Larry washed the phone off himself, then scrubbed down the desk all over again, poured more benzine on it, and lit it. He was ready to begin his day.

Walter Oleksy also remembers Mike Royko's musical tastes:

> Mike loved Beethoven. When he came on duty as night editor, he would check the WFMT listings and if any Beethoven was on overnight, he'd plan his work schedule around the symphony, concerto, or whatever. When the music would start, he'd tell me not to use my

typewriter and the teletype guy not to use his machine. The copy boy was to tip-toe around and not run the mimeograph machine or make any noise in the back-room. Mike would lay his head on his desk and just listen. The only thing he'd allow to distract him would be a 4-11 alarm on the fire alarm box. He'd have whoever handled the incoming calls disturb him only if it was a big story. When Beethoven was over, Mike would get back to work.

Larry Mulay, incidentally, says that he noticed that Mike had a strong flair for features, and when the *Daily News* took him on, Larry suggested that they try him as a columnist; he had a hunch he would do very well at it.

Mulay went after money-making ideas for the bureau. Although the public relations wire service was instituted under Issac Gershman, Mulay considers it his baby. He built it into a lucrative thing, and he also extended the bureau's service to Northwestern University, and to magazines like *Newsweek, Time* and *US News and World Report*. Mulay is proud to say that he is the only editor and managing director who was ever able to return one dime to the newspapers. Before his time, he says, the bureau was an orphan or bas-tard organization, which was never able to carry any of its own weight.

Mulay's tenure as managing director of the bureau spanned ten revolutionary years, from 1964 to 1974. He ran head on into what might be called the "youth rebellion" of the late '60s which changed many social attitudes in the country, probably for good. Walter Ryberg remembers that reporters had to be clean-shaven and wear suits. Larry Mulay had a deep aversion to beards, and Ryberg himself remembers chiding a teletype operator who came to the office in Ber-muda shorts: that was not proper attire, he told the man, and he should be wearing a necktie too. Bernie Judge recalls that he wore a suit when he was running from the police and from protestors in Grant Park during the Democratic convention in 1968.

It was perhaps inevitable that some disaffected youth would wander into City News and wander out again, to record his jaundiced view of the bureau for posterity. Such a one was Ed Zotti, who wrote an article on City News for the *Reader* in 1976. Zotti had worked for the bureau for three months in 1974. The origins of City News, he said, at least for the purposes of his story, are lost in antiquity: he adds parenthetically that Jim Peneff, who was managing the bureau in 1976, and whom he intended to ask about the bureau's origins, "declined to speak to me, no doubt having an accurate premonition that I intended to write an 'honest' story about his organization."

Zotti had quit another job in December of 1973, had "spent a couple of weeks in Florida visiting friends" and now he "was back in the grey city, and getting a little itchy." He also had "an uncle with clout" who put in a good word for him. His initial interview, he says, "should have given him a clue as to what [he] was getting into." This is a somewhat mysterious remark, which is never fully explained, but he goes on to mention that this interview was with the "bureau's then-general manager, a venerable gentleman who had done work in his day but who was, at that late date in his career (he retired six months later) a little, ahh, out of it." This venerable gentleman was, of course, Larry Mulay, who, says Zotti, treated him "to a long rambling exposition on the place of City News in the history of world events." If he had listened, perhaps Zotti would not have had to phone Jim Peneff to ask about the history of the bureau; it is perhaps indicative of the kind of reporter Zotti was that Peneff "declined" to speak to him.

Mulay told Zotti the story of the bureau's scoop on Pearl Harbor, and Zotti comments graciously in his article: "Some months later, after observing the bureau's propensity for running stories on the basis of no facts at all, it occurred to me that only City News would bulletin a story they'd gotten by phone on a Sunday morning from some crackpot with a three-tube RCA Victor." The "crackpot" was, of course, a veteran City News reporter with an expensive short-wave radio. To Zotti, 1941 would have been in the age of the crystal set.

Mulay also told Zotti that "City News had trained a lot of famous reporters"—however, Zotti says, he later learned that "Yellow Kid" Weil, a "successful confidence man of the '30s" had been "another of the bureau's famous alumni," a fact which apparently negated all the others. Mulay then suddenly asked Zotti whether he had ever been a member of the SDS, or had participated in a demonstration. Zotti mumbled "something noncommittal like 'not lately,' " and was told to get a haircut and sent on his way. He had applied for the job in "blue jeans and a raggy old lumber jacket", having placed his faith in "the power of clout," which, not surprisingly, did not work in this instance. Apparently the venerable gentleman could still see.

After three months of unemployment Zotti threw in the towel and got a haircut and what he calls "some clothes" and went back and was hired.

The haircut was traumatic enough to warrant three paragraphs of discussion.

His five day training period he found enjoyable, because he worked with reporters his own age or just a little older with backgrounds similar to his. But after that he was on his own, and he hated it—not the hours or the pay, or even the fact that he "wasn't good at being a reporter." He was offered no balm by the bureau—no gossip with fellow reporters, no sympathy from the desk:

> You are subjected to the quirks of demented deskmen, who want to know the color of the murder victim's underwear and the name of his orthodontist, and who think every staticky squawk they hear over the police radio means another body in the lake.

Checking out coroner cases he found unappealing:

... it is the delightful task of the City News reporter to call up the grieving relatives and ask them, as subtly as possible, if the departed was important enough to write a story about. Almost without exception he was not. The idea behind this, as far as I could tell, was that the bureau would find out in case somebody like Nelson Rockefeller croaked incognito while visiting his relatives who lived in a bungalow on Archer Avenue next to the body and fender shop. It was without question one of the most inane, barbaric, intensely mortifying jobs ever conceived.

Sometimes you got to call up relatives who didn't know little Johnny was dead yet.

Toward the end of his three months at the bureau, Zotti says he was getting "pretty insubordinate," so he was constantly being assigned to south side police as punishment. He finally told himself that if he was assigned to the south side one more time he would quit. He was, and he did. He did not want to be a reporter anyway. So he tore up the pages of his notebook into small pieces and stuffed the spiral binding into a trash can. He had had enough of "guys getting killed with nails driven through their hearts. Little kids getting stabbed and stuffed in garbage cans. Women getting raped in the motorman's compartment of subway trains by sex-crazed ex-CTA employees." And the final touch: "All happening at once, a half-hour before your shift is supposed to end."

Worse than anything else to Zotti, however was the fact that the newspaper job market was bad, and the "purgatorial period" at the bureau could stretch out "to two, three or even four years." Bernie Judge told him that he hired only "one reporter from City News during his two-year tenure at the *Tribune.*"

Zotti's comment that the bureau runs stories "on the basis of no facts at all" might gain support because City News material, when it is printed in the newspapers, does not carry a logotype, like AP or UPI. About the only time the existence of City News is acknowledged publicly by the newspapers—barring anniversaries and deaths—is when, despite its strivings for accuracy, the bureau sends out an incorrect story. The papers which printed the story then usually run retractions, which end: "The erroneous information was supplied by the City News Bureau." People who read several such retractions, and never see the bureau mentioned in any other context, probably assume that the City News Bureau exists only for the purpose of making mistakes.

And some public figures use City News as a convenient scapegoat for their own errors. A news item to this effect appeared in the *Tribune* on October 4, 1979, the day scheduled for the arrival of the Pope in Chicago:

> An erroneous radio report Wednesday that Pope John Paul II's visit to Chicago had been cancelled resulted in a flurry of telephone calls and some red faces.
>
> Steve Dahl, a disc jockey at WLUP-FM began it all while reading news reports of the Pope's visit to New York City. Dahl was "joshing" when he announced the pontiff's visit to Chicago would cause no troubles because it had been cancelled, said Les Elias, station general manager.
>
> Elias said Dahl immediately told the audience the announcement was false, but Mayor Byrne's office reported three dozen telephone calls on the special hotline for the Pope's visit.
>
> Officials at City News Bureau said two of their employees heard WLUP erroneously attribute the report to City News, which supplies information to newspapers and radio and TV stations. City News demanded a retraction from WLUP and the station later apologized to the mayor's office and the news service.

In a sense, Hecht and MacArthur addressed themselves to the same point as Ed Zotti, when they put into Hildy Johnson's mouth in *The Front Page* the words:

You steal pictures off old ladies of their daughters that got raped in Oak Park. And what for? So a million shopgirls and motormens wives can get their jollies. And the next day, somebody's wrapping that front page, with your deathless prose on it around a dead mackerel.

This point was raised by Harrison Salisbury in a Public Broadcasting System panel discussion of *Front Page* journalism. Other members of the panel were Herman Kogan, Mike Royko and Clayton Kirkpatrick, all veterans of the City News Bureau. Herman Kogan commented that Ben Hecht always talked about today's newspaper being what you wrap tomorrow's herring in. At City News, Kogan said, there were of course no reasons to steal pictures, but the picture-stealing mentality obviously existed at the bureau. Mike Royko commented on that: it was that attitude, the crossing of "certain ethical lines in order to get the story" that achieved certain reforms. One of the most telling examples was Seymour Hersh's war reporting:

I just read Sy Hersh's account. . .of how he got the My Lai story. And, of course, Sy was a City Press reporter. And I was delighted when I read it, to see that one of the really most important news stories of our time. . .developed just the way you'd go after a good local story. He just went from point to point in the country, chasing down every lead, used a few side-door tricks, a little con when he needed it, and a tremendous amount of aggressiveness. And that's really what that tradition is about. And he wasn't doing it because he was on any type of personal cause against the war, he was doing it because that was a good story and he wanted to get that story. And I think. . .that's an important part of Chicago journalism is getting the story because that's your job and you want to do it well; and you're aggressive rather than having any personal axe to grind.

All the newsmen agreed that the gathering of news was a little more responsible than it had been in the *Front Page* era. Harrison Salisbury said that he had been told by a reporter named Bobby Laughren, who worked at the UP in Chicago at the same time as Salisbury, that Laughren had a tip that Mayor Cermak was going to be assassinated on the steps of City Hall. The tip came from a reliable gangland source. Laughren made plans to be present when the assassination occurred. He planned to leave the office on a break, and keep open a phone line to Salisbury in the UP office from a tobacco store which was right across the street from City Hall. He foresaw a world-wide UP scoop. He was consequently very upset when Cermak was shot in Miami.

It never occurred, Salisbury said, either to him or to Laughren that they had any obligation to warn the mayor. Everyone agreed that if the situation were to come up now, the mayor would be warned. But in the '20s and '30s the name of the game was crime; as Walter Ryberg says, if there were no crime news in those days there would have been almost no news. A divorce was news then; an automobile collision was news. Because possibly of the bigger picture in reporting, reporters themselves have a larger view of events, and this inevitably has made them less irresponsible.

As an example of the bad old days, Mike Royko recalled something that Buddy McHugh had done. When Roger Touhy was killed in Chicago, Royko was a bureau reporter who reached the scene and checked out all the surrounding buildings. A group of newsmen went door to door in all the buildings, interviewing everyone. And Royko himself went into the basements of all the buildings. The next day Buddy McHugh had an enormous exclusive in the Hearst paper: he said he had found the place where the assassins had waited for Roger Touhy. There were photographs of the place, a basement, the floor littered with cigarette butts.

Royko had been in the basement after the shooting. And there had been no cigarette butts there then.

21

Criticism

Another young reporter who viewed the bureau with a critical eye is Greg Small, who is now in the Honolulu bureau of the Associated Press. Small worked at City News from May of 1974 to March of 1977. He was the next to last reporter hired by Mulay before his retirement. He noted some differences between the way in which Mulay operated and the way in which Peneff operated.

Mulay's office, which was in the southeast corner of the building, had an unused air. "The furnishings were old and worn," says Small, "but the room looked more like a stage set than like an office used every day." This impression was later confirmed for Small by bureau veterans, who said that Mulay spent most of his time in a partitioned area with some older employees who, it was assumed, handled accounts and payroll and so on. Peneff, on the other hand, spent most of his time in the corner office with the door closed. Bureau veterans told Small that Mulay came into the newsroom to take charge of really big stories, but that Peneff never did that. Small, after his police assignment, worked most of the time in the newsroom as rewrite or radio desk editor and he recalls that Peneff did come into the newsroom a few times.

Small noted another area of difference between the two managers. Mulay told him during his initial interview that he preferred to hire college graduates who had majored in English, or in political science and history, rather than in journalism. He said, "English majors know how to write *a* sentence, and political science majors know what *a* fact is, but journalism majors don't seem to know much about anything." Small noted this, because he was himself a political science major. Peneff seemed to hire only journalism majors. Small came to think, after working at the bureau for a while, that it made no difference what the cub had majored in. The personality of the individual was all-important. Both journalism and non-journalism majors succeeded or failed at the bureau depending upon how well they were able to handle the demands upon them.

At the time that Small was there, the city newspapers were not hiring CNB graduates, who were going to the wire services, radio and television stations and out-of-town or out-of-state newspapers. The Chicago newspapers were hiring journalism majors who had just graduated from school. Those graduates whom the papers did not want were told to go to City News for training. When Small left, there were said to be 2000 active applicants on file at the bureau. During his three years, he remembers only one CNB reporter landing a job with Chicago papers: this was Mike Powers, who had City Hall, the premier beat at the bureau. He was hired as a legman for *Tribune* columnist Jack Mabley.

Three incidents stay in Small's mind. One involved a faulty elevator in the 188 W. Randolph street building. Paul Zimbrakos sent Small to find out about it: he watched as firemen pried open the doors to the elevator shaft and lowered a ladder into the car. The occupants climbed out, shaken but unhurt. They said the car had suddenly dropped from under them and fallen three floors before its automatic braking system was activated. Small's story which said that the elevator had "plunged" three floors, was taken by Zimbrakos to Peneff—an unheard of step. According to Small, Peneff never read copy before it went out. Peneff then summoned Small, and went over the story with him, questioning the use of the word "plunged". When Small defended it, Peneff sent him to show the story to the building's owner, who was somewhat put out that the story was being written at all. Finally a compromise of sorts was reached: when the story went out over the wire, the elevator was said to have "descended rapidly"; it had not "plunged".

On another occasion City News ran a story about someone who had walked along a north side street smashing car windows as he went. Police arrested a teenage suspect and identified him as an employee of an auto glass repair shop. The next day the attorney for the glass shop called Zimbrakos and insisted that the teenager was not employed there. He asked for a retraction. Zimbrakos assigned Small to investigate: as it turned out, it was the stepfather of the suspect who worked at the shop, not the suspect, and the stepfather paid the teenager a few dollars to clean up now and then. Small dutifully wrote this down, and Zimbrakos suggested he talk to the attorney about it. The attorney did not care for this version of events, either, and spoke to Zimbrakos, who consulted Peneff. The correction was sent out saying that the police had given CNB misinformation. The suspect was not an employee of the shop.

On the third occasion, the bureau sent out a story on a multimillion dollar lawsuit that had been filed in Chicago against one of the two daily newspapers. Reporter Ronni L. Scheier had written the story about the suit, which had been filed by a man involved in the California assassination attempt on Gerald Ford, against newspapers which had reported he was a homosexual. The suit stated that his sexual preferences had been private, and he had suffered because of this revelation. Ronni's story was edited and sent out by night editor Wayne Klatt. The next day Zimbrakos and Peneff were again closeted, and a KILL was sent out on the story because it was inaccurate. But no corrected story was sent out. The inaccuracy lay, apparently, in the statement in the story that the Chicago suit was the first to be filed. It was not the first suit. The young reporters surmised that this story was embarrassing to the Chicago daily, and was killed for that reason.

"Criticizing City News was one of our favorite pastimes as reporters," Small says. There was resentment about the pay, which they considered ridiculously low, about the heavy workload, and about desk decisions which they thought ill-advised. There was also resentment, according to Small, over the bureau's Scrooge-like attitude toward reporter's illnesses. "We had to put up with Paul moaning and groaning each time one of us would call in sick," Small says. "There was so much psychological pressure that we made it into the office any way we could, no matter what our condition may have been." Small himself went to work after a wisdom tooth extraction, looking as though he had a baseball stuck in his cheek.

Like Zotti, Small disliked the practice of calling the bereaved to find out if the deceased were worth a story. "It didn't matter if the dead person's address was Skid Row," Small says. "Calls had to be made before the story could be 'cheapened out'. (Any happening is a story, but one that isn't worth writing about is 'cheap'.) More psychological stress, because children die too. And fetuses are born dead, and the death is reported to the coroner. When I asked Wayne how a dead fetus could possibly be worth a story, he told me to call the home to find out if the father was important enough to warrant a story."

Small resented also the fact that City News reporters were responsible for all the news in Chicago and major stories in Cook County, and that they were criticized often for missing something that had been picked up by a veteran reporter who had had the luxury of covering far fewer stories. And the help that he was given was not by veteran bureau workers, Small says:

> The teaching that goes on at City News is provided by the more experienced young reporters, not the "lifers". Gene Grant taught me how to cover coroner cases, Mike Powers taught me how to edit radio wire copy, Greg MacArthur taught me how to get quotes and how to use the teletype machine. And in my turn, I taught Sal

Cinquegrani, Price Patton and others. We all helped each other survive City News.

The clue to some of the difficulties Small encountered perhaps lies in his statement:

I used to sit in the newsroom at City News and think, 'We're kids. We're just a bunch of kids.'

The "kids" had to cope with bureau stories of international significance during the sixties: the West side riots, the 1968 Democratic National Convention, and the resultant Conspiracy trial; states attorney Edward Hanrahan's raid on the Black Panther's Chicago apartment and its tragic aftermath... More recently and on a somewhat lighter note Paul Zimbrakos points out that it was the bureau which released the story of Nancy Reagan's reference at a Chicago fund-raiser in February, 1980, to "all these beautiful white people." No local papers covered the speech so it was CNB's story which made national news.

22

More of the Same

When Larry Mulay retired in June 1974, after fifty-five years at the bureau, he was succeeded by Jim Peneff, who had not come up through the ranks of the bureau as earlier managers had. A tradition was broken with Peneff, who had been at City News in 1944, and had then gone to the *Sun-Times* (then the *Sun*) where he had spent thirty years, rising to the post of city editor.

Peneff brought the bureau into line with current newspaper practice by increasing coverage of labor-management disputes, consumer problems and various other matters previously considered too controversial for the bureau to handle. In addition, Peneff extended the geographical area of coverage, which had formerly been limited to Cook county except in "list" stories, to most of northern Illinois. A copy desk was set up to winnow out errors from the bureau's writers; previously this had been an additional burden for the deskmen. And salaries were raised again.

In the summer of 1982 City News left 188 W. Randolph St., where it had been for thirty-two years, and moved to larger more modern quarters at 35 E. Wacker Dr.

The big story of the Tylenol murders broke just after the bureau moved to their new quarters. They were covered for the bureau by John Flynn Rooney, Ed Rooney's son:

> On Wednesday night, September 29, 1982, I was working in the press room at police headquarters [11th

257

and State]. At about 10:30 p.m. my editor, Dianne Banis, called me and asked me to check on a medical examiner's case from Arlington Heights. I had already placed a call to Northwest Community hospital, so I waited for them to return my call. The hospital public relations director returned my call about 11:30 p.m. to tell me that the case I had originally called about was a death from natural causes. I asked her about the Janus case, and she immediately read me a long press release. I asked her about the circumstances of the deaths of the two brothers and she said that the medical examiner was investigating them. I called the medical examiner's office and was told that the investigation was still going on.

I called Dianne Banis back at midnight and told her what was going on, before she left for the night. "Sounds like a good story," she said. I began to call the neighbors of the Janus family and all any of them could tell me was that the house had been sealed off. I called the Arlington Heights police, and they confirmed that the house had been sealed off by the medical examiner's office. Earlier in the evening I had called the Elk Grove Village police to ask about the death of 12-year-old Mary Kellerman. They said they were awaiting the result of an autopsy to determine the cause of death.

At about one in the morning I received a call from the midnight editor Rick Baert. He had just received an anonymous call from someone at Passavant hospital who attributed three deaths on the 29th to tainted Tylenol. He asked me to start checking all over again. I called back the hospital with the new information and pleaded with the nursing supervisor to give me any information which she had. She said she knew nothing about the Tylenol theory. I called the police department again, to be told the medical examiner was still investigating. Again I called the medical examiner's office: they were still not ready. By the time I went home at 2:30 a.m. I was beginning to think the whole thing was a hoax.

When I heard the news later that morning I realized the "hoax" was a nightmare, and the nightmare was real.*

In March 1983 Jim Peneff retired and his place was taken by Bernie Judge, who had spent 1965 as a bureau reporter and had gone to the *Tribune*, rising to city editor. Moving into the computer age, City News plans to put on line in 1983 its new state of the art Atex Text processing system with 18 in-office video display terminals and five portable terminals for beat reporters.

"With computers," Peneff says, "we can send new copy to the *Tribune*, the *Sun-Times* and our other clients at speeds up to 1200 words a minute compared with the old 75 w.p.m. rate. These other clients include the major wire services, as well as 30 odd radio and TV stations in the area. Copy backup will be all but eliminated."

Bernie Judge says that CNB is like "a college newspaper run by grown-ups" and that there is a strong sense of community among graduates of the bureau. Many national media people, he says, had their training at CNB and numerous Chicago assignment editors were CNB trained. One of the most noticeable benefits of the bureau is the quality of news broadcasting in Chicago, he says. "CNB is the reason Chicago TV news is more professional than TV news in other cities, where there's a dearth of lead-news and where each news staff has to develop its own, with a few stringers helping out."

Charles McKelvy gives a relevant story from a bureau worker:

It was three p.m. on a slow news Sunday afternoon— seventy-six, I believe—when a messenger arrived from a TV newsroom with a press release embargoed for 9:58 p.m. The station's political reporter had uncovered a big

* For the first time in its history, City News entered a contest and won the prize: the Peter Lisagor Award (which it shared with AP of Chicago) for the Tylenol story.

scandal in the Governor's office, and he must've thought City News was such a rookie operation that we couldn't touch his story. But we had the last laugh on him. Our city editor had his own sources in the Governor's office, and we not only recovered the entire scoop in a couple of hours, we came up with a whole new angle on the story. We put our story on the news and broadcast wires at nine-thirty that night and ran his on the PR wire at 9:58—just the way he ordered. Of course the other TV stations picked up our story and ran it on their ten o'clock news shows. Jeez, was he mad. But it served him right. He never worked at City News.

McKelvy distributed a survey at a gathering of more than one hundred City News alumni, asking whether they believed City News was important to the Chicago editorial community and whether their training there was helpful to them in their present positions.

Twenty of them responded [McKelvy says] and they expressed strong support for City News. All but two stated there was a continued need for City News. Sixteen said they learned more about reporting and writing at City News than in school and eighteen said that City News training was helpful to them in their present positions. Respondents included reporters and editors at Chicago's two remaining dailies, UPI, AP, Chicago's three network television affiliates, business people, a public-relations consultant and a freelance writer.

Some criticized the bureau for not teaching the cubs to write. They had found that if you wanted to learn to write, you had to leave the bureau. Jim Peneff's response is that "City News, despite all the stories you hear, is *not* a finishing school or a training ground. . . We expect our people to know how to write when they get here."

On the question of the value of the bureau to newspapers, McKelvy quotes Marti Ahern, a former City News reporter who went into the assignment class at WBBM-TV and then to WLS-TV.

If it wasn't for City News...every newsroom in this
city would have to double and in some cases triple its
staff to be able to cover the amount of news that City
News puts out every day. If there was no City News, the
news media coverage in this city would be a lot more
shallow and incomplete and the "little stories" that
sometimes come to light through City News would
never see the light of day.

There are few organizations like the bureau. There is a City
News service in Los Angeles, which was established in the
twenties. Its coverage is similar to City News. The Bay City
News Service was established in San Francisco in 1979 covering nine counties in the Bay area. In the Chicago area there
is Community News Service set up by Earl Bush and Herbert
Brin in order to cover news for weekly community and suburban newspapers and the *Defender* in the same way that
City News covers the city. Brin went to California in 1947
and Bush worked full time servicing 50 newspapers. Community News was the first service to supply news to the radio
stations; gradually City News pre-empted that service. Bush
says:

...in 1954 the Chicago newspapers put me out of the
(radio) business. They initially refused to permit the
radio stations to subscribe to the...City News Bureau
which covered the basic beats for them and provided
pooled election coverage...But as station after station
subscribed to my service...the publishers offered the
complete CNB service to radio and TV stations at half
my price. I had 20 employees and operated 18 hours a
day, six days a week. City News had more than 100
employees and operated 24 hours a day. After I was out
of the business, the publishers boosted the price.

Bush became press secretary to Mayor Daley in 1955 and
Max Sonderby took over Community News which he still
operates.

Finally we can give the podium to Paul Zimbrakos, city editor of the bureau, who has been there since 1958:

> Our methods of training have not changed much over the years, and, according to those who have gone on successfully, it does not need to.
>
> However, those who worked at CNB when the tubes were still being used had a slight advantage. In those days everyone started as a copy person.
>
> The advantage was that as a copyperson in the office, they were able to learn about style, procedures, could read the copy and talk to the writers and editors. Thus when they went out on the street they knew what went into a story, knew what the office wanted, had a "beat book" filled with important telephone numbers and, to avoid being relegated back to cranking out copy, really hustled for the stories.
>
> Now when a person is hired, he or she is put right on the street to begin training.
>
> The recruit is put out one week with other reporters to work the three police beats: north, south and central. After that they are on their own, under the stern and watchful eyes of the rewrite staff and editors.
>
> Although the pay is meager, there is no college or university that can teach a journalism student how to talk to a hardened homicide detective or tough desk sergeant, or do the legwork necessary to put together a story like CNB can. It is tough, like basic training in the military, but important in the making of a good journalist.
>
> Once on the street, the apprentice is watched closely for accuracy...is told what else is needed for the story... and told who else to call. Sometimes they must make two or three calls to one source to get additional information.
>
> The basic assignments are given out by the city desk, but the reporters also have an established "beat check" that they are required to make at least twice on a normal night, by telephone.

The normal route of progress is police reporter, re-write, and then department reporter. The departments are City Hall, County, State, Federal, Education, Circuit courts and Criminal courts. It is essential that each person get writing training and experience before working a department beat because there all stories are dictated. Unlike the police beats where the facts are turned in and writers put the stories together. The top beats are the State of Illinois building, the Federal building, and City Hall.

Some of the better people also get a taste of editing.

CNB has never closed, so the staffers can expect to work days, nights, overnight, holidays, and weekends during their stints.

There is only one time that I can recall our front door being closed and that was only for a short while in the early morning hours. We identified the main character in a story as a nephew of a Chicago Bears football star. The football player heard the story on the radio and called the office to demand the story be corrected. . . because he was not related to the man in the story. The editor on duty called me at home and said the gridiron star told him that if the story was not corrected he would come to the office and straighten the story out himself.

"What should I do?" the editor asked me.

"Set the phone down," I said, "and go shut the door. Lock it, and then put out his correction."

By the way, the wrong information had been supplied to us by the police.

I am frequently asked to say whether our past reporters were better than our present ones. There is no way I can say. We have had outstanding people throughout our history—witness how far former CNBers have progressed, both in the old days and now.

I can say, though, that those hired nowadays are less patient than those in the past. After a few months on the street they feel they are ready to go on to better things, even though in many cases they have not received all the training available to them at CNB.

The refrain I hear almost unanimously from former CNBers is that the discipline and training they received with us was an invaluable tool they were able to use toward their success.

The bureau has been treated recently as a source of official news for the city. Jane Byrne, when she was mayor called CNB to announce that she and her husband were moving into the Cabrini-Green housing projects. This story, which also made national news, originated with City News, as did another story when, on February 14, 1980, called the bureau at 2:25 a.m. to say that there was going to be a firemen's strike. And when Mayor Byrne removed bodyguards from the family of former Mayor Michael Bilandic, his wife Heather came herself to the CNB offices to give a statement.

Let's return for a moment to that bullet-splashed saloon in Beirut, where we left some journalists talking about the old days at the bureau. The blonde from Philadelphia is murmuring,

" 'The more things change, the more they remain the same.' Its almost five o'clock. . . What time it is in Chicago right now?"

"About eight a.m.," someone says.

"Eight o'clock," the wire service man says. "The day side editor is probably yelling at the last watch desk man for leaving something out of the court case schedule. . . Something really important, like 'Smithson Larceny. Stole shoe laces. Felony Court. 11 a.m.' "

"Yeah," says the man in the burnous. "And the north man is typing out an excuse about why he missed that big story about the chop shops. He'll say that Sergeant Peesnayvitch gave an exclusive to the *Tribune* because his son works there as a copyboy. That's the way I always did it."

In the general chatter, the blonde reporter says thoughtfully, "When they're computerized, I hope that machine can spell real well. New people at City News always have trouble spelling words with more than four letters."

Appendix

The following is the style book given to reporters at Saylor and Leckie's bureau.

A Reporter's Note-Book.

Compiled with special reference to the
requirements of the City Press
Association of Chicago
1897.

Introductory

The reporter's note book is a fiction clung to by the layman and for brief periods converted into a reality as new men find corners in the local room. Beyond the first few days of the young reporter the notebook does not exist—in actual practice there is no such thing. The style of newspaper work in the United States is due, in no small measure to this, and it would be hard to imagine anything more antagonistic to everything the American appreciates and demands in his paper than the English idea of dependency on the note book. The reporter of today uses his memory, with the assistance only of a shirt cuff, the back of an envelope or a business card as a record of names and dates.

In consequence, the title of this pamphlet will at first glance be misleading, but it is a "note book" nevertheless, and one which some experience at the copy desk indicates will come amiss neither to the veteran nor to the novice, for whose use it was originally designed.

In preparing the matter contained in its pages, an effort has been made to call attention only to those errors most frequently found in reportorial copy. The list of these is by no means complete, but a careful reading of those presented will do much, it is believed, to raise the standard of copy. Many of the suggestions seem almost ridiculous, but they touch on forms of carelessness that are common and all the more objectionable by reason of this.

I

A Few Guide Posts.

It should not be necessary to warn the beginner that the hints given refer only to the formation of a general style. He is not the judge of what is to be printed in the paper on which he is employed, and his first duty is to study the requirements of his employers and write his matter in a vein consonant with the ideas that have been adopted without his views having been consulted. As a base, a plain, but forceful, style should be acquired and little difficulty will then be encountered in coloring it to meet any exigency.

Intelligent, individual action, necessary as it is, must always be subject to the equal necessity of informing your office of developments in the news field. Important news events must invariably be reported to the office at once. Remember that the individual reporter is but a portion of one machine, the parts of which must act in concert. Do not absent yourself without informing your city editor of your whereabouts. The telephone removes all excuse for such action. This should be carried so far as to urge upon you, after having received a day assignment the previous night, to report to "the desk" that you have actually started upon the work. Another point too often overlooked is that it benefits your office little that you have a good and complete story if you do not get it in. Singular as it may seem, reporters have been known to fall back on the statement: "That messenger must have gone to sleep." Your responsibility ceases only after the copy is in the city editor's hands and you have been told that no additional information is needed from you.

Read the newspapers. No reporter can enter on a day's work and do justice to his office and himself unless he is prepared to handle any assignment intelligently. He should be conversant not only with the local news from commerce and finance to sports, but he should know what Congress is doing and what events of interest are taking place in other parts of the United States and the world. He should be able to talk intelligently, if not profoundly, on British politics and make proper distinction between Count Kalnoky and Premier Sagaska. Above all he should never be led into the constantly set trap to induce him to write as news something that has been printed weeks or months before. Don't say you have no time to read the papers. Take time or prepare for a brief newspaper career.

Old reporters do not assume any special privileges or license by reason of their craft and they rarely attract attention to themselves by demanding any other treatment than that accorded to any gentleman in search of information. The man is not necessarily the most competent reporter who imagines the open sesame to all privacy is the phrase "I am a reporter." The glamour that once hung over the reporter of the pseudo Bohemian days of newspaper work has long since faded and the most useful successor to the old school is the tireless, politely persistent young man who makes news gathering a profession. Remember always that the newspaper writer is in no sense different from any other gentleman and that his duty to himself demands that his bearing shall be such that he will be welcomed a second time in any office or home. Firmness and a recognition of the privileges and conventions assigned to the modern newspaper are not to be elaborated into insolence. The amateurish explanation of the policy of his paper is always in bad taste and no experienced reporter will attempt to explain at what the paper for which he is working aims or means to do. In the first place he rarely knows what is going on in the managing editor's room, and if he goes further than his immediate work is concerned, it is none of his business. Anything else is presumption, and it will be quite sufficient if he simply takes advantage of what he may know of the inside plans of his office and shapes his work accordingly. Let the paper speak for itself, so far as you are concerned, and never, under any circumstances, entertain those with whom you may have business with pretentious talk of what "we" propose doing.

The men who collect news in remote districts and suburban towns lying within the local news field are not the less reporters because they are not so frequently seen in the office. Their work is of special importance in that they are usually the links uniting their territory with their office. Not only must they get the news, but they must take the place of fire alarm signals, police reports and many other mediums through which news "tips" reach an office. Since those who are responsible for the securing of news always like to shape and direct its preparation from the start, it follows that the greatest value of a "suburban" or "country" reporter is the celerity with which he acquaints his office with the news of his district. He cannot too quickly notify his office of promising matter. There should be prompt notification of anything out of the ordinary. To do this by mail should be a last resource. The telegraph, except where the service is special and extensive, means frequently long delay. The quick and sure method is the telephone where it is available. A good man at each end of the telephone wire will dispose of brief and ordinary matter while copy is being made for the telegraph. Even if the telephone is used only to transmit a bulletin, personal communication is infinitely better than a telegram.

II
Getting Up Copy.

The question of what constitutes news has been discussed from every standpoint with results more or less satisfactory. A general definition which for present purposes will suffice is, "News is the earliest presentation of an occurrence which is of the greatest interest to the greatest number of readers." In the newspaperman there is an intuitive appreciation of news value, largely governed by local circumstances, only one of which, however, is outside the general rule laid down. That circumstance may be debatable, but it is generally accepted and a competent reporter, his first duty being to obey instructions, will measure his story largely by the office standard: "Is it exclusive?" According to the general rule the story worth 200 words if possessed by competitors is swollen to a front page display for a column and turn when it is measured by this special circumstance of "Is it exclusive?"

The value of a story after all depends much on the writer. The reader, untrained in such matters, will frequently decline to become vitally interested in an event, no matter how many novel features it may present, or how great its latent interest, unless these are made prominent and his attention skilfully and quickly directed to them by the reporter who prepares the story. On skill in this direction, more, perhaps, than any other one thing, depends the success of the newspaper writer.

The story obtained, the first problem to be confronted is the opening paragraph which even to the veteran reporter assumes proportions that become more formidable as the importance of the story increases. But on this paragraph depends in a great degree the success of the article. In events of the greatest importance when simple dignity of expression is imperative, there is little choice: "Chicago was destroyed by fire yesterday." "President James A. Garfield was assassinated at 3 o'clock this afternoon." Such events require no elaboration or introduction and any effort in that direction would be as brilliant as the artist's essay to paint the lily. In the narrative of more commonplace occurrences, however, graphic opening sentences are permissible, even desirable, if used with judgement. It must be borne in mind, though, that the opening of a story must be as honest as the headlines. Do not promise the reader a sensation your story does not fulfill, and do not exaggerate for the purpose of attracting attention. An account of a fire undoubtedly increases in interest with the amount of loss; an accident with the number killed or injured, and a murder with the uniqueness of the details or the prominence of the victim, but to falsify facts to bring these conditions about is the cheapest sort of journalism and a style not to be the less avoided because it happens to be just at present somewhat in fashion. The beginning of a story usually sets forth these important details, but they should not be distorted in an effort to secure a striking introduction, and even if the story afterward tells the truth, the reader is apt to resent the misleading first lines as an affront to his intelligence.

As a suggestion of how not to begin a story it is well to remember that inversion no longer shows originality, and to begin by writing, "Stunned and bleeding, James Smith----," or "Crushed beyond recognition, the body of----," is to use a feeble artifice. The briefer the item the more conventional must necessarily be the beginning of it, but hackneyed phrases such as, "As a result of a street car accident----" ought to be avoided when possible.

In preparing your matter, be careful to continue the conservative policy outlined. If necessary to speculate, draw a distinct line between surmises and the statements of fact. Do not mislead the reader in this direction nor indulge in speculations which your judgement indicates are improbable. The care devoted to your work in news gathering will tell in your copy. Complete information on the part of the writer, plainly and concisely placed before the reader, is much better than the wild, florid narrative of the "genius" who will not trouble himself with the work of research. Of course your story must be well told and style is almost as important as information. The proper combination marks the valuable man.

Because the afternoon papers do not go to press until after 2 o'clock is no reason why you should allow copy to accumulate in your possession until that hour. The combined efforts of a score of reporters exerted in this direction will "swamp" any existing force of copy readers or compositors. A ten line item at 10 o'clock in the morning from each of twenty men means a column disposed of before the "rush" hour, and by preparing a few pages of copy at the earliest possible moment you will materially aid the office. In very few instances will you find it necessary to delay writing until you have collected all the details of your story. A little ingenuity and care will generally permit you to submit your matter even when its full value may depend on the finale. In this case, of course, your copy must be marked: "Lead to follow." Reporters have too little idea of the value of time and of the men who economize it. This necessity for prompt work is particularly the portion of the afternoon newspaper, but the application of the same principle to morning paper work will readily be seen.

To hasten this dispatch of copy, it is desirable to write it in sections or "takes." When doing so, mark the first section or "take," "Lead—Snell Murder." At the end of this "take"—at the bottom of the last page—write this, "(more)." The second "take" must be marked "1st Add Snell Murder" and closed with, "(more)." Number your copy by pages consecutively and do not begin renumbering with each "take."

In many cases it is necessary to sacrifice everything but accuracy to speed. On such occasions it is necessary to tolerate poor copy. But the reporter who can combine neatness with dispatch is a valuable man. Generally speaking, too little attention is paid to the preparation of copy. It is no mark of genius to possess a chirography as illegible as that of Horace Greeley. It only requires care and persistence to cultivate a plain, neat style.

Having notified the office of an important piece of news, do not assume that the information you have supplied will be written in the office. Get specific instructions at the time how you are to handle the story.

Never, unless you are so instructed to do so, write an "add" to a story of which you have not yourself written the "lead." Do not assume that some one else is writing a "lead."

Having turned in a story, and discovering later that it contains an error, notify the office at once. When you write a new version of an incomplete story, be certain that you call attention to it. Failure to do so may lead to duplication.

Ordinarily when uninstructed as to space, do not "pad." With the amount of news matter now available, condensation is the general rule. Your judgement, based on a study of your paper's style, must be your guide. The story which tends to uphold an editorial policy of your paper may be worth columns to it while its value to another newspaper might be but a few lines.

If you cannot write plainly and neatly, by all means learn to use the typewriter: it is a good idea to master this useful machine in any event. Unfortunately the typewriter is not so constructed as to aid in composition. It is even easier to leave out a word or letter when using the machine than when the pencil is employed, and this is only a reason why more care should be used and why every reporter, whether he uses the machine or not, should read his copy carefully before submitting it.

In newspaper work, the best period, or full stop, is a small cross, thus, x. Where it is possible to mistake the letters, mark the "u" with a dash beneath and the "n" with a dash above.

Denote a new paragraph by indenting the first word of it. If you have failed to do so in the hurrying of composition, use this mark to distinguish the place where the paragraph should begin,

It is well to end a paragraph at the bottom of a page whenever possible. If you make a paragraph at or below the middle of a sheet and there is not room for another on the same page, commence the next one on a new sheet.

Avoid breaking a sentence at the bottom of a page of copy. When possible always end the page with a complete sentence.

III
Machine Made Matter.

The constant use of hackneyed expressions shows not only a lack of the inventive faculty but it has a tendency to make copy commonplace. Try to use English as a person of average intelligence would use it when exactness is the aim. The distorted phrases of the police, of gamblers, or of those who use "society" talk, may safely be left for department editors. Notice the following objectionable phrases: "Mistress Black poured," "Pinched his man," "Jumped his bond," "The bird has flown," "Plans are on foot," "Run to earth," "Much in evidence," "Time and again," "Times without number," "To try and find," "Take stock in," "In a blaze of glory," "Wide berth," "Nipped in the bud," "Quite a stir," "Good thieves," "Good arrest," "Up in arms," "Eke out a miserable existence," "Fire fiend," "Dull thud," "Incipient blaze."

One objection to the indiscriminate use of these conventional phrases is that they rarely express the shade of meaning one has in view and tend to take all the vigor out of the story. For instance, the man who wrote, "They united in giving him a cordial farewell" did not mean just that, but the phrase came easily. Other forms of objectionable phrases are especially frequent as "snappers" to short paragraphs in the form of, "Despondency is supposed to be the cause," "the matter was reported to the police," "where the physicians said he would die," "a large number of guests was present," and many similar ones. They all mean something but it can be told in a way to avoid the constant iteration of the expressions.

Like complaint is to be made of a large number of conventionalisms in which the superfluous words are italicized. There seems to be no reason why the expressions are not just as full of meaning with the indicated words omitted. "Failed to *put in an* appear*ance*," "while *in the act of* picking pockets," "whether *or not*," "while *engaged in* stealing."

The elimination of superfluous words from copy does not always improve the style and, in some instances, it may not help the sense: it comes from a natural impulse to do away with that which is unnecessary and the writer ought to feel this as strongly as the corrector of his work. More illustrations of the use of the superfluous words and phrases follow. They are italicized (underlined) as examples of that are certain, when they are used, to mark the trail of the blue pencil. Men from eight *different* states. Thrown *a distance of* fifteen feet. Confidence *reposed* in. Showed no desire *at all*. Gave him *the sum of* $50. Between *the hours of* 8 o'clock and 11 o'clock last evening. During the breakfast hour yesterday *morning*. He spoke of the *various* members. On both *of the* bills. Who soon arrived *on the scene*. Several years *past*. Would not say what *the nature of* the clue is. Both *of them* jumped.

Note, too: "Averaging about $50" for "nearly $50." "Lodged behind the bars" for "locked up" or "imprisoned." "On hand" for "present" or "show his hand" for "reveal." "Regulation fine" for "usual" or "customary fine." "Acted in the capacity of treasurer" for "acted as treasurer." "Proceeded to begin" for "began." "Came to" for "became conscious." "Balance of his life" for "rest of his life" or "natural life" for "life."

The phrase, "fears are entertained for his recovery," is frequently used in such connection as to make it ridiculous. It is unnecessary to use it in connection with injured persons in whom the public has no special interest and more especially in the case of criminals shot while endeavoring to commit crimes or escape arrest. "Fortunately his injuries were not of a fatal nature" is a similar expression seeking, apparently, to convey an impression of deep personal interest on the part of the writer.

If one attempts to profit by these suggestions, he will be inclined to be honest in what is written even at the expense of decorative detail. In doing so he will not write "the police are looking" for a man unless he knows it; or "the residents in the vicinity were greatly excited," or that "a panic was narrowly averted" or that "the wound is probably fatal," or that "he is well known to the police," and like phrases unless they are true and mean something.

Finally, revolver balls "crashing through skulls or timber" only makes work for the copy reader. "The bullet went wide of its mark" is a phrase which has outlived its usefulness. Do not use it.

IV

Names and Titles.

The natural inclination of the American nation to use titles may be a cause, in part, of the growth to its present ridiculous proportions of their indiscriminate bestowal. Colonel, captain, president and secretary are illustrations of a class of titles concerning the use of which there is, of course, no objection, as there can be none concerning the use of professional terms such as attorney, doctor and professor. When a semi-professional class is reached, such as an engineer or motorman, doubt arises. But when titles are coined to express "Fireman Brown," "Dog-catcher Jones," "Grocer Smith," or "Newsboy Johnson," the limit has been passed and these latter expressions should not, ordinarily, be used. Their introduction is doubtless caused by the desire of the reporter to conceal the fact that he has not secured the Christian name or initials and in the necessary process of elimination and substitution the copyreader is left to struggle with them and the directory. Many a "service no longer required" note in the box Saturday night has been based on this kind of work.

The use of the title "Mr." is regulated by no very well

marked rules. It should not be used when the Christian names or initials are used: "John H. Smith" will be sufficient. Further than this it is difficult to formulate a rule. In speaking of prominent citizens or those of sufficient importance to be speakers at banquets or meetings, or to be entitled to obituary notices or other attentions other than in the criminal or sporting columns of the newspapers, the title may generally be used, always, however, as a substitute for the Christian name. It is probably well to err on the safe side if doubt exists and use the prefix. In this connection it is well to understand that unless it is in accord with the explicitly defined policy of your paper, you will not write " 'Baron' Yerkes," "Old Hutch," " 'Deacon' Bisbee." Instead, refer to "Mr. Yerkes," "Mr. Hutchinson," "Attorney Bisbee." Undue familiarity is not to be encouraged. H.C. Mc Donald is not a social leader nor was his wealth acquired in the most approved of way, yet the careful reporter will refrain from calling him "Mike" Mc Donald.

Because a man's name is Fitzgibbon or Mayer, it does not follow that he wants to be called Fitzgibbons or Mayers. The directory is the bible in reference to proper names and where this is available, there is no justifiable excuse for the smallest error. Get names always at first hand and have the owners spell them letter by letter. Don't take the word of those who think they know, and above all don't take a police or coroner's report except in desperation. In lists of pallbearers, committees, and in all cases where there is not positive knowledge, consult the directory. It is a good rule to print proper names.

Above all do not write "one Lowenstein" meaning a man of the name of Lowenstein. Ascertain his full name while you are about it, if possible. William McKinley was not "named McKinley," he was named "William" and he is "of the name of McKinley." Think of this.

You never write Mister Smith; then why say Professor Smith, Captain Jones, Colonel Brown or Reverend John Robinson? As a prefix, the title should be abbreviated, as Prof., Capt., Col., and Rev. Note, however, that in other cases the title is spelled out, as "the colonel ordered the captain."

Never write "the newly married couple;" make it "Mr. and Mrs. De Lacy."

Do not, under any circumstances, in ordinary news narrative use the Christian name of a person except in quotation.

V

Words to Think About.

While warning you against the use of "none" in the plural it is understood that there is competent authority for its employment. Webster and the "Century" both grudgingly admit it, but both in limited connection and barely permissible. "None were" is convenient and is used in constantly growing proportion by modern writers. As a means of avoiding awkwardness it is frequently passed by the careful copyreaders, but it still seems bad form in view of the construction of "none" from the words "no one."

Occasionally the reporter is obliged to use words he would not speak in polite society. In cases of the kind make your copy as clean as possible. Unpleasant and indecent matters must be merely suggested when referred to at all. In this line be careful never to use "adultery," "rape," "bastard," "seduction," or words of that class. Of course, "accomplished his design" in a criminal assault is never permitted.

Do not confuse "night" with "evening." The former means any time between sunset and sunrise, but usually suggests a later hour; any time, for instance, between the usual bedtime and morning. "Evening" means the "beginning" of night. Receptions and meetings after sundown are nearly always spoken of as occurring in the "evening." Fires and murders after 10 o'clock, say, are by the same argument referred to as occurring "last night."

Since "conspire" means to "plot together" there is no more reason to say "conspire together" than there is to say "separate apart." Speaking of "separate" do you know it is not spelled "seperate?"

You can not "telegraph" nor "telephone" a man. The message only is sent. Always use the word "to" as "telegraphed to" or "telephone to."

"Whence" means "from what" or "from which place." Therefore, when you say "the body was taken to the County hospital from whence—," you are saying "from which place." "Whence" should never be preceded by "from."

Dead men do not leave "wives," but they may leave "widows."

The relative pronoun "that" is used about three times superfluously to the once when it helps the sense.

Avoid the use of the word "above" as: "in the above mentioned house," "the persons above mentioned."

Such adverbs as "tastefully," "beautifully," "elaborately," "neatly," must never be used except in quotation or indirect discourse.

With "neither" always use "nor." With "either" always use "or." Never write "neither man or woman."

"Etc." is a resource for the careless or slipshod. The best newspapers do not use it in narrative writing, preferring to specify in detail what is meant.

This office spells it "programme."

"Burglarize" is a good word. It is recognized by the most advanced authorities and may be used.

"Riding" and "driving" are words that are frequently stumbling blocks. It is plain that one rides on a horse or in a wagon and that one may drive a horse while riding a vehicle.

"Very" is a word often used without discrimination. It is not difficult to express the same meaning when it is eliminated.

Never use "ere" and "tho" unless you have an assignment to write poetry.

"Worthless" is better than "bogus" when referring to checks used by swindlers.

"State, stated and statement" indicate a formal communication. Do not use them indiscriminately. "The police say" not "state;" "Mr. Jones said" not "stated."

A prisoner is not "brought" into court or the police station, neither does he "come" there. He was "taken" or "went." One may be "brought" or may "come" to life or his senses, or to America, the United States, Illinois, Cook County or Chicago. An infant comes or is brought into the world.

The past tense of the verb "to lead" is "led." That of "plead" is "pleaded."

It is ordinarily unnecessary to use profane words. "D--d," "blank," "dashed" and other evasions are no longer permissible. If utterance is of sufficient importance to demand its use do not quibble; write, "The public be damned."

When you write "the loss was nominal" the English of the expression means, of course, that the loss was only one "in name" and by inference, a small one. But why not write "the loss was a small one"?

Most men and Dr. Mary Walker wear "trousers" not "pants."

If there are any "young gents" on the staff they will please treasure the appelation as one not to be parted with, at least not in their copy.

Most women are very properly proud of that name and you will seldom find favor, where favor is desirable, by referring to them as ladies. In some instances this may be necessary, but you will find it is seldom that the word "woman" will not apply with as much grace and far more dignity.

Hotels are kept, not "run." The same rule applies to gambling houses, saloons or resorts of any kind. Technically a person cannot "run" an engine, but long usage makes the expression permissible in this connection.

"Shall" and "will" as auxiliary verbs are frequently confounded without excuse. The difference between them is not too fine to be made in ordinary writing where exactness is desired. "Shall" indicates a duty or necessity whose obligation is derived from the person speaking. In the second or third person it indicates a command, a threat or a promise. "Should" is everywhere used in the same connection and in the same sense as shall, as its imperfect. "Will" indicates futurity—in the first person, willingness, consent, promise and, when emphasized, determination, a fixed purpose. In the second and third person it denotes simple certainty.

VI

"Caps," Dots and Dashes.

Punctuation varies, to some extent, with different newspapers, but there can be no question concerning the use of the period, comma, colon, semicolon, and interrogation point as taught in the grammar schools. A little study of such matters as hotel arrivals or lists of guests will be of much benefit. The average reporter can use the period and comma properly, but is in sad confusion when asked to handle a few colons and semicolons. These are forms generally used:

Among the hotel arrivals yesterday were: Virgil P. Kline, Cleveland, at the Annex. Harvey P. Miller, St. Louis; George F. Ferguson, Albion, Mich.; J.E. Rahsdale, Gibson City, Ill., at the Sherman.

For lists of officers:

The officers of the council are: Moderator, Dr. Little, Boston; scribe, Rev. Dr. Bradley, Grand Rapids, Mich.; councilmen, Rev. Arthur Little, Rev. J.B. Silcox.

Names to be printed in one-half or single column form are followed by periods, as:

W.W. Clark.   W.A. Waterman.
J.W. Perkins.   Philip Krohn.
John Brown.   Harvey N. Hollister.

The rules for capitalization vary widely. The following examples cover many of the doubtful points and the style outlined will be followed in this office:

Board of Trade.
Board of Education.
Sanitary district.
First National bank.
First Methodist church.
Cicero Town band.
President John Smith.
Secretary Samuel Jones.
John Smith, president of the bank.
Samuel Jones, secretary of the association.
Joseph Kipley, chief of police.
Chief of Police Kipley.
Illinois Central Railway company.
State street.
The West side.
The west side of the city.
The North town.
The county building.
The city hall.
The Circuit court.
Steinway hall.
Passavant hospital.
Merchants' and Traders' Loan association.
The democratic party.

The invariable rule for forming the possessive is to add an apostrophe and "s"—'s; as the man's coat, the woman's flowers, Cranes's paper, Burns's poetry. But the "s" in cases similar to the last two illustrations is nearly always omitted as a matter of taste. This is especially true when the additional syllable so formed makes an unpleasant sound, as the words in the plural such as girls' hats and boys' school, when the apostrophe alone indicates the possessive. In these words the apostrophe and "s" are added, the latter being, however, dropped to secure euphony.

The proper use of the abbreviations is a matter to which too little attention is generally paid. The names of states when used in conjuction with those of cities are always abbreviated, thus: "Chicago, Ill." When used alone the name must be spelled out as: "The senator from Illinois," "Illinois spent $50,000."

It is generally unnecessary, when the city is of any great importance, to mention the name of the state in which it is situated. For instance, do not say "New York, N.Y." "Chicago, Ill.," "St. Louis, Mo.," "Omaha, Neb." Of course, St. Louis, Miss., must be so designated as must Lockport, N.Y., the latter because while it is important enough to come under the first section of the rule, it shares its name with so many other cities in different localities.

It is troublesome, but not the less necessary, to write in full the names of railway and other corporations. Do not write "C.B. & Q. Ry." but write "Chicago Burlington & Quincy railway."

As for the interrogation point, there is a reporter of six years' experience, a university man, who insists on writing " 'Will you take any action,' Mr. Smith was asked?" Note the location of the point. The use of the single quotation mark as illustrated in the preceding should be studied. It is a necessary evil encountered less frequently than before the use of a smaller body of type for extended quotations, but when used at all it should be used correctly. Even the double quotation mark is not universally understood. There is a man in Chicago who in spite of years of experience, writes: "I will go to New York tomorrow, said Mr. Smith." This rule can be depended upon in the matter of the use of quotation marks:

Except when matter is set in a small body type to indicate that it is direct speech, it must always be enclosed in quotation marks and these marks must never include more than the direct speech. When this direct talk makes use of the language of other than the speaker, the incorporated matter must be enclosed in single quotation marks. Mr. Gladstone then said: "As the poet expresses it 'we are but the playthings of Time.'" Be careful also of your tenses in quotations. Do not write: The speaker said: "He was inclined to the belief" when you mean to write "I am inclined to the belief." English publications use indirect discourse in quotation, but it is not permitted in American newspapers.

VII

For the Police Reporter.

Much criticism has been evoked by the use of the old fashioned phrase: "it is alleged," with its various ramifications, yet it is difficult to see how it can be dispensed with. For instance, John Smith is arrested not "for robbery" but on "a charge of robbery." The reporter must not assume as in the first instance that Smith committed the robbery. Again, "Jones, who is in a cell, stole a purse." This won't do: "it is alleged that Jones, who is in a cell, stole a purse." The allegation of crime is a statement of fact; you must stand prepared to prove your charges if necessary. You can easily show that Smith or Jones was charged with the crime, while it might be a difficult matter to prove his guilt. This is apart from ethical considerations and primarily involves the principles of self protection.

Every criminal charge preferred is of the highest significance to someone, usually the defendant, and, whatever that allegation, remember there are two sides to the story; that the defendant is yet to have his day in court and must never be assumed guilty. Your own impression counts for nothing except in overt acts concerning which, as they relate to the guilt of the defendant, there can be no reasonable doubt. Give the defendant the benefit of every doubt.

Do not write, perfunctorily, "he will be arraigned this morning," nor "an inquest will be held this morning," unless you know where and when. In the case of inquests this is impossible because they are not often arranged for until the next morning. The phrases suggest that you are short on information and are writing against space.

The police like to assert that persons arrested by them are members of the "Market Street gang," the "cowboy push," the "Shevlin gang," and other half mythical bodies. These are, by imputation, serious charges and must not be made without investigation. "The police say" will not be taken as an excuse in case of trouble. Better avoid the "gangs" altogether unless you are sure of your ground.

"Trials" in criminal cases are never held by justices. These officials have no jurisdiction except as committing magistrates. They only examine into the probable guilt or innocence of the accused. Do not, therefore, say, "John Smith was tried before Justice Jones." He may have a "hearing" however.

"Alias" is a word which is frequently misused. The police are fond of it as establishing a presumption of guilt. Hence we see Thomas Jones alias "Texas," or William alias "Long" Smith. Neither of these is an alias in the meaning of the word. Both are nicknames not borne with any intent to disguise identity. As well say Richard alias "Lionheart." The general use of the word may well be curtailed, especially when it is realized that the subject is being branded through no fault of his.

There is no such thing as a "4-11" fire. One may speak of a "4-11 alarm;" the fire is not the result of the alarm. There would be less of the conventional in the story of fires if there were fewer references to the alarms and the extreme haste with which they are turned in. A fire story in which "Marshal Jones immediately responded and at once turned in a 4-11 alarm" was not a prominent statement, would be refreshing.

Do not write "James White and John Brown, 'two men'" nor "Willie Wall and John Green, 'two boys,' eleven and twelve years old respectively." Leave something to the common sense of the reader. When you have named the persons you are writing of, it is not necessary to count them for the reader nor to inform him that male persons of tender years are "boys." There is also a superfluity of information in the common phrase, "John Jones, five years old, living with his parents."

There is no reason why the caliber of a revolver in murder or suicide stories should not be mentioned except that it has been overdone and every copy reader wastes time in displaying the allusions to the rest of the staff when he encounters it. Consequently, do not designate the weapon further than to say whether it was large or small. Of course this does not apply in stories of such magnitude as to demand trifling details.

Instead of meaning to write; "He was charged with stealing a coat in Judge Smith's court" you probably intended "he was charged in Judge Smith's court with stealing a coat."

"Placed him under arrest" is apparently a tasty morsel for the new reporter. "Arrested him" will save space and answer all other requirements.

It is not necessary to inform the reader that casualties resulted "before they could be avoided." Omit the italicized words in such uses as the following: "The horse ran and *before Smith could stop him*, threw the rider;" and "*before the firemen could extinguish them*, the flames caused damage amounting to $5,000." Of a similar nature is the allegation regarding the arrest of an employee: "Smith and Co. say that Jones, *while in their employ*, embezzled money."

The police have discovered so many "finest sets of burglars' tools" that the expression is meaningless. There is no cleverness in making a safe blowing outfit out of a hammer and a cold chisel.

It is not often that the use of names of police officers adds to the interest of a story and never unless for some special act or in reports of extraordinary news. New reporters like to write: "Officers Brown, Dick and Fitzgerald yesterday arrested Tommy Atkins on a charge of larceny."

There is no particular news in designating the nationality of a person unless something depends on it. The police report which says "Ole Olson, Swede, 25 years old, and living at 492 West 13th street" contains a superabundance of information and it is not the best literary model.

There has never been a lynching in Chicago. Whenever you hear loud cries of "lynch him," and find men with ropes ready to commit this act, get the names and addresses of the enthusiasts. This is the only condition under which we will use a lynching story.

Every person is known to someone: therefore, while a newly found body may be "unidentified" it is not "unknown." A traveler may discover an unknown lake, but he can't discover an unknown man.

It is better to write "the engine struck" or the "engine ran over" than to use the words "ran down." To "run down" implies a chase which is probably not often true in railway or other accidents unless the person injured is racing with the colliding object.

When you write "he stole $200 in cash" or "in money" the words "in cash" and "in money" are superfluous because if the amount is in checks or notes these are invariably named.

When a person disappears from his home, you write "he has not been seen since" you probably mean he has not since been seen by his friends, or family or those in search of him.

When economizing in words do not carry it to the point of leaving out the word "station" after "locked up at Desplaines" or "Harrison street."

Do not write "was held" when you mean "was held to the grand jury," nor "the case went over" when you mean "the case was continued."

A police magistrate, like any other justice of the peace, is a "justice" only, not a judge. The latter title, in its legal connection, belongs solely to the judges of courts of record.

"Hold up men" for robbers, is an expression so bad that its condemnation here should be unnecessary.

VIII

General But Useful.

"Sang a vocal solo" includes a needless repetition.

Do not write "this city" when you mean Chicago.

In narrative writing the abbreviation "vs" is abominable.

Do not write "No. 112 State street," "112 State street" is sufficient.

Use "half a block," "half a mile;" not "a half block," "a half mile."

Don't write "aged 30" if you mean 30 years old. "John Jones, aged 9," may mean 9 years or 9 months.

When you do not know the cause of a dispute do not say "they quarreled over some trivial affair."

This sentence frequently occurs: "The dead man was seen on the streets the day before." How is it possible?

Time, when used in narrative, is to be expressed as "2 o'clock yesterday afternoon," not "2 p.m. yesterday."

Perhaps Mr. Jones did marry Mrs. Jones in 1884. You probably mean, however, that he married Miss Smith.

When you mean a person stays or boards at a hotel, do not write "stops" or "puts up," and never say "hostelry."

If several persons "meet to discuss" a proposition it is unnecesary to say they "met for the purpose of discussing" it.

One may visit a museum "with" relatives, but one does not go to another's home to visit "with" the person.

A glance is "a sudden darting of the sight." A "hurried glance" must be a "hurried sudden darting." Glance is sufficient.

To "pick" is to "take with the fingers." Avoid "the policeman picked up the prostrate woman." It is better to "assist" or "help."

Does not this tell the whole story with the indicated words omitted: "George Jones, *a* colored *man*? If it does, remember it.

"Opened up" is a phrase for which there is no excuse. Is there an occasion when "opened" does not fully cover the ground?

Clark street north of the river is known as "North Clark street." South of the river it is "Clark street." Never write "South Clark."

In describing locations such as "Clark and Jackson streets," do not precede the phrase with "at." Never use "at the corner of."

The preposition "on" is superfluous in designating dates as, "on Tuesday," "on Aug. 18," "on the day he was arrested." Cut it out always.

In ordinary funeral assignments we will accept copy that does not mention "Rock of Ages," "Lead Kindly Light" or "Just as I am Without One Plea."

"It will be remembered" is only permissible in editorials. "It appears" should also appear only on the fourth page with which you have nothing to do.

The death of celebrated men, an eclipse of the moon, are usually timed to the minute, but it is not necessary to record minor accidents as occurring at 7:20 or 8:15 o'clock.

You can, socially, repay a call made upon you, but you cannot well "pay a visit to the scene of the murder." At least you can go there, or make a visit, more consistently.

"Palms and potted plants" is an indefinite, conventional phrase; it suggests that the writer does not know what the decorations were. If these decorations are worth mentioning describe them.

Avoid "the" grocer at 82 Madison street or "the" hatter on

Wabash avenue. If he has been in business long enough to be so well known, he ought to pay for the advertising. "A" grocer makes him no better than others.

If you are seeking brevity you will possibly find "which was" and "which were" used oftener than the sense demands. For instance: "on a warrant *which was* sworn out" and "recovered the article *which was* stolen."

Never write "a quiet but elegant wedding;" there is nothing consistent in the coupling of these words; the affair can be both quiet and elegant. Do not use the name of the orchestra or the caterer employed at social affairs.

Please remember this: When it is written, "he struck the man with a *blunt instrument*" the copy reader is put on the rack at once. He may substitute "a club" for the phrase but he has as much right to make it a "brick."

In speaking of the time of events, except when using "today, tomorrow or yesterday," give only the day of the month and avoid subsequent confusion. It is not necessary to write "June 21st" or "Aug. 3d." "June 21 " and "Aug. 3" tell the same thing.

"Gertie were not returning home" even if there were others with her as in this: "Gertie, accompanied by two companions, were returning home." Gertie and George "were;" Gertie, who knows George, or Gertie, who saw George, or Gertie, accompanied by George, "was."

Never, under any circumstances, express a sentiment, feeling or judgment except when quoted from a genuine personal source. If a murder is "horrible" the narrated facts make it plain. A programme may be "well rendered" but it is no concern of the reporter.

It is barely possible that the pickpocket was caught as he "started to run." It is not absolutely beyond reason that the dog was shot as it "commenced to bark." It is much more probable, however, that the thief was caught while running, and the dog was shot while barking.

It is "$7," not "seven dollars," "7 dollars" nor "$7.00." In expressing sums of money it is not usually necessary to use the decimal. For newspaper use it is generally sufficient to say $864 when the actual amount is $864.32. Of course, this is only a general rule not to apply where exactness is essential.

In interviews do not have the man talking address you with "yes, sir" and "no, sir." "Sir" in its best usage suggests a conferred distinction and it is a kind of title a modest reporter may well avoid. The same objection applies to "your city" and "your town" with which phrases the person interviewed invests the reporter with unnecessary personality.

A "dose" is a quantity of medicine given at one time and to say "he committed suicide by drinking a dose of carbolic acid" is to write a ridiculous thing. Nor is it correct to say suicide was caused by an "overdose" of morphine which implies just the reverse or an accident. Persons committing suicide do not take "doses."

There is a distinction, which is not finical, between "reside" and "live" in referring to a place of residence. To reside in a particular place suggests permanent habitation; therefore, boarders do not "reside" in apartments or flats. To "live" in one place means only a dwelling there which may be long or short.

If a well known church or public building burns, or is the scene of a panic or other great news event, it is well to go into details which would otherwise be unimportant. But when the women of the Epworth league give a colonial tea party it is unnecessary to write: "The entertainment was given in the Hyde Park Presbyterian church, *Washington avenue and 53d street*." The italicized words may be omitted.

There is a "yellow" newspaper maxim to the effect that "all sudden deaths are cases of suicide until proven otherwise and that all cases of suicide are murders until shown not to be so." But you will save grey matter and subsequent explanations if you do not work on this line. Because a man stays away from home over night, don't say, "his friends suspect foul play." Do not use the words "foul play" in any connection.

The advertiser is always lying in wait for the unsuspecting reporter. The theater press agent is tireless in this direction and there are others. "Considerable damage to the stock by water" as a confidential confession by the merchant will probably be followed in a few days by a fire sale. In this connection avoid the use of proprietary names as "Rough on Rats," for rat poison, "Winchester" or "Colt" rifle, "Smith & Wesson" revolver, bottle of "Mumm's."

That John Smith had his leg broken is usually misleading information. It implies that Mr. Smith voluntarily submitted his leg to the operation. There are occasions in surgical annals where this has been the case. Under other circumstances it is well to announce the fact in some other way: for instance, "John Smith's leg was broken." Please bear in mind also that while Mr. Smith may "receive" the full force of the blow or of a charge of shot, he does not "receive" the injury which breaks his leg. He "was injured."

IX

Some Verbal Don'ts.

Don't use "less" when you mean "fewer."

Don't use "eye sight." "Sight" will be sufficient.

Don't use "all of the witnesses;" of is superfluous.

Don't use "locate" meaning "to discover" or "to find."

Don't use "party" meaning "person," except in court stories.

Don't use "gutted." It is a good word, but there are better.

Don't use "ad" for "advertisement" or "photo" for "photograph."

Don't use "employ" for "employment." It is a poetical license.

Don't confuse "partial" with "part." "Partial" also means "biased."

Don't use "scare" and "scared" in the sense of "fright" and "frightened."

Don't use "mooted" meaning debatable. It means "much talked of."

Don't under any provocation use "scab" meaning a non-union workman.

Don't use "grocery store" and "grocery man" meaning "grocery" and "grocer."

Don't use "chew" or "spit" when you can substitute "masticate" or "expectorate."

Don't use "claim" meaning "say, allege, assert, insist." To "claim" is to "demand as a due."

Don't use "post mortem" as synonymous with "autopsy." Write "post mortem examination."

Don't use "old veteran" meaning only "veteran." This is as superfluous as to write "widow woman."

Don't use "den" or "joint" in referring to a place where opium is smoked. "Resort" is the word.

Don't use "goodly" as suggesting a large number. It is an adjective meaning "pleasant" or "desirable."

Don't use "patrol" when you mean "patrol wagon" or "a habeas corpus" when you mean "a writ of habeas corpus."

Don't make "tough" mean "difficult" as "tough task" or "tough problem." Nor does it mean "rough" or "rowdy."

Don't use "male" or "female" in place of "man" or "woman." A female may mean a human being, a fish or a fowl.

Don't use "institute" or "inaugurate" for simple "begin." Of a like nature is "converse" for "talk" and "donate" for "give."

Don't use "nolle prosequi" except in important cases. "Discontinued" or "dismissed" do not express it exactly but they are near enough.

Don't use "communicate" in fire stories when "spread" is meant. You don't say the rushing water rapidly communicated to the adjoining banks."

Don't use "lengthy" meaning "long." A speech or resolution may be lengthy, a rope, a pole or a string may be long.

Don't use "people" in referring to a specific number. It should be "one thousand persons were present" and "the people are of one accord in the matter."

Don't write "burly negro" any oftener than you write "burly" in referring to other races—which is probably never.

Don't write "Board of Trade man," or "cattle man," or "hardware man." Make it "member of the Board of Trade" or "cattle dealer" or "hardware merchant."

Don't use "lecture" for "reprimand," "censure" or "admonish." Police court justices do not deliver "lectures" from the bench, although they may sometimes think they do.

Don't use "mob" meaning only "a curious crowd." "Mob" means "a riotous gathering for an unlawful purpose" and is not synonymous with "a number of excited persons."

Don't use "laundry " meaning "linen" or "laundered clothes." The word is possibly permissible, but it confuses the "linen" with the place where the work is done.

Don't believe "done" in green means the same as "decorated" with green for it does not, except to a few who have agreed on this perversion.

Don't write "badly injured." That means "unskillfully" or in a "bad manner." Nor is it better to write "seriously" for that means "in earnest" or "solemnly." The word is "severely" which means "gravely" or "painfully."

Finally, "don't" is not an abbreviation of "does not" but of "do not." Just recall this when writing "he don't," or "the officer don't" or "health don't."

X

Clear Copy.

Nothing is more annoying to a copy reader than to find

errors in the matter before him that the writer himself would have corrected had he taken the trouble to carefully revise his copy. The reporter who is not as careful in the revision of his work, up to his ability, as the copyreader who follows him, does not appreciate his responsibility. Copy that does not represent a reporter's highest ability is inexcusable, because it presumes someone else is to do a portion of his work. If there is not time for examination, this does not apply, but there is little newspaper work that cannot be run before the eyes a second time. Mechanical blunders in typewriter work, missing words, mispelled proper names, contradictions, and the many little things that are quite apart from quality, extent and policy—with which the copyreader is primarily concerned—all contribute to make the least satisfactory and most unreliable reporter.

Use every effort to have your story in such shape that the reader will not be obliged to analyze the sentences to grasp your meaning. Observance of the hints in this chapter will accomplish a great deal in this direction, but there are many situations due to clumsy composition to illustrate, which would require too much space. These must be avoided by the reporter's own observation and care. Do not say: "I know I didn't get that fixed just right but the copyreader can fix it." At least if you do say so once, watch to see how he "fixes it" and avoid a repetition of the error. Everyone can learn by careful observation; it is the man who does learn that succeeds.

Matter is frequently made obscure by the improper use of nouns, pronouns and verbs. For example: "John Smith and Edward Jones engaged in an altercation. Smith struck Jones who returned the blow, blackening his eye." This is a simple illustration of an error which often assumes more complex forms and befogs the meaning. The fault is in the substitution of the pronoun for the proper noun. Here is another illustration in which the pronoun and verb are slighted at the expense of clearness; "John Jones and Harry Brown were frustrated in an attempt to hold up the saloon of David Bates, 621 State street at 9:30 o'clock last night, and (they were) captured with great difficulty." The omission of the words "they were" makes it possible that the men were not only captured but were also frustrated with difficulty. The omission of "they" and the use of "were" might make sense, but it is advisable to use both words. This confusion is less likely to arrive if the relative pronoun and qualifying clauses are placed as near their subject as possible.

"The latter" seems to be easier to write than the name of the person alluded to and this form of word economy is attended by its own troubles. Note this: "As the man, accompanied by his wife, walked upon the bridge, the latter fell breaking her arm." Of course the sentence is ungrammatical unless it is intended to personify the bridge as one might personify a vessel and indicate that she (the bridge) fell, breaking some part of her (it) known as the arm. It is probably safe to conclude that what was meant was that the woman's arm was broken; but did the woman fall or did the bridge drop on her?

XI

A Frightful Example.

Finally, it must be understood, this compilation is an unpretentious affair, designed in the main for the admonition of careless newspaper workers. Literary critics may examine it in vain for enlightenment on the mysteries of plural pronouns as used with collective nouns, the separation of the subject and its predicate, and similar points of contention. Like the old time temperance lecture, the notes close with the exhibition of a frightful example, a symposium of inexcusable errors noted within a few days in manuscript arriving at one copy desk. He who reads it and does not at once detect fifty-five errors of expression or examples of bad taste can, it is believed, well use half an hour in going over the pages of the notebook again. The example:

At half past three p.m. yesterday afternoon, as exclusively announced in an extra edition of this paper, a fearful panic occurred on State street. The sidewalks were thronged with the usual crowds who assemble on bright afternoons on the busy thoroughfare, when some unknown but dastardly miscreant turned in an alarm of fire. In an instant pandemonium reigned and a panic ensued which narrowly escaped having awful results.

The dead:

Skidds, Mrs. Seraphina, died at her home in Oak Park last night of heart disease.

The injured:

Mrs. Sarah Jones, 2345 Wooly avenue, ankle sprained and supposed internal injuries. Will probably recover.

Unknown woman, almost prostrated by nervous shock. Taken home.

In answering the alarm of fire the engined dashed rapidly around the corners, scaring the occupants of Marshall Field's, Carson & Pirie's and other stores. The scene that followed can better be imagined than described. Women fainted and strong men turned pale while children ran screaming for their parents. As soon as Chief Sweenie arrived he immediately turned in a 4-11.

On top of the Fair store Mr. and Mrs. Smith were preparing to take the elevator to make their descent to the street below but when the car started down neither of them were ready, an event which proved most fortunate for both of them.

The rapidly descending car was crowded with people when three panic stricken pedestrians ran in from the street in feverish haste crying "fire" at the top of their voices. The elevator man lost his head and with carelessness a little short of criminality, loosened his hold on the cable. Mr. and Mrs. Jones were preparing to leave the cage when the latter fell, spraining her wrist so badly that medical aid had to be summoned.

In the meantime Mr. and Mrs. Smith on the top floor were devising means to try and make their escape. They could not agree and finally each went their separate way, making a date to meet later.

By this time the mob had learned that their fears were groundless and the panic began to give signs of subsiding. It was discovered later by police that one young man who had been keeping company with a light-complected young saleslady had in the confusion left for parts unknown.

Another incident was the hasty exit and successful escape of a thief who stole a purse containing $5 and a marble clock.

It is considered little short of miraculous that so few casualties occurred. Had the alarm been raised an hour later when the tide of shoppers had set toward home the death list must have been greatly swollen.

Alan Mueller, who worked at the bureau from May 1972 to September 1976 has provided a description of the working arrangements at the bureau:

> Day reporters worked either 8 a.m. to 4:30 p.m. or 8:30 a.m. to 5 p.m. Midwatch reporters followed them and the overnight reporter who worked at central police headquarters [11th and State] was the only overnight reporter.
>
> During the day there would be four rewrite persons, during the evening three rewrites and overnight two or three rewrites. For the busiest part of the weekdays, there were two news editors and one radio wire editor. The second news editor worked from about 10 a.m. until 6:30 p.m.
>
> Someone was on the radio desk from about 8 a.m. until 2 a.m. the next day. Here CNB copy was written for the ear, to make it easy for listeners to understand. In the early morning when the desk was unattended, they received the same copy the news side did, except for one summary which was written by the evening editor before he/she left.
>
> Daily news operations were under city editor Paul Zimbrakos during the day and Wayne Klatt in the evenings. Sports editor was Phil Weisman, assisted by Steven Foltin.
>
> The second daily and weekend city editor changed frequently as people were either put on other shifts or moved to other jobs. Some women held this job, including Sharon Cahill and Anne Hennessy. This was the top of the ladder.
>
> The police reporter at central police headquarters covered the Loop and near south side plus all the suburbs. At first this included only Cook county, but was later expanded to Lake, DuPage, Will and McHenry counties, and Lake county, Indiana.
>
> The Hyde Park person covered an area roughly south of Chicago avenue. The North person got the rest.

Reporters came first to the CNB office where they got copies of stories their predecessors had worked on. Then they went to a police station the balance of their shifts unless they were sent out on a special story.

Rewrites stayed in the office and took notes from police reporters and dictation from all others. Stories were typed on six-part carbon copy paper. They were then edited and sent by teletype to clients.

The regular daytime beats are city hall, county government, civic center courts, criminal courts and the Federal building. Also Education and the State of Illinois building. O'Hare was a regular beat at that time.

CNB published a daily schedule of items it expected to cover. Reporters were expected also to dig up stories on their own and re-cover stories which appeared in the three or four other dailies which existed when I was there. Police reporters got their tips from beat checks, reports heard or misheard over the police radio in the office, and from the coroner's office.

Bibliography and Notes

Most of the information on the history of the City News Bureau from its inception to the late thirties came from Tom Vickerman's unpublished thesis. Minutes of publishers' meetings, and letters from Ballantyne, Leckie and Saylor are from the files of the City News Bureau.

Chapter 3: The New Bureau

P. 16.

Details of negotiations with the transportation companies are to be found in a letter from John Ballantyne to the Executive Committee of the City Press Association, dated September 11, 1890, and in a follow-up letter to Victor Lawson dated September 18, 1890. CNB files.

As an example of the sort of thing to which Ballantyne was reacting, here is a letter to him from Montgomery B. Gibbs, city editor of the *Evening Post*, dated December 31, 1890:

Please permit me to call your attention to the enclosed clippings—one the report of the South Chicago bank robbers in the Evening POST; the other the report from the NEWS. The one (the latter) is a report; the other (the former) is a mockery, a delusion, and a snare. I could have covered this case myself quite comfortably to-day; but inasmuch as you scheduled it we hoped that you had made arrangements for something not worse than a perfunctory and insufferably harassing piece of bungling.

The Evening POST is not infallible—and occasionally perhaps it will get the worst of it; but even to you it must now be painfully apparent that the three scoops which we have suffered in the past eight days are wholly attributable to the incompetency of the Bureau's service. And outside the courts (which are remarkably well attended to) there appears no way for us to save ourselves except by doing over again what you pretend to do.

Is it too much to expect that you will henceforth furnish me each morning with a schedule of what you can and will cover *well*; and that I be informed of events that you attend to in such an inadequate manner as to give me a case of heartache.

An answer to this letter, with replies to the requests herein contained, is expected and will greatly oblige Yours, etc....

Chapter 6: Love Feasts and Scoops

Pp. 49-50.   The comments from Charles Carpenter were incorporated by Tom Vickerman in his thesis.

Chapter 7: Hard Times in the Nineties

P. 64.   "Note to City Editors." A discussion of some of these "Notes" is to be found in William T. Moore, *Dateline Chicago: A Veteran News-*

man Recalls its Heyday (N.Y.: Taplinger Publishing Co., 1973), 163-164.

Chapter 8: Sayler's Bureau

Pp. 84-85.   Details of the Lorimer affair can be found in Lloyd Wendt, *Chicago Tribune: The Rise of a Great American Newspaper* (Chicago: Rand McNally & Co., 1979), 368-371.

P. 88.   "Leaving the Tribune..." from John J. McPhaul, *Deadlines and Monkeyshines: The Fabled World of Chicago Journalism* (NY: Prentice-Hall, 1962), 107-108.

Chapter 9: Journalists Bootcamp

Pp. 104-105   "Every morning, Buddy McHugh..." from Edward Doherty, *Gall and Honey: The Story of a Newspaperman* (NY: Sheed & Ward, 1941), 27-28.

Chapter 10: World War I

Pp. 108-109.   The letters from reporters about Walter Brown were incorporated in Vickerman's thesis.

Pp. 110-111.   "...he could not have punched..." is from George Murray, *The Madhouse on Madison Street* (Chicago: Follett Publishing Co., 1965), 296. "On one occasion newspaper readers..." from Murray, 297.

Pp. 112-113.   For Wanderer stories see McPhaul, 227, and Murray, 232-241 and 298.

P. 119.   "Sgt. Francis (Jiggs) Donahue..." see McPhaul, 123-124.

P. 123   For an account of the 1919 race riots see Dempsey J. Travis, *An Autobiography of Black Chicago* (Chicago: Urban Research Institute, 1981), 26.

Chapter 11: *The Front Page* Era

Pp. 122-124   Kurt Vonnegut, *Slaughterhouse Five* (New York: Delta/Dell, 1969), 7-9

Pp. 133-134.   For information on Buddy McHugh see Murray, 248ff.

Pp. 139.   For information about Jake Lingle, see Wendt, pp. 527-536.

Chapter 14: Labor Problems

Information for this chapter came from interviews with Walter Ryberg and Ed Eulenberg and letters from Bob Kennedy and Frank Walsh. Other material is from CNB files.

Pp. 181-182.   The sheriff's name was Babb.

Chapter 15: Gershman

Information for this chapter came from an interview with Ed Eulenberg and a letter from Jim Mundis.

Chapter 16: The War...and Women

Glady's "Ruby" Ryan Wherity provided information on pp. 188-190. Other information came from Shirley Lowry Haas, Marjorie Minsk Kriz, Gera-Lind Kolarik, Walter Ryberg, Larry Mulay and Paul Zimbrakos.

P. 194.   "It was Mary Faith who..." McPhaul, 125.

Pp. 196-197.   For Terry Colangelo, see McPhaul, 123-124, 191-199.

P. 202.   "When Gera-Lind Kolarik..." Morris Yanoff, *Where is Joey?* (Chicago: Swallow Press, 1982), 180.

Chapter 17: Legendary Dividends

Information for this chapter came from letters from Tom Abbott and Jim Mundis.

Chapter 18: The Fifties

Information on the Our Lady of Angels school fire came from a letter from Walter Oleksy and an article in a City News Newsletter by Ray Bendig. The John Murphy sketch is from the City News Newsletter.

Chapter 19: Larry Mulay

Pp. 249-250.   WNET *Behind the Lines* transcript of "Whatever Happened to Front Page Journalism?" April 9, 1975. Copyright 1975, Educational Broadcasting Corporation.

Chapter 20: Criticism

Paul Zimbrakos remembers Greg Small as the bureau's all-time worst speller, who left an obscene farewell to the bureau in the City Desk log. Ed Zotti, of course, quit without notice.

Chapter 21: More of the Same

P. 256.   Celeste Huenergard in *Editor and Publisher* for October 9, 1982, p. 33, gives full details of the Tylenol story:

> It was a routine telephone call to the... Northwest Memorial Hospital that tipped a young City News Bureau reporter that something was up.
> "I just happened to mention that I had this 'unknown causes' death and the pr director said she would have to read me a

release on it," 23-year-old John Flynn Rooney recalled...

It was 11 p.m. on the Wednesday night before the Tylenol-cyanide stories broke across the nation the following morning.

The release concerned the deaths of Adam and Stanley Janus and the critical condition of the latter's wife. The statement attributed the deaths to cardio-pulmonary collapse.

While his other three colleagues on duty that night were busy tracking down what they thought would be a bigger story, the shooting of a suburban policeman, Rooney called the police and the medical examiner's office. The only information he could come up with was that they had sealed off the Janus house.

At 1 a.m. the bureau received an anonymous tip from "someone who said they worked at the hospital and that they had three deaths involving Tylenol."

"We called the medical examiner's office and it was the first time those guys ever laughed in our faces," the bureau's midnight editor Rick Baert said. "They flat out denied it."

Baert said he and his reporters debated whether or not to go with the tip. "I thought at first, what the heck, then I had visions of a Johnson & Johnson lawsuit with my name on it. Here we even have to verify middle initials because a lot of our clients don't have newsrooms—especially the radio stations—and some disc jockey spinning 45s isn't going to know how to verify a story."

...At 3:01 a.m. on Thursday, City News sent a bulletin that six members of the

Janus family remained hospitalized after two brothers had died and that their home had been sealed off. At 7:33 a.m. the bureau ran an insert connecting the death of 12-year-old Mary Kellerman to those of the Janus family, but could not list the cause.

A telephone note was sent to subscribers at 8:20 a.m., informing them of a press conference scheduled by the medical examiner's office for 9:30 a.m. to warn the public that "an over-the-counter drug...is linked to three deaths in Arlington Heights."

At 9:10 a.m. the bureau ran an insert saying the deaths were caused by cyanide contained in an "over-the-counter headache remedy." After the press conference, the wire carried another insert at 10:21 a.m., confirming the Tylenol connection.

Rooney said afterwards his office caught onto the story early simply "because it's part of our job to call the medical examiner's office at least three or four times a day to check on unknown deaths."

Meanwhile, a few miles away, the city's all-news CBS radio affiliate WBBM received a similar anonymous tip around 1:30 a.m. on Thursday, and hit the air with the two Janus deaths "from some kind of medication" 20 minutes later.

A CBS newsman said that while the medical examiner's office refused to verify a medication or Tylenol connection, the police admitted that "some kind of medication" was involved. The station referred to it as a "headache remedy" in its 7:10 a.m. broadcast that day, finally identifying it as Tylenol at 10:06 a.m. after the medical examiner's press conference.

Chicago Tribune started work on the

story after its assistant city editor crawled out of bed at 4:45 a.m. on Thursday, listening to a radio report on the policeman's death in the suburbs and a "couple of strange family deaths in Arlington Heights."

Since the *Tribune*'s newsroom is dead from 3 a.m. until 6:30 a.m. with the exception of a wire editor, Steven M. Pratt called his police reporter.

"I was really more concerned about getting the cop story...but I did tell him to check the thing in Arlington Heights," said Pratt.

At 5:45 a.m. the reporter phoned Pratt to tell him that "somebody took some Tylenol."

The city editor then started assigning reporters to investigate. The story made the paper's first edition, that afternoon.

Across the street, at the *Chicago Sun-Times*, city editor Alan Mutter also woke up with the radio. "I heard something on the news around 6 a.m. about some suspicious deaths. I thought it might be furnace fumes."

When Mutter got to the office, a stringer telephoned with a tip that a death in Elk Grove Village might be tied with those in Arlington Heights. It was around 7:30 a.m.

"We still didn't know what it meant," Mutter said.

The paper then got a call from the morgue telling them about the medical examiner's press conference scheduled for 9:30 a.m. A reporter called the morgue back around 8:30 a.m. and a source attributed the deaths to cyanide contained in some Tylenol capsules.

Mutter began assigning reporters to background pieces so that "we had our ducks in a row," when the news was announced at the press conference for the paper's first deadline that afternoon.

The Associated Press ran the complete story at 10:06 a.m. after the press conference, prefacing it at 8:58 a.m. with a story about "three deaths in the suburbs," and the suggestion of possible contaminated medication.

United Press International sent its first bulletin out at 10:45 a.m. "We didn't send anyone to the press conference because the medical examiner is always calling press conferences," a UPI spokesman said. The wire service had run a general story earlier about the three suburban deaths.

Pp. 258-260.   Charles McKelvy, "J-schools or jobs? Local news bureaus are a little of both" in *The Quill* (February, 1983), 24-26.

Index

A

B

C

E

I

L

N